The Real George Freeman

Tony Reeves was an investigative reporter of many years standing, having worked at the ABC, *Nation Review*, the *Sunday Telegraph* and the *Sunday Australian*, investigating Australia's underworld. His reporting helped bring about the 1973–74 Moffitt Royal Commission into organised crime. His first book, *Mr Big, Lennie McPherson and his life of crime*, won the 2005 Ned Kelly Award for True Crime. His other books include *Mr Sin, the Abe Saffron Dossier* (2007). He died in 2014.

To Kamala, for her continuing support and generous assistance.

THE REAL GEORGE FREEMAN

THIEF, RACE-FIXER, STANDOVER MAN AND UNDERWORLD CRIM

TONY REEVES

HYBRID
PUBLISHERS

Published by Hybrid Publishers

Melbourne Victoria Australia

© Tony Reeves 2013

This publication is copyright. Apart from any use as permitted under the Copyright Act 1968, no part may be reproduced by any process without prior written permission from the publisher. Requests and enquiries concerning reproduction should be addressed to the Publisher, Hybrid Publishers,

PO Box 52, Ormond, Victoria 3204, Australia.

www.hybridpublishers.com.au

First published by Penguin 2011

This revised edition 2013

Reprinted 2024

National Library of Australia Cataloguing-in-Publication entry

Reeves, Tony, 1940-2014 author.

The real George Freeman: thief, race-fixer, standover man and underworld crim / Tony Reeves.

3rd edition

ISBN: 9781925000016 (paperback)

9781742982892 (e-book)

Includes index.

Freeman, George, 1935-1990.

Criminals–New South Wales–Sydney–Biography.

Book-making (Betting)–New South Wales–Biography.

Organized crime–New South Wales–Sydney.

Sydney (NSW)–Biography.

364.1092

Contents

Prologue		1
1	Getting started in the trade	4
2	Taking a peep at the big time	15
3	Stealing or gambling? George has an each-way bet	24
4	Reaching for the top – into deals with Mr Big	35
5	Hospitality repaid – showing the Mafia our bright lights	42
6	Only a dope would've missed it: drugs make a big hit	45
7	Odds to die for: betting on the drugs trade	53
8	Crims give peace a chance, all meet in same room	63
9	Drugs not the only racket: racing gets a fix, too	69
10	Chips are down as casinos raided: punters take a short break	77
11	A shot in the dark: Freeman cops it in the neck	89
12	A new top cop, the same old game	100
13	Punting is easy when you know the winner!	110

14	The doc prescribes drugs to ease the pain of his debts	126
15	Tall poppies mown down in killing fields	136
16	NCA targets Freeman – and misses	149
17	Building a new deal in extortion	160
18	The slaughter goes on	167
19	The hit man becomes the target	176
20	McCann clan blown apart	192
21	Crims play law games: win more time for crime	196
22	Illegal bookie suffers amnesia, writes life story	204
23	Death of a drug addict	210
Epilogue: unfinished business: Freeman's bequest lives on		215
Notes		224
Index		230

Author note

Throughout the book monetary amounts are expressed in their contemporary values. For events prior to February 1966, before decimalisation, the amounts are shown in £/s/d (pounds, shillings and pence); after that in $ and ¢ (dollars and cents). To help readers assess the values involved, I have included updated (to 2012, the latest available in the system) amounts based on the Reserve Bank of Australia's online inflation calculator. These updated amounts are shown in parentheses and italics, for example (*$120*).

I hope this is of assistance.

Prologue

> Crime is a fact of the human species, a fact of that species alone, but it is above all the secret aspect, impenetrable and hidden. Crime hides, and by far the most terrifying things are those which elude us.
> – Georges Bataille, *The Trial Of Gilles De Rais*

Australia's 'Sin City', Sydney, has always been subjected to waves: the second-most common after those that pound its beaches are the surges of criminal activity. Over the last two centuries of our nation's history, crime has regularly ebbed back to a neap tide, as perpetrators have slunk off to dark crevices, only to violently pitch forward again. From the beginning of European settlement, the ties between 'goodies' and 'baddies' have been strong and lasting. It is not irrelevant that the earliest official 'constabulary' – a night-watch patrol – formed in 1789 by Australia's first governor, Captain Arthur Phillip, was manned exclusively by the best behaved convicts.

Yet strangely, some Australians will always praise the nefarious, glorify the inglorious – it's the 'Ned Kelly syndrome'. As the nation matured, criminals came to be held in awe rather than fear, their names whispered among those in the know, their feats becoming the stuff of legend from the playground to the local pub. More recently, criminals and crooked former cops have become fêted media celebrities, their offences against society worn as badges of courage, their ghost-written books, filled with less than the truth, given prime media attention and sitting at the top of bestseller lists.

It should not surprise us then that some set out from an early age to pursue a life of crime, fantasising about the rich rewards. So it was for this book's subject. While other boys were thinking of becoming firemen or sailors, George David Freeman as a young lad decided he wanted to be a criminal like his idol – legendary Sydney felon Darcy Dugan. This dream became a reality: Freeman was one of Australia's most successful and powerful criminals, a man with a place at the top table, where decisions of life and death were made. He was sufficiently respected and supported – and feared – to have been a major player in the crime scene of the 1980s and to have shared in the huge benefits of being one – and some say the biggest – of the Mr Bigs in Australia's history.

George David Freeman's image as the charming rogue of the Australian crime world, as depicted in a popular 2009 television series, revealed little of his true character. In real life he was part of a powerful gang of three who robbed, raped, bribed and blackmailed their way to the top of Sydney's underworld, a scene they ruled for more than three decades.

Some writers – and others loyal to their old friend – have fostered the idea of Freeman as a tough but friendly man who dabbled in illegal SP bookmaking and occasionally race fixing. George's admirers dismissed as fantasy the small-screen scenes of Freeman doling out money in Kings Cross backrooms and savagely beating the 'Mr Asia' drug kingpin Terry Clark. Ironically, for all the gloss of his television portrayal, these are the images that actually hit closest to the mark. He was obsessed with power and greed and was willing to do anything to protect his valuable empire.

An equal of Lennie McPherson and Abe Saffron, George Freeman was part of an elite group of gangsters, crooked cops and corrupt politicians who shaped the criminal milieu and decided the fate of many men. He was a key player in the vicious gangland warfare that erupted in Sydney in the 1980s and was directly involved in at least three murders during that period. The massive bribery and blackmail that was the lifeblood of the Sydney crime scene ensured he did not face prosecution for his major crimes.

Freeman hired as his bodyguard a man reputed to be a notorious gun-for-hire and was later implicated in the disappearance – and undoubted murder – of that man.

He even evaded scrutiny from the nation's top crime-fighting body, the National Crime Authority, despite a brief from the federal and state parliaments to place Freeman at the top on the NCA's investigations.

And while Freeman – like all criminals – publicly decried the illicit drug industry, he sympathised when a close friend was jailed for organising drug importation on a massive scale. Freeman himself became a drug addict, a habit that eventually killed him.

This story, based on detailed research, creates no fictions about this major criminal: the real George Freeman was a violent, venally corrupt gangster who lived a life far removed from the glamorous existence portrayed in the TV series.

1. Getting started in the trade

*Destiny. A tyrant's authority for crime
and a fool's excuse for failure.
– Ambrose Bierce, The Devil's Dictionary*

The mid-1930s was a volatile time. Countries the globe over were slowly and painfully extricating themselves from the shackles of the Great Depression. In Germany the sabre-rattling of Adolf Hitler and his gang of thugs grew louder as world leaders looked on in awe at this brutal political phenomenon. Back home, in 1935, unemployment was running at around 16 per cent, down from the 1932 peak when close to a third of the entire workforce was on the breadline.

Though the year was still young, 1935's most dramatic crime took place on 22 January when a petty thief, John Kingsley Clarkson, aged 24, fled Cootamundra prison, NSW. When confronted by a gun-toting constable at nearby Gagandra sheep station, he shouted, 'I am not a gunman; it hasn't come to that yet!' Clarkson was soon back in the custodial embrace of his jailer.

In Sydney police were gaining the upper hand over local criminals (or so they claimed). A report issued the same day as Clarkson's recapture stated there had been a marked decrease in night assaults and other violent crimes. 'As many as five assaults a night were reported a few months ago. Now there are no more than two cases of thug violence reported each week,' came the gloat. The report pointed to more frequent and visible police patrols and severer penalties being handed down by judges as the main reasons for the cut in incidences of night-time thuggery.

That same date, Sydneysiders who could afford a wager on the horses – many with their illegal Starting Price (SP) bookie at the local pub – had backed Emily Rose and Regal Son as favourites for the upcoming AJC Challenge Stakes and Anniversary Handicap respectively, which would take place the following weekend.

On that hot and sultry summer Tuesday, another son was in the making. This one was not at all regal but would certainly go on to develop an interest in both racing and SP betting. Rita Eileen Freeman, then aged 30, had gone that morning to Annandale's Queen Victoria Hospital for Women and Babies – later to be known as the Holy Family Convent. She left her son and daughter in the care of a neighbour in the family's dingy single-storey cottage at 43 Westbourne Street, back south across the Western Highway in Stanmore. Rita gave birth to a second son, George David.

Rita Cooke had married William David Freeman, a plasterer, in 1931. Six years after George's birth, William left the family for good, divorcing Rita, and remarrying in 1941 to start a new family in Five Dock. He had little contact with Rita and their children from that point on, although George later recalled as a lad going to Five Dock to pick up a meagre amount of pocket money. Rita and the three kids moved north across the highway into another tiny house at 67 Young Street, Annandale.

A year after the police had boasted about their efficiency in dealing with thugs, things had taken a turn for the worse. Now they were having difficulty fighting violent crime, particularly among armed criminals. Police destroyed all the unlicensed pistols they could find but, as they were reported in the *Sydney Morning Herald* as saying, 'the supply is constantly being augmented by smuggling, by robberies from gunsmiths' shops.' It's tempting to think that George Freeman's mere arrival in the world was enough to trigger a crime wave, but it's unlikely. There would, however, be plenty of time for him to achieve that in a more hands-on way.

* * *

George's earliest recollections were of him and his brother, Les, sleeping in the hallway of the Annandale house on kapok-filled mattresses, the two existing bedrooms being taken up by his mother and sister respectively. Each morning the boys would roll up their mattresses before breakfasting on bread and dripping. Rita formed a relationship with a Balmain knockabout, Ernest, a man with a small-time criminal history who died of natural causes not long after they got together. No record could be found of their marriage.

School held little interest for George – he was tossed out of two in Annandale before he attended the junior technical school in neighbouring Glebe – but getting a conventional education was not part of his life's plan. There was fun to be had: he and his young mates would go 'scaling' on trams, jumping onto the running boards and leaping off before the conductor came to claim a fare from them.

Sometimes the tram driver would spot them in his rear-view mirror and bring the tram to a squealing halt. The kids would then unhook the sprung arm to the overhead powerline, disabling the tram, and run away.

Like the other kids he hung around with in those years, Freeman got into stealing – small items from shops, biscuits from a local factory, all very petty. It was the sort of behaviour many boys indulge in – and most grow out of. But George never really let the habit go; for him, this was the start of his chosen career path. In his own words: 'Looking back on those early days, one thing sticks out clearly in my mind: right from the start there was only one thing I wanted out of life. I wanted to be a crook. Not just any crook, but the crook, the biggest – the man with money, power, influence. Working for a living never entered my head.'

Hanging around the streets of Sydney's inner-west – he called them a 'survival zone for battlers' – Freeman met a few like-minded people.

One of the first of this sort was a lad a year younger than him called Stanley John Smith, who was also destined for a senior rank in the local crime scene. The two formed a loyal and lasting friendship.

There were other connections that would come to influence the young George. His short-lived de facto stepfather, Ernest, was great mates with another local rogue, Richard Dugan. Dugan's brown-haired, grey-eyed son Darcy was well on the road to gaining notoriety as a thief and murderer. Dugan junior was destined to spend much of his life in jail and – sometimes successfully – trying to escape from it.

Before Ernest died, he introduced George to the young Dugan, who lived only a stroll away from Freeman's home. Although Darcy was 15 years older than George, the pair got on famously, and for many years Freeman looked on his new mate as a hero. 'He was our model: a crook who was really making it,' Freeman wrote.

Dugan was to leave the local kids to their own devices for a while.

On 18 May 1941, he called in to the army-recruiting centre in nearby Leichhardt to do his bit in the fight against Hitler. They checked him in as healthy and standing five feet six and a quarter inches in his stockinged feet.

Dugan quickly came to the view that the army was not for him.

The fourteen months of rigorous training at the Kapooka base near Wagga Wagga in southern NSW were more than enough, it appears.

On 22 July 1942 he shot through, returning to his suburb of grime and his life of crime. A military court of inquiry three weeks later came to the obvious conclusion that Dugan wanted nothing further to do with the military forces, and having declared himself absent without leave 'is still so absent'. The army rubberstamped a dishonourable discharge and Darcy went back to his younger mates and to stealing, only to be rounded up by the cops soon after. In the Sydney Quarter Sessions on 10 October he was convicted on a charge of robbery and received a sentence of two years' hard labour.

George Freeman was just nine years old when Dugan was back

on the streets. George, Stan Smith and others Freeman called the 'wild kids' spent little time at school, much more time in the snooker rooms and pool halls, where a good player could earn a bit of spare cash. A week after his twelfth birthday Freeman made his children's court debut. He was hauled before a magistrate in the old brick-and-sandstone building in Albion Street, Surry Hills – in those days conveniently located around the corner from the police's Criminal Investigation Branch (CIB) headquarters. In the basement were the small cells of the Metropolitan Boys' Shelter – the 'home' for boys awaiting trial.

In his first court appearance Freeman was charged with possession of an unlicensed pistol. His police record suggests that he had stolen an unattended parked car and removed some crockery and ornaments from the boot, which he sold to a receiver he regularly dealt with.

He was clearly well-organised even at that young age. When he was arrested, police found the gun in his coat pocket.

Despite the frequent expressions of concern from police about the growing prevalence of guns, the magistrate of the day went quite easy on the lad. He ordered the pistol be forfeited, of course, and then found the charges proven but didn't formally enter a conviction. With a stern lecture from the bench, Freeman was placed on a good-behaviour bond of £10 (*$606 in 2012 values*) for two years. If he broke the bond, he would face conviction – and a custodial sentence – on the firearm charge.

Freeman went back to petty theft and poolroom hustling, ensuring he would resolutely not 'be of good behaviour' for the next two years.

At the end of October 1947, just nine months after his first appearance in the stern Albion Street building, he was back before the beak.

This time he appeared at the Ashfield Children's Court, charged with stealing a sheath knife, fountain pens and some cash. The terms of his earlier bond were somehow overlooked, the gun charge forgotten, it appears, as he was placed on four years' probation to once again 'be of good behaviour'.

In his own tinted version of his life Freeman made it clear that over the following years he remained driven in his quest to become a major criminal, and kept on stealing as a way to reach that goal. But for a while at least he stayed out of reach of the law's long arm. He left school after he turned 14; he'd attended long enough to discover that he was a numbers whiz – a facility that would serve him well.

His mother, no doubt concerned by her youngest son's wayward lifestyle, found him a job. It was with a horse trainer named Charles McLoughlin, and George quickly took to it, even with its hard work in the stables, long hours and solitary day off a month. He found working with the horses exciting, and later claimed he could tell if a horse was fit just by looking at it. After a while, his equine knowledge helped him to pick winners at the races. His first winning bet, he said, was on Lady Rosetta, one of McLoughlin's horses, which won at the old Moorefield racetrack. It wouldn't be his last flutter.

Two years on and George had left his first – and only – steady job.

He'd reverted to his bad old habits with his bad old mates, hustling in the pool halls and stealing, and this time the law was quick to catch up with him. In 1951, at age 16, and within the space of 28 days, he had clocked up three convictions, two of them a long way from Sydney.

The first of the charges, this one for stealing, was heard in the Children's Court in Melbourne. Freeman must have experienced déjà vu when the magistrate gavelled and announced the penalty: a £10 good behaviour bond running till January 1953. A fortnight later George popped up in court at the NSW coastal town of Coffs Harbour charged with evading the fare for the train trip that brought him there. 'Fine: one pound, plus the unpaid fare,' snapped the judge. Another fortnight, another town, another court appearance. This time, back in the familiar surrounds of the Sydney Children's Court, he was fined £3 for 'using insulting words'. These counts were all relatively minor, recalling that his first case involved an unlawful pistol.

Just as an apprentice builder might think of grazed knuckles as signalling their initiation into the trade, one measure of an aspiring criminal's success is a term of imprisonment. George Freeman was to achieve this gong at the end of his hectic round of court appearances in 1951. He had been the unlicensed driver in a smash-and-grab raid, and on 28 December he faced the court charged with breaking, entering and stealing, illegal use of a motor vehicle, and stealing a car radio and electric fan.

He was sent off on a two-year term to the 'naughty boys' home', the Mount Penang Training School, situated on the big hill overlooking Gosford, just north of Sydney. It was a hard place for lads, with the longer-term and older inmates – and even some of the warders – known to bully and sexually assault new arrivals. George may have escaped the worst of the 'initiation' rites. He had little problem with the other inmates, it seems. What is clear is that he started a campaign of absolute disobedience with the officers, which ensured he copped his share of harsh punishment. As he later wrote:

> By now I was completely rebellious. I was rebelling against the system as soon as I arrived at the home. If the officers said to walk along this line I'd walk across it. If they'd order me to say that black was black I would argue all day that it was white. I was cheeky and I wouldn't work. I wanted to be a crook, nothing more, nothing less.

When the punishment regime inflicted on Freeman failed to curb his insubordinate behaviour, officials stamped 'Transfer to Tamworth: continual disorder' on his record and put him on the north-bound train to serve out the rest of his sentence at the brutal and brutalising Institution for Boys in Dean Street, Tamworth, in northern NSW.

Former criminal Bernie Matthews, author of *Intractable* – an account of his time in various boys' homes and jails – recorded an interview with a one-time Tamworth inmate, Keith Higgins.

> It was a cruel place. The screws were sadistic animals and attacked without warning. We were bashed and starved for no reason whatsoever. I remember one time

I was forced to stand with my nose touching the wall for some minor infringement of the rules. My arms were outstretched in a crucifix. After an hour or so my arms got tired and began slipping down. The screws got stuck into me. They bashed me every time my arms slipped. They eventually knocked me out and dumped me in a cell. They used to take our meals and halve them as punishment. Sometimes we didn't get a meal at all for 48 hours. Bouncing they called it, or being unprivileged. We were always hungry.

Bernie Matthews added, 'Tamworth Institution for Boys remains the Frankenstein monster of a bygone era. It was a monster the NSW Child Welfare Department cloaked in secrecy to brutalise and emotionally scar children in its care. It served no other useful purpose.' In 1976 the Tamworth facility was renamed 'Endeavour House' but continued to be used to lock up truants and other naughty boys, albeit with a somewhat improved policy for dealing with its inmates.

The time George Freeman spent at Tamworth only consolidated his determination to become a criminal, as it did for so many of its young prisoners. In a desperate attempt to be moved to another home, he ate a lump of laundry soap. Freeman became so ill that the warders called a doctor, who diagnosed George as suffering from acute appendicitis. He was taken – under guard – to the local hospital and operated on. But four days later he was again in the dreaded institution and within a month he was back to the usual demoralising slog of hard work and beatings. Towards the end of his sentence, two weeks before his 18th birthday, Freeman was sent back to the Mount Penang reformatory, presumably to prepare him for a return to 'normal' society. But now, more than ever, he didn't aspire to normality,

* * *

On the beat once more, Freeman teamed up again with Stan Smith and, with their gang, got back to the business of stealing. On Friday afternoons, if they weren't 'booked' for a job, they would often scale a tram into the city and join the great clan of thieves, pickpockets, touts and spivs that gathered for end-of-week drinks at the Marble Bar in the Pitt Street entrance of Adams Hotel (now the site of the Hilton Hotel, where the old bar was reinstalled – without its traditional clientele).

It was a lively spot: patrons would be offered the same watch at a bargain price twice in the same evening – by different hawkers. One would sell it; another would steal it from the buyer and flog it again.

It was that sort of a crowd and casual visitors were wise to protect the contents of their pockets – and what they wore on their wrists. Being a year or so underage rarely stopped lads from buying a beer or two in those days; George, who later claimed to be a non-drinker, and Stan were among the regulars there during the mid-1950s. Their fun and games in the ornate bar would end at six o'clock every evening when the pubs closed, but on 1 February 1955 the anti-social 'six o'clock swill' hours became a thing of the past. The bars were now legally allowed to stay open until 10 p.m.

Freeman in this period stepped things up a notch, graduating to breaking into premises in order to steal things. While the rewards were greater, it was a higher risk strategy, with the penalties being more severe than those imposed for pinching from local shops and parked cars, as he was about to learn.

On 3 February 1954 a young Queen Elizabeth II and the older Duke she had married arrived in Sydney at the start of their two-month-long royal tour of Australia. The large crowds that crammed into the city to see the couple alight from the royal barge at Farm Cove contained few if any of Freeman's cohort. Stan Smith for one was far too preoccupied: he'd been arrested that morning and charged with assault, for which he was later convicted and fined.

Freeman also had other engagements. He had been caught, charged and committed in the Magistrates Court to stand trial for some seriously bad behaviour. In the Sydney Quarter Sessions that took place in early February, a jury found him guilty on break-and-enter and auto theft charges. The judge, appropriately named Holden, sent him down to Long Bay Gaol at Malabar, the state penitentiary 11 kilometres south of the city, for a week while he pondered an apt punishment for this miscreant. Freeman recalled the experience:

> Going through those big green gates at 'the Bay', I felt a mixture of excitement and dread. Gaol: this was the big time. A bit like, I suppose, the way other kids thought of going to university. Yes, there was some cockiness, even a touch of pride. But there was fear. This was the big time. This was not a boys' home, this was a place for men.

Indeed, he was no longer a boy: he was now, at 19, a five-foot-eight-inch (1.7m)-tall man. In the prison records he is described as being of medium build, with a 'fresh' complexion, brown hair and hazel eyes.

On the final day of the royal visit to Sydney, 19 February, the city was recovering from its hottest day in eight years, when the thermometer had pushed past 35.5 degrees Celsius. As the Black Maria drove Freeman from Long Bay to again face Judge Holden, the day already had the makings of another scorcher. Back in court for sentencing, Freeman was given his first adult prison sentence by the judge, who clearly had not been impressed with the criminal's lean-faced good looks nor the polite demeanour with which he had faced the man on the bench; Holden packed him off to jail for three years.

Freeman was sent to Parramatta Gaol to serve the time – and there caught up with his teen years' idol, Darcy Dugan. With remissions, Freeman was out in 12 months. It had been a time of learning new skills – mostly from other inmates – including that of safe-breaking using oxyacetylene torches and explosives. 'Suddenly a whole new trade was opening up,' he wrote later. On his release and as a condition of his parole, Freeman was sent to work in the state abattoir at Homebush, but before long he started putting his new-found burglary skills into practice. His entry in the *Australasian Criminal Register* – a yearly catalogue of the region's top criminals produced by the NSW Police Fingerprint

Department up until 1976 – notes a few of his post-prison activities.

> Perpetrated numerous robberies from clubhouses, hotels and shops in New South Wales and the Australian Capital Territory, stealing property valued at many thousands of dollars. At times safes were opened on the premises or transported away and later opened in bushland with explosive charges. Stolen motor vehicles were frequently used as a means of transport.

In 1955 Freeman paid another visit to Melbourne. He probably thought later that he'd have been better off staying at home: George was nabbed and convicted for possession of house-breaking implements and sent off to Pentridge Prison for three months. Back in Sydney, having broken the terms of his earlier parole, he was locked up again to complete the full term of the original sentence, which had been set to end in February 1957. He was moved around from one prison to another during this stay, and it was at Long Bay Gaol in 1956 that he met the man the kids in the street referred to only in whispers: Leonard McPherson. The stage was now set for George Freeman to really move into the big time.

2. Taking a peep at the big time

Small crimes always precede great ones.
– Jean Baptiste Racine

Leonard Arthur McPherson was *the* name among the young criminals in Sydney's inner suburbs. By the mid-1950s Stan Smith had already spoken to George Freeman in glowing terms of the tough man from Balmain. The way Smith painted him made McPherson seem every bit the leader. He stole cars for fun and was the first of the gang lads to have his own motorbike. Stan had met him a few times, and even been tagged with a moniker by McPherson. It was a coming-of-age moment for 20-year-old Stan, and the tag was to stick to him for life: the brown-haired, brown-eyed wannabe gangster was from then on referred to as 'Stan "The Man" Smith'.

McPherson was 14 years older than Freeman, and the two had strikingly similar criminal histories. Lennie was 11 – a year younger than Freeman had been – when he'd first fronted up at the Children's Court on a charge of stealing, earning his first good-behaviour bond.

McPherson was back in Albion Street for stealing 18 months later. His bond was renewed for a year, but within 35 days he was back again, facing two further charges of stealing. This time he was sent to Mount Penang boys' home. He was just 13; Freeman had been 16 when he was sent there. McPherson was 25 when he first entered an adult prison, convicted for stealing – again – in February 1946; Freeman had been 19.

Their early police records bore similarities, but McPherson differed from Freeman in significant ways. Lennie had married and started a family at a younger age, albeit in a dysfunctional manner. In early 1939 he met Dawn Joy Allan, then 15, who lived with her parents. She fell pregnant to him and they ran away, but soon returned and were persuaded – chiefly by the Allans – to get married. They visited the Sydney Registry office early in 1940, after their baby was born. A police report written on 31 January 1940 described the situation:

> McPherson is a married man, has one child aged eight months and prior to being married he ran away with his wife, then Miss Allan of North Street, Balmain, and since his marriage he has frequently quarrelled with his wife and her parents. He is a man of peculiar disposition – he is not addicted to drink and is regarded as a reasonably good worker but he believes that his wife's people are tempted to do him some injury and when in this frame of mind he is most peculiar in his manner.

The long-suffering Dawn put up with his brutish violence for 20 years before finally leaving him.

In 1941 McPherson had developed a skill that earned him the awed respect of the local street kids: bomb-making. In November of that year, while working as a driller at the Mort's Dock shipyards in Balmain – then providing maintenance to Australian wartime naval vessels – McPherson had made three bombs using galvanised pipe and homemade chemical explosive.

He had taken the bombs to his home nearby at 21 Roseberry Street, where one of them was exploded – by a mate of his while McPherson was out, he later told curious police. He had taken the remaining two bombs and hidden them in a cleaner's hut at the works, where they were found by a leading hand. Police were called and McPherson was arrested and taken to the local police station, where a detective took his statement and rattled off an urgent message up the line to determine whether McPherson should be dealt with under wartime Regulation Number Eight of the National Security (Firearms and Explosives) Regulations. Lennie had stayed in the Balmain lock-up until Deputy Director of Public Prosecutions George Watson notified the police that 'the Commonwealth does not propose to proceed in this matter' and that 'McPherson should be released'. No further explanation was given. Had Watson's advice gone the other way, it would have certainly meant a long jail term for Lennie.

There was a further achievement that placed Lennie McPherson head and shoulders above Freeman and other local aspiring crims: in 1951 he had visited America and made contact with a few minor US Mafia figures. McPherson had long idolised the Chicagoan gangster Al Capone, and so after his 30th birthday, he embarked on a US 'study tour'. On his return to Australia he was fined £100 ($3,867) for using a false passport – made out in his brother's name, 'because with convictions you can't get a US visa,' he told the court – and was placed on a £20 ($773.40) three-year good-behaviour bond. But that had proved an impossible ask as two years later he was back behind bars. McPherson had been jailed again, for three and a half years on a break, enter and steal conviction. He was then 32, and it was while serving out this sentence that he met Freeman at Long Bay.

His release on 19 October 1956 marked a hiatus in McPherson's jail sentences that would last for many years, and apart from a few overnight stays while awaiting court appearances, he would never again spend time behind the harsh bluestone walls of Long Bay Gaol.

It was around then that McPherson, through associations with some corrupt senior cops, began to experience the benefits of being a police informer. One of the plusses of ratting to cops about the activities of fellow crims was immunity from prosecution, and this would protect McPherson for almost the rest of his life, despite the fact that over time he'd prove to be a mass murderer.

His new fan, Freeman, had not yet reached such elevated criminal status; he had more time to spend in the clink before he would make the same sorts of professional associations as McPherson. It was only a couple of months after his 1957 release from jail that he was again caught on the job. This time, with two fellow felons, the Rowntree brothers, he had broken into and robbed two H. G. Palmer electrical shops, one at Campsie, the other at Marrickville. They had taken the safes from each shop, and using George's newly acquired facility with oxyacetylene to open them, shared the spoils – £8000 ($225,282.23) – between them. They then dumped the safes on disused land at Bankstown, and police later found traces of paint from one of them in the boot of Freeman's car. Freeman claimed the police planted that evidence, but never denied he'd organised the robbery.

In the ponderous way in which the law operates, it took ten months for the case to come to court – during which time George had been refused bail – and in 1959 he was sentenced to a three-year jail term.

It was during this latest stretch behind bars that someone approached Freeman 'to do a McPherson' – to become a police informer, known in the trade as a 'fizgig', a term that's been part of Australian vernacular since the goldfield days. The offer came from a notoriously corrupt detective, Frederick Krahe, who ran his own organised-crime operations from within the NSW Police department. Freeman rejected Krahe's proposition – probably on advice from McPherson, who was dealing with another crooked faction in the force. When he wasn't released on bail while awaiting trial, Freeman blamed a 'false' police record of interview, in which Freeman had purportedly confessed to his crime. It had been Krahe who tendered the document to the court.

Freeman explained how Krahe operated a 'pricing scheme' in his dealings with crooks:

> After he'd arrest you, the paying began. You'd pay him to get bail, you'd pay some more later for a reduced sentence, you'd pay for remands, you'd pay for whether or not he gave verbal evidence against you, and you'd pay again if he decided not to give evidence against you at all.

Another copper who would have a profound impact on events in George Freeman's life came onto the scene in 1961. Roger Caleb Rogerson, then aged 21, had been appointed to a police division that was to become notoriously corrupt – and remain so for many years – the 21 Division (Gaming Squad). The division

Fred Krahe, killer cop

Frederick Claude Krahe was born in the northern NSW town of Kyogle on 16 November 1919. At the age of 18, on April Fools' Day 1937, he was one of 17 local lads to sign up for the NSW Police Force. No one in the same intake would make such a name, or as unsavoury a reputation, for himself as Fred Krahe.

Over his career he developed close associations with detectives Ray 'The Gunner' Kelly (also known as 'Verbal' for his creative and forceful work extracting criminals' confessions) and Don Fergusson. Under the corrupt leadership of Commissioner Fred Hanson, these rogue police took control of most major criminal activities and extorted massive graft payments from gangsters, who preferred paying the cash rather than doing the time. Krahe was particularly involved in extracting graft payments from illegal abortionists.

By early 1970 Fergusson had fallen out with Kelly and Krahe. Shortly afterwards, Fergusson (by then a superintendent) was found shot dead in the toilets at the CIB, his service revolver by his side.

A morgue worker told me that the first autopsy showed that Fergusson had sustained two bullet wounds to the head, and that they'd been shot at a range of three metres. 'He must have had very long arms and very quick reflexes,' noted my source. A second report was quickly prepared and adopted as the official version.

According to the latter account, Fergusson was known to be deeply depressed and had fired a single shot to his head from his own revolver at point-blank range.

In 1971 Krahe's association with a prostitute, Shirley Brifman, was exposed. He allegedly killed Brifman (or organised her murder) in March 1972 by forcing her to take an overdose of sleeping tablets. He was never charged or tried for this crime.

Shortly after Brifman's murder, Commissioner Fred Hanson approved Krahe's early retirement, complete with full pension, on health grounds. Krahe claimed to have thrombosis in his leg. (Premier Neville Wran later joked with me that Krahe's 'health problem' could have come from 'kicking too many people to death'.) Krahe was later engaged as a security adviser to developer Frank Theeman in Kings Cross, helping to evict squatters from houses slotted for redevelopment and using more than a modest amount of violence. Infamously, anti-development campaigner Juanita Nielsen was murdered in 1975. Lennie McPherson later told a senior federal policeman that he had rejected the contract to kill Nielsen, but that it had been taken up 'by the man that killed Don Fergusson in the CIB' – a clear allusion (so the source told me) to Fred Krahe.

Writer Barry Ward and I in 1976 made a statutory declaration that Krahe had 'committed or organised' with three others the 1975 murder of Kings Cross activist Juanita Nielsen, but few in positions of authority wanted to hear such information about this vicious man.

In the mid-1970s Krahe was briefly employed by *The Sun* newspaper in Sydney, although his main contribution was to prevent stories exposing police corruption from seeing the light of day. He died of cancer on 6 December 1981.

had responsibility, among other matters, for prosecuting illegal SP bookmakers. Rogerson quickly became close to Freeman, an association that was to last a long time.

* * *

It's maybe appropriate that a man as keen on making money as Freeman became a dough-maker at Parramatta Gaol. Freeman, who had by this time stopped fighting the authorities, had been sent to work in the prison bakery; after a couple of years he was even promoted to head kneader. He was also the jail bookie, taking bets of 'a shilling, half an ounce of tobacco, food, whatever was available'. He would expand of this line of work once he was released.

While George was serving this latest sentence, a change occurred in the outside world that he'd later have to come to terms with. Norm Allan took over as NSW Police Commissioner. Stepping down was Colin John Delaney, who was retiring after having held the top job for ten years. Biographer Garry Wotherspoon noted that Delaney 'never really solved the problem of institutionalised corruption within the force.'

Freeman was only back on the streets for a year before he was arrested in 1962 for stealing stockings from a shop (presumably

Norm Allan's promotion: 'Foreman' gets the boss's job

Norman Thomas William Allan was born at Lithgow, west of Sydney, on 3 June 1909.

Allan signed up to become a cop when, at the age of 20, he'd been retrenched from his first job as a junior telephone technician.

He spent the early 1930s as a police prosecutor at the central Criminal Court, transferring to police headquarters in 1938. Known as 'Norman the Foreman' to some and 'the mushroom' (kept in the dark and fed on bullshit) to others, he took over as police commissioner on 28 February 1962, having served for 18 years as assistant to three former commissioners. Ten years later when Sergeant Philip Arantz accused Allan of falsifying crime clean-up figures, Allan tried to have Arantz declared insane. That failed, but Arantz left the force without a pension.

In Allan's biography, Evan Whitton suggests that a long-established culture of corruption had become more deeply entrenched during Allan's term as chief commissioner, and that NSW Premier Bob Askin supported Allan because 'they had established an arrangement under which thousands of dollars weekly in bribes and payments were handed over by the gambling clubs'. After ten years in the job, Allan retired with a generous pension and successfully recommended that Fred Hanson take over his job. Allan died on 28 January 1977, aged 68.

to sell, not to wear). He had teamed up with Australia's infamous international shoplifting team led by Arthur Delaney, a dapper man eight years older than Freeman. By 1973, the year of his last Australasian Criminal Register (ACR) listing, Delaney had a long history of shop theft and 110 arrests in NSW, Victoria and Queensland, and in England to his credit, mostly on stealing charges.

Delaney operated under the protective hand of an old-fashioned criminal and corrupter of police and politicians, Charles 'Paddles' Anderson (the nickname referred to his extra-large feet), but that did not stop the cops putting details of Delaney's exploits into their records.

'He is Australia's – and possibly the world's – most active thief,' the ACR reads. 'Delaney has been expert in forming large gangs of thieves around him to perpetrate large-scale robberies. He is a criminal of international repute, known to police in many countries as "The Duke".' An earlier listing in the 1967 edition described him as 'an incorrigible thief, addicted to liquor, and associates with prostitutes and criminals'. When Freeman teamed up with the Duke, he joined a colourful group of thieves, including:

Cecil Lloyd, then aged 40, who had just pulled off his biggest heist, snaring diamond rings worth around £10,000 ($259,038) from a jewellery shop in Geelong, south of Melbourne. His fingerprints were already on file in New Scotland Yard and at police headquarters in Paris and Zurich, where he had been on shoplifting sprees with Delaney.

Richard Jarvis, originally from Victoria, was 36 when Freeman joined the gang. From 1946 he was a regular before the courts on stealing charges. A year before Freeman joined up, Jarvis had failed to appear in a Victorian court on a larceny charges and a month later was convicted in Sydney's Paddington Court of possessing stolen goods.

James Roland Wilson, then 35, had been in the stealing game with Delaney for around seven years when Freeman came on board. He had a lengthy record as a thief, with one of his biggest hauls being the theft of a load of clothing, blankets and liquor from a railway-goods truck in Henty, Victoria.

Harold O'Brien, known as 'Rastus' to his mates, hailed from New Zealand, and at 58 was the elder statesman of this gang of thieves. His police file describes him as a confidence man, forger, thief and shoplifter. One of his strategies was to fly interstate for a stealing spree, before quickly flying back to Sydney and deliberately drawing police's attention for a minor matter, seeking to create an alibi for the interstate job.

There appears to be something of a 'keystone cops' farce about the gang: members of this crew – including Freeman – were frequently arrested during the 1960s yet have gone down in

Australian criminal folklore as 'the great international shoplifting gang'. This is yet more evidence of the public's perverse fascination with and glorification of criminals.

On 5 February 1963 Freeman made another 'team' commitment: he got married. Marcia McDonald had six years earlier married at Marrickville, but that partnership failed and they were later divorced. Now she was throwing in her lot with George Freeman in an exchange of vows at the Sydney Registry Office. It was a move that may have fatefully persuaded the groom to consider a change of business.

3. Stealing or gambling? George has an each-way bet

Another great evil arising from this desire to be thought rich, is the destructive thing which has been honoured by the name of 'speculation'; but which ought to be called gambling.
– William Cobbett, British journalist, reformer

By the mid-1960s Freeman's rather inept attempts at thieving and shoplifting were being supplemented by another activity, albeit one at which he showed greater talent. He became involved in illegally taking bets on horseracing, known widely as starting price (SP) bookmaking, which for the rest of his days would be his major business interest.

SP bookies paid winners on fixed odds, those at which the horse had officially been backed at the start of the race – hence 'starting price'.

The only lawful form of gambling in those days took place on the course or racetrack, so the SP game was no less illegal than stealing. It was, however, an industry that enjoyed widespread support from and protection by police, most of whom earned a few quid on the side – or a free bet on a Saturday races winner – for allowing the trade to continue at pubs in suburbs and towns all over the country. But George Freeman's foray into bookmaking and a government move to stamp out the practice were to profoundly affect how SP gambling operated over the ensuing years.

In 1963 George Freeman had gone into a partnership with an

SP bookie at the Henson Park Hotel in Marrickville, investing some of his ill-gotten gains. The venture was not an immediate success, however, and this was Freeman's excuse for not giving away his other activities.

As he puts it, 'Everybody thought I was out of the stealing business because of the SP. The truth was, more often than not, I was forced back into safe robberies and shoplifting because I was doing my money SP betting.' For more than three years he worked with the bookie, whose regular pay cheque came from being the local butcher. Freeman became the bookie's bodyguard when there were big collections to be made from losing punters, and claimed the man taught him how to pick winners.

His earlier experience with horses at McLoughlin's stables now also came in handy. When his SP mentor died, Freeman teamed up with a big-time bookie, 'Melbourne' Mick Bartley (also known among winning punters as 'Deaf Mick'). The relationship was to last for some years. The money began to roll in, but Freeman still had the stealing bug itching away. He paid for his and Marcia's first house not from the proceeds of SP wins but from those of a pre-Christmas robbery of a large city store.

He and an offsider had hidden themselves in the shop before closing time and after midnight cracked the safe. He later told a mate the safe had contained 'more money than you've seen in your life'.

Had Freeman made an actuarial assessment of his new line of business he would have been impressed: a decade earlier, in 1951–52, NSW SP bookies had made a profit estimated to be around £17 million (*$657 million*). By 1962 this figure had risen to £28 million (*$725 million*). The industry's turnover was ten times these amounts. There had been, however, a shadow looming over SP gambling. In 1962 Supreme Court Justice Edward 'Ted' Kinsella started his year-long royal commission into off-course betting – an inquiry into the illegal SP industry.

The Kinsella inquiry estimated there was one SP bookmaker to every 700 people in the state. In an effort to stymie the growth of underground betting Kinsella's report recommended, among other moves, that a state-run totalisator agency board (TAB) be established.

While there were many forces working against this – not the least of which was Liberal MP and soon-to-be-Premier Bob Askin – the first off-course TAB branches in NSW opened for business on 9 December 1964, after a determined effort by Labor Premier Robert 'Bob' Heffron.

However, this did not toll the death knell for the SP bookies as many had predicted. The racket continued to survive, sometimes as large telephone set-ups in suburban offices but most usually in the pubs where it had always thrived, in the corners of bars close to the phone, up and down the country. The SPs had a distinct advantage over legal gambling outfits in that they paid no tax to the state. But in the face of legal competition for SP, its main supporters quickly realised that what they needed was an improved protection system – a better insurance policy. This would come from on high.

Robert (born Robin) Askin had run an SP bookie operation in his wartime army unit between 1942 and 1946, and in a civilian job at the Rural Bank, where his gambling interests earned him the nickname 'Slippery Sam'. Askin had won the leadership of the state Liberal Party in 1959 but failed to oust the Labor government in the March 1962 election. Gearing up for his next chance to win government, he campaigned heavily to legalise SP telephone betting, which would legitimise Freeman's main line of illegal business. Although Askin failed in this, he would go on to directly support Freeman and others in the illicit trade.

In the run-up to the state election on 1 May 1965, Askin received significant financial backing from illegal SP operators and the legal on-course bookmakers, who were concerned about their business being cannibalised by the TAB. As Freeman says in his book, 'You'd have to be a fool not to think that someone was being paid off.' Askin won the 1965 election.

Author David Hickie said of Askin in the ABC-TV documentary *The Track*, 'He understood the fact that in every suburban shopping centre there was SP betting activity going on every Saturday afternoon. And he understood that this was a very good source of campaign funds for anybody who allowed them to operate and, more importantly, there was a bit of a no-win situation in trying to crack down on it. He "encouraged" the connection between ... the SP bookies and the government.' On-course – and often controversial – bookmaker William 'Bill' Waterhouse acknowledged on the same program that bookies 'gave generously to his [Askin's] election costs and encouraged their clients to vote for him'.

Well-known professional punter Arthur Harris provided more colourful detail: 'Askin, as the Premier of New South Wales, really looked after the SPs. Instead of all the SPs having to pay the local cop – they now had to only pay one man. And the bag-man used to go into City Tatts, and I've seen this, and the bag person used to collect the tribute from the SPs, once a month.'

* * *

While he was working with Mick Bartley, Freeman's friendship with Lennie McPherson grew. They met frequently and, sensing an opportunity, the older man took the younger under his wing. The 'corporatisation' of the SP business under Askin had aroused McPherson's interest, and he could envision a role for himself under the new arrangements, one which would result in a significant increase in his 'commission' payments. McPherson would have been quick to see that George Freeman – who had already established himself as a major force in the SP business and set up substantial and protective links with a few grafting cops – was ideally placed to secure even greater control over the tide of illegal gambling dollars.

In grooming Freeman for a more involved role in the Sydney underworld, McPherson revealed details of his working relationship with certain corrupt police – how his unique 'insurance policy' worked.

In a dangerous game where information is used as currency, McPherson's kickback for ratting on fellow crims eventually became total immunity from prosecution: he and his favoured mates were left alone and even encouraged in their enterprises as money found its way into the pockets of crooked cops – and those of their political supporters.

McPherson's rise from the mid-1950s onwards to become the undisputed Mr Big of the Sydney crime scene came about after he did deals with a rough, tough man, one who was on his way to becoming the copper who controlled most of a very bent NSW Police Force: Ray Kelly.

Ray Kelly, killer cop Raymond
William Kelly was born on 3 February 1906 at Wellington in central western NSW. At the age of 27 he married Mary Barnes, a salesgirl. Two years later he signed up to the police force and started patrolling the inner-Sydney suburbs. He soon earned the moniker 'The Gunner' thanks to his heavy-handed style. Five months into the job, he chased down a stolen car on a bicycle and fired five shots into the vehicle, killing one of the occupants and injuring the other two.

He was promoted to detective in 1941 and from then on chiefly worked out of the CIB. It was Ray Kelly who in 1950 had arrested Freeman's boyhood idol, Darcy Dugan – and who would do so three more times after Darcy's repeated escapes from jail. By 1953 Kelly had become head of the Safe-breaking Squad (described as 'aptly named' by one wag, who reckoned in those days the cops broke into more safes than the crims). In March that same year Kelly shot and killed fleeing bank robber Lloyd Day, strengthening his reputation as a ruthless killer.

Throughout the 1950s and '60s Ray Kelly was quite open about his friendships with renowned illegal abortionist Dr Reginald Stuart-Jones, illegal gamblers Perc Galea and Joe Taylor, and leading Sydney gangster Paddles Anderson. Kelly rose to inspector rank in 1960 and retired in 1966. He used criminal informants and ensured that while some were protected, arrest rates remained high. A former Crime Squad detective told me that 'Kelly ran McPherson for many years. He ran a lot of other criminal activities but McPherson was his main point of contact with the crims – his major fizgig [informer]'.

Ray Kelly died on 11 August 1977, aged 71.

For McPherson, the arrangement with Ray Kelly had a dual advantage. As well guaranteeing him immunity from prosecution, by reporting to the cop on the activities of other crims, Lennie could finger opponents – and rising threats to his own leadership – ensuring their arrest and incarceration. Kelly once said to a couple of younger cops who had arrested Lennie after catching him red-handed in a break-and-enter robbery, 'Leave McPherson to me in future.' The set-up had inherent dangers; it created a great many enemies for McPherson, and over the years he developed a deep paranoia about his personal safety.

At the start of their relationship, Kelly and McPherson would meet at the Hollywood Hotel, just down from the old CIB headquarters, which had for years been located in 'temporary' premises, a former hat factory in Campbell Street, Surry Hills. Other trusted cops would join them for a beer-soaked afternoon in which McPherson would pass on pieces of intelligence to Kelly, who would immediately direct his juniors to take prompt action against those named.

Over time the operation became more sophisticated, and McPherson used a reel-to-reel tape recorder to compile a monthly report on activities taking place on the bad side of town. One low-level crim told me he once saw a uniquely marked tape reel in McPherson's home, and a week later spotted the same identifiable reel on Ray Kelly's desk at the CIB. Kelly had grinned at my informant and said, 'That's McPherson's monthly report on you lot!' During the long McPherson-Kelly alliance, which lasted until the cop's retirement in 1966, Lennie literally got away with murder.

At around eleven o'clock on the night of 27 July 1959, McPherson and his trusted offsider Louis 'Snowy' Rayner shot and killed a small-time crim, George Hackett, in Elswick Street, Leichhardt. McPherson himself revealed this in a remarkable letter to an accomplice, Chris Campbell, which he dictated while awaiting a court appearance in relation to the murder: 'We had to knock Hackett because he had a big mouth when he was drunk. We surrendered to Verbal [Ray Kelly] and there are no statements...' The murder case against McPherson failed when a key witness, Hilton Clayton, refused to testify. McPherson's letter had stated, 'Clayton won't talk, he's been seen.' On the night of his second wedding, 9 July 1963, using Freeman's mate Stan Smith as a driver, McPherson shot dead 26-year-old Robert 'Pretty Boy' Walker, a crim who'd upset a few of the in-crowd. Once again Ray Kelly took control of the murder investigation. McPherson and Smith were not even charged.

In 1965 Robert 'Jacky' Steele, aged 50, had been heard claiming to be the biggest, toughest crim in Sydney, saying that Lennie McPherson had nothing on him. Steele, who had started his criminal career at the age of 15, was gunned down by rifle and shotgun blasts from a car as he walked home from the Nelson Hotel in Woollahra on 26 November; he later died in hospital.

Eventually police charged John Andrew Stuart, who copped a ten-year sentence. He was not involved in Steele's death. Stuart was later also convicted over the Whiskey Au Go Go firebomb murders in Brisbane in which 15 people died on 8 March 1973. Till his end, he protested his innocence in that affair, claiming he was the victim of a police 'verbal'. He died in Brisbane's Boggo Road Gaol.

At around 3.10 a.m. on Sunday, 28 May 1967 revellers were still going at it at Sammy Lee's Latin Quarter nightclub in Pitt Street, Sydney, when Lenny McPherson shot and killed another loud-mouthed crim, Raymond 'Ducky' O'Connor. Two CIB detectives, Maurie Wild and Jack Whelan, were there looking on. It was to be reported as an unsolved gangland killing. Even 18 months after Kelly had retired, McPherson was still being protected. It wouldn't be the last time, either.

Freeman's close association with McPherson meant he would have quickly learnt about his friend's murderous history, and, as an aspiring criminal, he would have been in awe of McPherson's ability to avoid prosecution. Teaming up with a criminal the likes of whom had a good working arrangement with Kelly would have definitely seemed a step in the right direction.

Freeman recalled in his memoir that Ray Kelly had once

arrested him for a safe-breaking job; the crook denied his involvement. During questioning, Freeman claimed, Kelly hit him on the chin, and Freeman 'screamed abuse at him'. After an exchange of threats, another policeman warned Freeman that he could not talk to Ray Kelly like that. 'He was right,' wrote Freeman.

> A week later I was driving along the road, minding my own business when I was pulled over by the police. Before I knew it there was a gun found in my car that just wasn't there to begin with. I was convicted and fined but it could have been a lot worse. It was just a warning – and a pay-back for abusing Mr Kelly.

* * *

In 1965 an American gangster came to town. Joseph Testa from Chicago was a lower-level Mafia man. His visit marked the first known contact between American mobsters and their Australian counterparts since McPherson's visit to the US in 1951. The story goes that Testa was on a trip to Hong Kong, where he was given a letter of introduction to Sydney illegal gambling heavyweight Ronnie Lee. Ronnie was then a partner to Joe Taylor in the Kellett Club – a favourite Freeman haunt – and later ran the Forbes Club, just across the road from the ABC newsroom in Darlinghurst, and a stone's throw from Kings Cross.

In comparison to later visits made by Testa, this appeared to be a low-key affair, though that could simply be because little official surveillance took place during his seven-day stay. Indeed an unidentified federal police officer later stated that the immigration department had not even alerted them to Testa's arrival in the country. There is no detailed record of his activities in Sydney, but he was shown around the illegal gambling clubs, and would have undoubtedly met leading criminals like Paddles Anderson, then just 50 but already suffering the ravages of alcoholism, and Lennie McPherson, and probably Freeman, Stan Smith and a few others.

Ronnie Lee and Testa regularly corresponded after the Mafia man had returned to Chicago, but at that stage, the big American gangsters showed little interest in developing business in Australia.

As we will see, time changed that view, and Testa would develop a lasting relationship with members of the Sydney criminal milieu, particularly George Freeman.

* * *

In mid-1966 Freeman and McPherson discussed the idea of expanding their criminal activities into the Far East, but Freeman, possibly feeling bound by his commitment to bookie Mick Bartley, declined the offer of an exploratory ocean cruise. They decided Stan Smith should take the trip with McPherson, and in July the duo shipped out to Japan, planning to call in at a number of Asian ports en route.

It was a fiasco: Ray Kelly had retired by that stage, and McPherson's main contacts within the police were Jack McNeill, then head of the newly formed Armed Hold-up Squad, and Roger Rogerson, who was with the 21 Division, which 'looked after' illegal gambling. Between them, they failed to do what Kelly would have done: prevent a routine police alert from being sent to the forces at each of the crims' ports of call.

McPherson and Smith were met by the boys in blue at every stop and blocked from going ashore to meet their local contacts. An extract from one police report sent back to Sydney said of the duo, 'They seemed rather proud of their criminal background and somewhat boastfully admitted that although they had come to Hong Kong purely for a holiday, they would have seized any opportunity to "get in on the big time" (as they put it) smuggling gold and narcotics.' The two returned to Sydney empty-handed, any opportunity for global expansion stymied – but certainly not abandoned.

Freeman had had his own problems to deal with: his wife Marcia, concerned that her husband was 'cuddling up' to a cold-blooded killer – and a few warm-blooded young women at the casinos he frequented – decided that husband number two had been a bad choice.

The pair separated. Helping her reach the decision was Freeman's predilection for late-night visits to Joe Taylor's Kellett Club in Kings Cross, where he'd arrange liaisons with the young attractive women who worked as croupiers and escorts. As Freeman writes of this period:

> At the time playing the horses wasn't my only pastime. Joe would say to me: 'Why don't you take one of these broads home with you?' referring to the croupiers and other workers in the club. I'd joke with him: 'Joe, I've had them all, get some new starters.'

After the split, Freeman tried a change of scenery, going to London for a six-week visit. He caught up with a few old mates: shoplifter Alexander Low and his associates Jack Callaghan and Dick Emont, who he joined on a few shoplifting expeditions in the city before returning home. His relationship with Marcia remained in limbo for 11 years, until in 1977 when the divorce proceedings were finalised. George would remain single – but presumably not lonely – until 1981.

* * *

George took a few days off from the SP business and he, Stan Smith and a few mates went to Western Australia for a hit-and-run shoplifting spree.

In this gang was his erstwhile London host Alexander Low, now back on home soil. The 44-year-old had been known to police from the time he was charged as a juvenile for stealing a car. He had gone on to an active life of stealing from shops throughout Australia and England. Unlike a lot of shoplifters, Low was considered by police to be a dangerous man; he was known go into jobs armed and was prepared to resort to violence.

Even more 'heavy' was team member William Joseph Stevens, listed in the ACR as an 'armed assailant, murderer, gunman, shop stealer and thief'. They teamed up in Perth with a local thief, Judith Shirley Campbell, who was used as a decoy to distract shop staff while the others stole whatever cash they could find in the office or cashier sections. In just two days they had raided 16 stores in the city area and nearby towns. They had netted around $7000 ($77,287), which they would have considered not too bad for a couple of days' work. The problem struck when they arrived at the airport for the flight home: the cops were waiting for them. They were all arrested and the money recovered before the team had even had time to buy celebratory drinks at the airport bar.

Freeman later wrote that the thought that crossed his mind as the men in blue marched them off was, 'Bugger this, there has to be a better way of making a living.' A short term inside the jail at Fremantle surely would have confirmed that view. It was to be his last stretch inside: his status would reflect his surname. He had graduated to become a protected person, under the indemnifying insurance that Lennie McPherson was able to extend to close and trusted friends, and George David Freeman had been slotted for a major role in developing McPherson's crime territory.

4. Reaching for the top – into deals with Mr Big

> Curst greed of gold, what crimes thy
> tyrant power has caused.
> – *Virgil*

Over the years Lennie McPherson declared many times that George Freeman was his closest mate. But it was more than friendship that brought Freeman into McPherson's inner sanctum. McPherson was constructing a crime empire to fulfil his aspirations not just to be a major criminal (as were George's) but to control crime in the region.

Freeman held a powerful position in the illegal SP racket and while McPherson had some influence in that area, he had not yet been able to wield much influence. Freeman, he reasoned, was someone he could trust who would provide the missing link in his territory.

One area where McPherson was already well developed was in standover activities. A standover man is broadly defined as someone of a thuggish demeanour who readily uses violence to extract money from people, an act generally described as extortion. The money might be paid as insurance, protecting the victim from those threatening them with violence. Another role for the standover man is to collect debts from slow-paying, losing clients of illegal SP bookmakers or casino operators, and McPherson was fully equipped to provide such a service to Freeman – and other operators. Indeed, in due course, McPherson's success with intimidation ensured he was the major collector of SP bad debts and protection money in Sydney. A mere phone call from the hulking brute, whose reputation was eclipsed only by his the size of his ego, was generally sufficient to produce a prompt payment to the waiting bookie. A generous commission would go to the debt collector too, of course.

In his days with Mick Bartley, Freeman travelled up and down the east coast of Australia carrying large wads of Bartley's cash (and plenty of his own) to wager on the gallopers, trotters and greyhounds. In his travels he made invaluable connections that enabled him over time to move into his own business. With Lennie McPherson but a call away for Freeman, Mick Bartley was not about to complain when George went his own way, becoming a direct competitor. For Freeman, with the flow of tax-free money and McPherson's access to the most venal cops in the force (which guaranteed them freedom in their choice of enterprise), it must have seemed like the power and the glory.

One old hand – who prefers anonymity – recalled a house in Maroubra Junction run by Freeman, where bets were collated from SP bookies all over Sydney. There were dozens of phones connected, and my source and some of his workmates from a nearby factory did an extra shift or two helping out Freeman's regulars on busy race days. Another source suggests that Freeman controlled up to 600 phone lines during those expansionary times.

In the 1960s communications networks were remarkably different to today's: there were no mobile phones, no internet and ordinary citizens often had to wait months for a line to become available before they could have their home phone connected.

How then could crooks like Freeman have 20 or more phone lines connected at one property? How could it be that after one place closed down (on the advice of friendly cops), another would be wired up with all the phone lines running by the next race day?

The telephone network up until 1975 was owned and operated by the Australian government, which had set up the Postmaster-General's Department (PMG) in 1901 to do the job. A former PMG union official confirmed that the 'line pairs' needed for each phone connection were in short supply in the post-Second World War years, and the situation improved only slowly throughout the 1960s. But middle-management PMG officers were in a position to keep bundles of lines available to meet the requests of people such as Freeman. And the price for making these multiple connections at short notice would have been high, the union organiser said.

There were bonuses for PMG workers lower down the rung, too: they would use the technicians' line-testing equipment to listen in on conversations between jockeys, trainers, bookies and the SP operators, ensuring that their days off at the races were invariably profitable.

In the post-TAB era the control of SP money became centralised. The punter would sidle up to the man in the corner of the bar and mumble his wager, something like, 'Five bob each way on Born to Lose.' He'd hand over his ten-bob note, the bookie would a make a coded scrawl on a scrap of paper and hand it to the punter. (The old lingo persevered for years after the Australian currency had changed to dollars and cents in 1966. For the SP bookies and their loyal punters a one-dollar note – since replaced by a coin – was long called a 'ten-bob note'.) After a few bets had been collected, minutes before each race, the bookie would make a phone call. I was once told that this was the operator 'laying off' some wagers with a bigger bookie. There could be a couple of layers between the small-time guy in the pub and the operator at the top of the tree, someone like Freeman, each passing on some or all of the wagers, all taking a bit of a punt themselves with the original bettors' investments. Big punters would have direct access to a central SP operation and would lay bets by phone. If a punter had a substantial win, the bookie would urgently call his next-in-line to arrange for cash to be brought to the pub for the payout.

In the mid-1960s at Riverstone, west of Sydney, I saw an SP operator working out of a tiny shed behind the pub; he had to lock the shed door each time he went to the phone to do his 'laying off'. The local copper, in uniform, was drinking at the bar. I asked him why the SP was working in the shed, and not in the public bar, nearer to the phone. 'That'd be illegal,' he said, without a trace of irony. In the fabled Phoenix Hotel, on the corner of

Wallis and Moncur streets in Woollahra – where cops and journalists swapped lies in the saloon bar, and the local knockabouts, pickpockets and ratbags, as well as the local SP agent, drank in the front bar – I watched a senior eastern-suburbs detective call out his bet to the SP bookie from the doorway between the two bars. He didn't pay cash for his wager; maybe, just maybe, he actually paid for his losing bets at the end of the day. The 'no losing bets to be paid for' policy was widely applied to appropriate people, it is understood, from Premier Askin down.

The operators in the pubs would invariably retain a few of the bets placed with them – their own little gamble – but all the rest of the money that had been lost by the punters, minus a percentage for the operator, was passed up the line. Some of it went right to the top. Freeman would take a slice for himself and McPherson before handing over the rest to the cops who provided protection for the racket and to Bob Askin, the politician who had once been an illegal SP bookie himself and now retained loyalty to those still in the game.

* * *

The SP empire was growing, but by late 1967 McPherson had more important duties for George Freeman. Sydney's illegal operations had become tightly controlled and protected by the corrupt police at the helm of the major crime squads, and the politicians who were collaborators or were blackmailed into acquiescence – and too much of the proceeds were going towards them. It was time for further talks with the Americans. McPherson was not prepared to again try to travel to the US: his previous conviction for using a forged passport in 1951 would complicate matters, as would, no doubt, his abortive 1966 Asian cruise. Somehow McPherson persuaded two people, both with criminal records, to make a trip on his behalf to catch up with the Chicago mobs. George Freeman and Stan Smith were going to the States.

The plan faced a minor hurdle. Novice cops from the Consorting Squad who were not aware Stan was a 'protected person' under McPherson's arrangement, had recently arrested him for carrying an unlicensed pistol. It only took a phone call from McPherson to resolve that problem, however.

Both Smith and Freeman needed forged passports to obtain their American visas and enter the US undetected, and these had to be produced by an expert. The best in Sydney in those days was the toupee-wearing Leo 'The Liar' Callaghan. Freeman had met Callaghan through his association with Arthur Delaney. The solidly built Callaghan, three years Freeman's junior, was a long-term member of Delaney's international shoplifting gang. He was an accomplished forger and in his spare time he supplied counterfeit drivers' licences, birth certificates, passports and other documents in high demand among criminals.

Freeman was handed a credible-looking document in the name of Kenneth Laurence Keane, complete with his photograph, description and details of tattoos (a heart, dagger, 'Geo', 'Maria' and 'Mother' on his right arm and the clichéd 'T-R-U-E L-O-V-E' on the backs of his fingers) and what might have just passed as an official departmental stamp. The sham passport had his vocation listed as 'labourer'. His mate Smith was provided with a similar work of art. It is understood that the ever-paranoid McPherson was not happy with Callaghan's forgeries, and persuaded the pair to apply for real passports using their adopted aliases. They were successful.

Illegal gambler Ronnie Lee was happy to let his mate Joseph Dan Testa in Chicago know that a few friendly visitors from Down Under were on their way. Another two men accompanied Smith and Freeman on parts of the trip. They arrived in Los Angeles in mid-1968, and the first stop for Freeman was a large department store for some pilferage – he just couldn't help himself. There, he noticed that a jewellery safe had been left unattended, with the keys nearby. The safe was quickly relieved of a considerable stash of gems, which were tucked into Freeman's shirt before he strode out of the shop into the warm Californian sunshine.

A quick phone call to Joe Testa and they were on their way to Chicago, nearly 2800 kilometres north-east, where their generous

Mafia host would greet them at his mansion just out of town. The guests were delighted by what they saw on their arrival. In Freeman's own words:

> It was a Sunday and all these beautiful women were just lazing around the swimming pool in bikinis. Testa wasn't there at the time but had left a message for us to make ourselves at home until he got there. When he arrived I put the question direct to him: 'Let's get something straight, Joe. We're all young blokes: what about the girls? Which ones are taboo?'
>
> 'My mother and my sister, and they're not here,' he replied.
>
> It was 'go for your life.' So I did.

Freeman and Smith enjoyed their taste of the mobster lifestyle and the special treatment it afforded them. They learned of Testa's close links with local cops when Freeman told him the next day about the stolen jewellery. Testa took him and the gems to the police station and handed the contraband over 'for safekeeping'. The booty was later sold for around $US200,000, of which Freeman guessed a part went to the police. Testa confided in them that he'd paid for the election campaign of one of the local police chiefs; it must have seemed like a home away from home to the Aussies.

They spent six weeks in the Windy City, with a three-day visit – at Testa's expense – to the Stardust Hotel in Las Vegas, where they met a few more Mafia figures.

The visit was judged a great success by McPherson and other persons of interest, as it successfully planted ideas of expansion in the American gangsters' minds. These seeds would bear fruit later on.

Freeman and Smith did however experience a hiccup on their return: they were charged with forging their passport applications and fined $200 (*$2,208*) each. Freeman later explained (to the 1973–74 Royal Commission into crime in clubs conducted by Judge Athol Moffitt) that he had gone to the US just 'for a holiday'.

If this were so, he was asked, why travel under an assumed name? He replied:

> Well, prior to us leaving for America, Smith went to Japan with McPherson on a ship on his own passport and was refused entry at each port they called at, so we assumed that going to America on his own passport they would not allow him in, nor myself, because of the prior history, so that is why we went on false passports.

And highlighting his awe-struck incredulity at the treatment he and Smith received in the States, Freeman went on to describe Testa's hospitality to the commission:

> I was amazed. It was like a house you see in the pictures. I have never seen anything like it, and he insisted we be his guests, and we accepted it, and we was [sic] informed we had no option: we didn't intend to stay six weeks with him but we was [sic] told the police knew we was there under the name of Keen [sic] and we thought we would have trouble leaving America and coming back to Australia.

Freeman appears to have done a fine job of selling Australia's potential to the Chicago hoodlums. Within months of Freeman and Smith's return, Joe Testa would make his second visit to Sydney, and Freeman would act as host on behalf of the local criminals.

For a man who started out as an inept thief, things were looking up.

5. Hospitality repaid – showing the Mafia our bright lights

*Crime expands according to our
willingness to put up with it.*
– Barry J. Farber, American trainer, speaker, author

By 1969 there were clear signals – for those who wanted to see them – that the US Mafia was taking a serious look at Down Under as a potential outpost. Among those aware of the moves were people in high offices of state or law enforcement who did nothing to interrupt the developments. Some went further than simply looking the other way. NSW Premier Bob Askin, who had won his second term election in 1968, valiantly tried to stop all forms of inquiry into the Mafia's overtures. A close friend of Freeman, Detective Jack McNeill, was eventually given the task of investigating the chorus of allegations that American criminals were infiltrating the local licensed-club and entertainment industries, with more than a little help from their Aussie mates. McNeill was castigated in Judge Moffitt's 1974 commission findings for his slack handling of these particular investigations.

Joe Testa was at the vanguard of the push into Australia. The Americans had a product they were eager to press on the Australian market: a poker machine churned out by a Mafia-controlled company, the Bally Corporation. A former officer from the US Justice Department, William Tomlinson, later told an inquiry in Sydney that Testa had a reputation in Chicago of being a 'lower-level associate' of the Chicago organised-crime scene, that he had a penchant for physical violence and always carried a gun.

When the 41-year-old Testa and his bodyguard, Nick Giordano, arrived on 10 February 1969 in Sydney for the second time, his Australian counterparts rolled out the red carpet. The aim was to persuade the Mafia ambassador that Australia's Sin City would provide rich pickings for his associates back in the US. Testa stayed 22 days, and while George Freeman played host, all the local crims chipped in to do their bit to make the visitors feel welcome. It was one of the rare occasions the various competing egos running the local little crime groups pulled together, all in the interests of making a bit more cash.

They booked their guest into the Chevron Hotel, just down from Kings Cross, which was then one of the 'in' places for visiting VIPs.

The first big party in honour of Testa was held at Chequers nightclub in the city, to which Freeman mustered Lennie McPherson and his second wife, Marlene, the thuggish Milan Petricevic – also known as 'Iron Bar Miller' – Stan Smith and Bill Delouney, Arthur Delaney, Joe Testa and their female companions. Little did they know that the roaming photographer who took a happy snap of the group was actually a federal policeman. This time around Testa's movements were subject to surveillance.

McPherson took Testa and his bodyguard on a pig- and kangaroo-shooting trip in north-western NSW, with one of McPherson's enforcers, Branko Balic, piloting the light plane for the round trip. Balic had joined the McPherson team just after his arrival in Australia from Yugoslavia in February 1966 under the assisted-migrant scheme. Once they were back in town, there were other festive nights out: sessions at illegal gambling dens, a feast at the Chevron with a huge iced cake emblazoned with the words 'Welcome Joe', and a party at the luxurious Watsons Bay home of Testa's original Sydney contact, illegal gambling supremo Ronnie Lee.

Freeman later dismissed suggestions he'd been showing a 'Mafia figure' around town:

> People meeting him, and meeting him in the company of myself and other people with criminal records, naturally

assumed that he was a crook, and he being American led to the word 'Mafia'. In fact, Testa was branded not only as a member of the Mafia but as one of its bosses, which was a joke, and anyone who had checked back with Chicago would have been able to verify it as a joke.

Subsequent investigation by federal police put the matter beyond doubt: Testa was indeed attached to the Chicago Mafia, and was in Sydney negotiating with local criminals about ways the Bally poker machine company could break into the Sydney licensed-club scene. Their intention was to become the exclusive supplier of the machines after driving the local manufacturer out of business.

The Mafia were coming to town, and McPherson and particularly Freeman had been major players in this success story. Crime was finding new profitable avenues, and in Sydney there was willingness, courtesy of a seriously corrupt state government and 'the best police force that money could buy', to put up with it.

6. Only a dope would've missed it: drugs make a big hit

> Australians initially became involved in the international narcotics trade in the mid-1960s ...
> – *Dr Alfred W. McCoy, American academic*

As the 1960s drew to a close, Australian criminals faced a number of changes to the way they ran their businesses. The Mafia-owned Bally poker machines infiltrated the market by way of hefty bribes going to the club officials who installed the machines, and to the politicians who lifted the ban on multi-coin versions of the one-armed bandits.

The Sydney thugs, however, weren't sure that they were gaining anything more than unwelcome notoriety from this new growth area.

The benefits were nearly all flowing to a wealthy – and very crooked – operator who sat outside the local crime cliques: Jack Rooklyn. Rooklyn was not a newcomer to the gaming-machine business: he'd cut his teeth operating a 'penny arcade' of pinball machines in Sydney in the 1950s. Now he was graduating to supplying sophisticated poker machines to gambling houses. Like SP bookmaking, poker machines had been used in NSW clubs illegally since the mid-1800s, with officialdom turning a blind eye. The state legalised use of the machines on 22 August 1956. Within three years there were more than 7000 poker machines in 1100 clubs.

Those like Rooklyn who sold the machines to the clubs turned handsome profits. The state government charged the club licence fees and initially claimed around 45 per cent – later reduced to around 22.5 per cent – of the money lost by gamblers, and the clubs kept the rest. NSW Treasury figures show the state revenue from poker-machine gambling in the decade of the 1960s was $153.7 million (*$1.79 billion*). The amount lost by gamblers in that period was roughly $683 million (*$7.95 billion*).

It has always been a no-win gamble for the players: clubs assure them they will get around 87 per cent return, which is a smart way of saying that, on average, they will lose 13 per cent of their investment.

One estimate suggests the chance of winning a big jackpot is one in 52 million.

By 2010 NSW had around 3000 legal gambling establishments and more than 95,000 poker machines. Government revenue was around $1 billion.

There were a few spin-offs for the locals as the US interests started influencing the entertainment side of the clubs' industry, but they were slim pickings compared to the big bucks Bally was capturing. Big entertainment acts with US Mafia connections were booked into the clubs – the so-called 'poker-machine palaces' – through agencies run by Sydney crooks who took three or more times the usual booking fees.

For a while Freeman encouraged his acquaintances to persist with the American connections, and in 1971 he played host to the second visit to Australia of Chicago gangster Joe Testa. During that trip, Freeman set up a joint venture company with Testa, calling it Grants Constructions – Grant being the name of Freeman's eldest son. The company had $350,000 (*$3.4 million*) to buy three old blocks of flats in Double Bay and replace them with high-rise units. It was a bum deal – the local council rejected their building plans and the flats were sold off at next to nothing – an outcome that could have been avoided had they simply checked the height restrictions for buildings in the area.

That said, losses on the enterprise would have seemed like small change to Freeman: in June of that year he had been part of a betting syndicate, including Mick Bartley and two others,

Jack Rooklyn: pinball hustler to global racketeer

Jack Rooklyn was born to Russian-Jewish parents in London on 11 March 1918. The family migrated to Australia in 1921 and by the Second World War Jack was organising access to illegal poker machines for visiting US soldiers. He owned a pinball parlour in the run-down end of George Street, near Sydney's Central Railway, and business was good. By the 1950s he had set up shop throughout southeast Asia, distributing machines made by Lion Manufacturing, the company the US Mafia took over, and which became the Bally Poker Machine Company.

When Bally started operations in Australia in the early 1970s, Rooklyn ran the show. The company offered bribes of a few thousand dollars to licensed-club secretaries for each Bally machine they installed.

Rooklyn and Bally were exposed in the 1973–74 Moffitt Royal Commission as being wholly controlled by the US Mafia. Judge Moffitt's 1974 report recommended to state and federal governments that the Bally Company be prevented from further trade in Australia, otherwise the country ran the risk of serious US Mafia intrusion into the nation's affairs. No action was taken against the company, Rooklyn or any of the major players in the Moffitt drama. Rooklyn died in July 1996, aged 78.

that broke the Canberra TAB with a half-million-dollar (*$4.86 million*) win on the jackpot tote. They had picked six straight winners in the Melbourne races.

During that visit, Joe Testa had been picked up by police. Interestingly, they were from the Consorting Squad – Jack McNeill's unit.

The cops proceeded to question the mobster about his associations with Freeman and McPherson. Testa had been arranging details of his Grants Constructions business deal at a solicitor's office at Bathurst Street in the city, and was nabbed as he left. At the CIB headquarters he was interrogated by Detective-Sergeant Doug Knight and an offsider. 'I was quite harassed by it. It was the first time in 43 years I had ever been to a police station,' he lied. 'He told me Freeman was this and Freeman was that, and he insinuated I was a member of the Mafia, and I got pretty upset about it.'

Testa claimed he knew neither that Freeman and Stan Smith had reputations as crooks, nor that local laws prevented him from consorting with known criminals. In the end it was a non-event: he was released without charge. It now appears that it was most likely a stunt orchestrated by Jack McNeill to up the ante in his dealings with McPherson. McNeill later whitewashed the incident, saying in an official report that McPherson had 'quite accidentally' met Testa on his first visit Sydney, and that Testa was 'a normal sort of a fellow who in all probability visited Australia for a holiday with no ulterior motive.' For that version to be put into the official records would have cost McPherson a tidy upfront sum; that's the way the system worked.

McNeill also rejected information passed on by the federal police from their Chicago sources suggesting Testa was a 'psychopathic killer' with Mafia associations.

While Testa admired the local police's relaxed attitude towards illegal gambling and breaches of liquor licensing laws, as well as the big bucks that flowed through the clubs' entertainment circuit, there is no evidence of his involvement in the drug trade.

* * *

The Sydney lads would eventually turn back to their traditional forms of making cash. The SP bookie racket was still booming, and George Freeman (with the okay from McPherson) brought a newcomer into their operation. The rookie bookie was Michael Hurley – known as 'Mickel' – and it was an association that would profoundly affect both their lives.

Possibly an omen of what would be in store for him, Michael Nicholas Hurley was born on the eve of Australia's most celebrated horserace, the Melbourne Cup, on 5 November 1945. It would take a few years, but Hurley certainly grew interested in racing, in particular the intricacies of SP bookmaking, becoming a willing pupil to a master of the game, George Freeman.

His was a working-class family living in Sydney's inner suburb of Pyrmont. Like Freeman, Hurley had left school when he was

14. He worked for a while in a distillery sticking labels onto bottles but went on to try his hand at a few illegal activities. Working on the wharves from the age of 18 had been an apprenticeship in stealing, and by the time Freeman took him under his wing, at age 24, Hurley had chalked up a police record that included 22 arrests for breaking, entering and stealing, car theft, assault, rape, receiving stolen goods and arson.

Five foot eight, with fair hair and blue eyes, Hurley had a habit of biting his bottom lip while he was talking. His most regular hang-out was the Pyrmont Bridge Hotel, a pub not known for having lace doilies on the tables. It was the sort of venue where you could place an order for, say, a television set, and collect it later that day for a dirt-cheap price; so long as you didn't ask any questions about where it came from. Hurley was a boon to Freeman: his stealing activities added to the gang's bottom line and he was a handy man to have around when serious money needed to be collected from late-paying punters.

Hurley would eventually acquire a heavyweight contact. He married Lena Muller, daughter of vicious gunman John 'Jacky' Muller. Freeman was an official witness at the nuptials. It was an intimacy he did not share with Muller, who was viewed by most criminals as a dangerous loner, under no one's control. Muller, however, once told a detective that he was on friendly terms with Freeman.

* * *

Among crooked industries, the business of importing, distributing and supplying drugs is the most difficult to track with any accuracy, as nearly all criminals will express moral outrage at the suggestion they deal drugs. People such as Freeman referred to stealing and illegal gambling fairly openly, but feigned shocked indignation when asked about drugs. McPherson, Smith, all of them, denied their involvement.

The firsthand knowledge we do have comes from arrests and court actions, and Stan Smith was the first of the group to face drug charges.

In 1970 Smith was charged with attempting to on-sell

John Muller: a lone gun for hire

John Marcus Muller was born in North Sydney on 30 November 1922. Many of the characters in these pages started their criminal careers at an early age. Muller beats most with his opening entry: he was convicted of stealing at the age of nine. Over the years he added convictions for break-enter-steal, consorting with criminals, offensive behaviour, indecent language and illegal betting to the list.

At 18, black-haired, hazel-eyed Jacky Muller did his bit for the military, enlisting in October 1941. He was classified as a gunner. While shooting might have interested him, military life did not, as with others in our story. By the following April he'd taken off; he was entered into the army's X-list, declared a deserter and dishonourably discharged. So, deprived of shooting for king and country, he took it up in civilian life.

In 1949 he married Esme Patmore at Burwood. They had a daughter, Lena.

Muller had worked on the wharves for years, and formally signed up with the Waterside Workers' Federation (WWF) in September 1950, sponsored by no less than the wharfies' famous communist boss, 'Big' Jim Healy. Within two months he'd been dragged before the Australian Stevedoring Board after viciously assaulting a wharf timekeeper. Muller was deregistered and thrown out of the industry.

Detective-Inspector Alfred Wilks of the Commonwealth Investigation Service dutifully reported this event to the newly formed Australian Security Intelligence Organisation (ASIO), which in those days was happy to open a file on anyone associated with communists, such as those who ran the WWF.

It was through his association with the criminal elements of the Painters and Dockers Union that Muller was to meet his future son-in-law, Michael Hurley.

Muller spent a number of stints in jail, and in 1975, fresh from a prison sentence, was one of three men hired by former detective Fred Krahe to kill Kings Cross activist Juanita Nielsen. At the time he was a regular doorman at one of the illegal casinos in the Cross.

A few months later he and a mate were charged and convicted over the theft of $50,000 (*$316,693*) from a mailbag in Port Macquarie, in northern NSW. For this hardened criminal, however, there was worse to come – much worse – and it all had to do with George Freeman.

amphetamines that had been stolen from a pharmaceutical warehouse in Waterloo.

While he pleaded guilty, Smith was obviously a beneficiary of the McPherson indemnity policy. Helpful police testified that Smith denied knowing drugs were involved in the warehouse heist. 'Smith was only there to make sure there was no trouble and, in fairness to the defendant, as a result of inquiries made by him, a large amount of the drugs were recovered,' the police prosecutor told Magistrate Walter Lewer, who fined Smith $1200 (*$11,020*) and gave him six months to pay.

His co-accused, James Randolph Sweetnam, however, copped a 12-month jail term. Lewer said Sweetnam should have known better, because he came from a good home, unlike Smith with his 'less favoured' background, and had attended the elite Newington College.

The whole exercise seemed to ignore the fact Smith was charged with selling the drugs, not just their theft from the warehouse.

* * *

In the ABC-TV documentary *The Track*, which first screened in 2000, former policeman Merv Beck said that money from illegal SP activities came into legal gambling and flowed on to organised crime – and inevitably into the drug trade.

The writer of the program, Keith Aberdeen, enlarged on Beck's statement: one of the links was George David Freeman, friend and business associate of a major – unnamed – mob banker. 'The dapper little man had risen, seemingly without trace, to the good life in a waterfront house he'd actually bought from [illegal gambler] Perc Galea's son. Yet he'd been a shoplifter, and an incompetent petty crim. Traditionally, the SP industry had been like a loved but shady uncle, the black sheep we fondly forgave. But drug money, and the likes of Freeman, made it something much less benign ... He was a hoodlum.' A decade on and Judge Athol Moffitt's 1973–74 inquiry into criminal matters in NSW would find evidence that big SP gambling syndicates (like Freeman's) had contact with major heroin smugglers and local drug distributors.

Being involved in the drug trade – and this refers to large-scale deals, not individual use – tends to distort reality. For instance, Lennie McPherson once said he liked Stan Smith but 'deplored his addictive use of drugs'. However, a former senior policeman, Clive Small, was adamant that while Smith was a pusher, he was not an addict. Stan Smith Jnr, Smith's son, was a heroin addict who died from an overdose at a young age. Another policeman, Consorting Squad detective Frank Charlton, suggested the friendship between McPherson and Smith eventually cooled because 'McPherson despises him to a degree over his drug habits'. Despising a person over their drug 'habit' would clearly indicate use of drugs as distinct from their sale. Many of the major drug movers were also users, and there is no evidence to support Small's argument that Smith was simply a pusher.

Smith's start in the trade was hardly a major haul compared to the large plantations of marijuana that other crims were growing around Griffith in NSW, and in remote areas of the Northern Territory. A more significant development in illicit drug supply would be financed by the Sydney crooks and their copper mates: the massive profits from SP bookmaking and illegal casinos were being funnelled into the importation of drugs. When the international drug trade erupted in Australia, George Freeman – despite his denials – was at the heart of it, as was McPherson.

The methods used to bring large-scale supplies of drugs into Australia during this time differed from the American Mafia's model. In the US the mob saw that bulk shipments cruised along routes regularly to maintain the constant flow of products onto the streets. As the trade exploded in Australia in the 1970s, there was no controlling body – no one 'Mr Big' – of drugs, and thus no real organising force or one main method of importing.

As the trade grew exponentially, so too did the greed of the criminals and dirty cops involved, and this was to prove a dangerous formula.

7. Odds to die for: betting on the drugs trade

> The expansion and sophistication of trans-national
> crime represents one of the most dangerous threats
> we confront in the next millennium.
> – Rand Beers: Assistant US Secretary of State for
> International Narcotics and Law Enforcement Affairs

Sydney is no stranger to violence, and its inhabitants have borne witness to a number of upsurges in organised crime. In the 1920s 'razor gangs' (so named for their preferred weapon) took control of the town's rougher streets, with the tension between rival gangs culminating in an all-out riot in 1929 – the Battle of Kellett Street. The blood was still flowing in the 1960s. Between 1963 and 1966 criminals were being slaughtered at the rate of about two a year, a record for the time.

In those times the fights were mainly over the control of prostitution rings, as this trade was illegal, and police who were grafting from the system would often take sides. The death toll fell a little as the new decade approached, when the crims and corrupt cops began fighting instead over the spoils of the drug trade. One factor that contributed to fewer gangland murders in the 1970s was a move to negotiate peaceful outcomes wherever possible. That ploy didn't always work, so killing rivals remained an alternative. During that time, however, there were a few near misses – and one of them would be George Freeman.

It would not be the only problem Freeman had to contend with. In early 1970 he was hit with an unpaid tax bill for $23,000 ($237,706).

Through his accountant, a man who was also engineering

international money-laundering and tax-avoidance scams for him, Freeman was able to negotiate a settlement of around $12,000 (*$124,020*) on the proviso that he pay up within seven days. It would have undoubtedly irked Freeman that federal investigators were nosing around his private affairs. But then it irked honest crime-fighters that the big-time crims were being hit with tax bills – which they could easily afford – rather than being brought up on criminal extortion charges. When the Taxman settled, there was no new entry on the crims' record-sheets: it was just a simple financial transaction.

Around this time Freeman's heavies became more 'assertive' in collecting bad debts. One of his enforcers, Bela Hejja, was later to tell of his gruesome work as a racing-loss collector. Hejja a was born in Hungary on 23 April 1939, and arrived in Melbourne in May 1957 under the Menzies government's Hungarian Refugee Scheme. A few years later he came to police attention for his work as an SP debt collector with the tough Victorian Painters and Dockers Union on the Melbourne waterfront. On moving to Sydney he teamed up with Freeman.

Hejja told how he would meet Freeman at plush Eliza's restaurant in Double Bay, where his boss would hand him a diary containing the names and details of indebted punters. For what he described as 'a small commission', around $1800 (*$18,603*) a week, he went collecting. If a punter was reluctant to pay, Hejja called in a couple of thugs. They would stand over the victim; one would point a revolver at the punter's head, the other would heft a tomahawk in his hand.

The axe-man would then chop off part of one of the man's fingers, by which time the terrified victim, knowing that more fingers could be lopped, would make – and keep – an agreement to pay off his debt.

The severed digit would be wrapped in paper and shown to others as a warning of the bloody consequences of running up bad debts with George Freeman. But the SP king faced none of these allegations at the time: out of 'loyalty' to his boss, Hejja waited until Freeman died before telling his dreadful story.

* * *

While tax bills might have lightened the wallets of a few, the 1970s also brought with it some good for the crims. The tough and deeply corrupt cop Jack McNeill took charge of the NSW Police Consorting Squad on 30 June 1970. McNeill took over from a man who did not fear or favour criminals: Detective-Sergeant Les Chowne. Chowne had actively enforced consorting laws, which stipulated that criminals could not be seen in public together. Under Chowne's direction the squad made it difficult for criminals to meet, and thus to do business. It was not a coincidence that a year before he was sidelined by McNeill, Chowne had achieved a consorting conviction against Lennie McPherson. Once in charge, McNeill went the other way, making special arrangements for Freeman, McPherson and Stan Smith to ensure they were not arrested for 'consorting with known criminals'.

A year into his new position McNeill advised Lennie McPherson to stop frequenting an illegal casino, the 33 Club on Oxford Street.

This move was later recast as McNeill 'put[ting] an end to McPherson's standover tactics' in the club. 'Although I have no proof of it, it was generally conceded that there was extensive gambling there,' McNeill told the 1973–74 Moffitt Royal Commission, 'and I could not see where gambling, associated with a man of his background and reputation, should go hand in glove.' So, he told Judge Moffitt, he had banned McPherson from going to the club. McNeill was never asked why he, a senior policeman, had no proof of illegal gambling on the premises.

However, when McNeill warned off McPherson from the 33 Club, he knew that another man – a McPherson associate – had already been arranged to collect the protection fees from the casino.

The real purpose of the meeting with Lennie was to check that McPherson, Freeman and Smith's social lives weren't being hampered by the consorting laws. While McPherson was told he should avoid that particular club, there were other places McNeill said he was happy for the trio to go together. He gave McPherson

Jack McNeill, a fair cop for the crims

After Ray Kelly retired from the NSW Police in 1966, there was a quiet power struggle to determine who would take over the major criminal operations the departing inspector ran from his desk at the CIB headquarters. Everything from breach of liquor licensing laws to big-time robberies, arson to illegal abortion, had provided a substantial income for Kelly and his trusted team. Fred Krahe and Roger Rogerson were touted as likely successors, but it was Jack McNeill who eventually became the most powerful of the bent boys in blue.

Born to Presbyterian parents on 11 May 1922 in Sutherland in Sydney's south, Jack McNeill failed the leaving certificate at Canterbury Boys High School and in February 1939 joined the police department.

In February 1944 McNeill signed up for wartime service in the RAAF, telling recruiters he had special skills in unarmed combat. In October that same year McNeill was lucky to escape when a Tiger Moth he was piloting as part of his flying course was involved in a collision. McNeill was discharged in June 1945 with a 'very good' character assessment. He resumed work in the police force and settled down with his wife, Mary, in Hurstville. He enjoyed a steady rise through the ranks, exerting, as one observer noted, 'authority in the organisation well beyond his rank … It seemed that his power came not from what he had, but from what people generally thought he had.' Under Ray Kelly's guiding hand, McNeill built up a network of criminals, in this way learning what was happening on the street and persuading crims to become fizgigs of the Kelly-McPherson model. It was McNeill who took over receiving the monthly reel-to-reel tapes produced by McPherson on criminal goings-on. Jack McNeill became very close to George Freeman, who regularly tipped him winners for the races.

McNeill stayed in the job until his retirement in 1982, at the age of 60. He died a year later.

the thumbs up to visit the Northside Polonia Soccer Club, provided he took his wife. 'As far as I was concerned, he could go there with another man who had a criminal background – provided the man had his wife with him, for just a social evening,' McNeill explained. He told the Moffitt inquiry how he had then spelled it out that the 'other man' could be George Freeman or Stan Smith, provided they too brought their companions along.

Another venue McNeill okayed for Sydney's top criminals in defiance of the consorting laws was the Sutherland United Services Club, which McNeill knew was a fun place as he himself frequented it.

The relationship between the senior policeman and these criminals was extremely cosy: the immunity insurance McPherson had taken out on their behalf with Ray Kelly survived intact. Lennie, George, Stan – the gang of three – and their favoured mates would, under Jack's watch, remain untouchable to members of the NSW constabulary.

Having a senior copper on your team as you moved into buying and distributing drugs on a large scale was an obvious plus. The problem in those days was that an insurance policy with one or two police officers would not provide protection against the newcomers on the scene, other criminal groupings, and their copper accomplices, all out to make a killing.

At this stage Freeman, McPherson and Smith were joined by another powerful ally, one who would prove to be a pioneer in importing drugs – former policeman and Olympic rowing gold medallist Murray Riley. He'd started working with McPherson's gang on a regular basis after he quit the NSW Police Force in 1962.

The growing drug trade was not without risks. Stan Smith was arrested in 1972 by NSW Drug Squad detectives working with federal narcotics agents for possession of a large quantity of drugs. Though Smith was under the insurance policy, the state cops found it difficult to refuse requests from the feds. However, evidence can get lost after the arrest and first committal court hearing have taken place. I could find no record of Smith being

Murray Riley: champion bent cop

Murray Stewart Riley was born on 5 October 1925, and joined the NSW Police in December 1943. He worked up through the ranks and was a favourite of Ray Kelly, who assigned him one of Lennie McPherson's hit men to look after. Ray Smith, a shonky poker-machine dealer, had had his car bombed at Pyrmont. As Detective Jack McNeill later explained, 'We had Riley protecting Smith for some months. He just went around everywhere with him as a bodyguard and I think at some stage he stayed in his house.' Two men were later charged over the incident, and Riley eventually returned to more normal police duties.

Riley was part of the rowing team in the 1950 and 1954 Commonwealth Games and the 1956 Melbourne Olympics. His sculling partner was Mervyn Wood, who 20 years after sharing the bronze-medal win in Melbourne, became Commissioner of the NSW Police Force.

Riley's association with McPherson saw him inducted him into Sydney's major organised-crime gang. Initially a collector of McPherson's standover payments and Freeman's SP debts, Riley did regular business with illegal casinos and SP operations across NSW. In the early 1960s reports emerged that he was importing drugs, using hostesses from the casinos he frequented to courier cannabis from Thailand.

In 1962, having risen to the rank of detective-sergeant, he resigned from the police force to take up crime – in particular the drug trade – as a full-time profession, in coalition with Freeman, McPherson and Smith. In July 1966 Riley was sentenced to a year's jail in Auckland, New Zealand, after he was found guilty of trying to bribe a policeman. He was deported back to Australia the following March.

tried on this charge, despite the fact the record of the arrest appears in his 1973 entry in the Australasian Criminal Register.

Freeman's friendship with Dr Nick Paltos – who, as we shall see, later became involved in the drugs trade – firmed in 1971. Paltos, an incurable gambler, became heavily indebted to Freeman, on whom he relied for racing tips. Freeman did not send his finger-chopping thugs after this man, though, for here was a client whose vulnerability could be exploited.

Doc gives Freeman a life-saver
Nicholas George Paltoglou, Nicholas George, was born on the Greek island of Kastellorizo, the youngest of ten children, on 21 July 1940. When he was seven he migrated with his family to Melbourne, where the family name was anglicised to Paltos. He moved to Sydney in 1955, worked in a metal factory and took up gambling. The boss of the illegal Thommo's Two-up School, Joe Taylor, persuaded him to further his education, and in 1968 Paltos completed a medical degree at the University of New South Wales. The previous year he'd met and married Marie Kratzis.

Within two years he was director of the emergency and casualty departments at Sydney Hospital. George Freeman had sought out Paltos to treat his severe asthma on the recommendation of ageing crime boss Paddles Anderson. Freeman wrote of Paltos in his memoir: 'Over the years he became not only my doctor but also my friend. I visited him many times when he was the head of casualty at Sydney Hospital. He had many commendations from all walks of life for his work in that casualty department. Make no mistake, Nick Paltos saved many lives in those days.' As we will see, later on Nick Paltos did a great deal to destroy lives, too.

Nick Paltos had been added to the list of crime suspects long before he did anything more outrageous than gamble at an illegal casino or make a few bets with an SP bookie. In 1971 state police had listened in on calls made on George Freeman's home phone with a bugging device of dubious legality. They recorded conversations with Paltos, and for the doctor it was a case of guilt by association.

Meanwhile Freeman (having moved on from the Duke Delaney gang), McPherson and Smith were assembling a cohort. David Kelleher would go on to make drug-trade history more than a decade later, but in these early days he was content to be a junior – albeit a difficult to control – member of the gang.

David John Kelleher was born in Sydney on 15 April 1951, and by age 22 he'd been arrested once for every year of his life. The blond-haired, blue-eyed, boyish-faced six-footer was a known associate of the Hells Angels, Galloping Gooses and the Finks motorcycle gangs.

Among the charges he'd faced were rape, forgery, possession of an unlicensed pistol, car theft, break-enter-steal and consorting with criminals. When he made the big time and was facing a jail term, he had his moment of insightful truth, saying, 'I have been a criminal nearly all my adult life. My ethics are in the gutter.' In hitching his lot to the Freeman-McPherson wagon in the mid-'70s, he found himself in appropriate company.

Kelleher later became the first person in Australia to be sentenced to life imprisonment under revised customs laws dealing with heroin importation after he arranged a ten-kilogram load of pure heroin to be brought into Australia.

* * *

The big shift in the country's drug use had come in the mid-1960s, with the decision to use Sydney as a 'Rest and Recreation' (R&R) venue for American troops fighting an unwinnable war in Vietnam. Until then, cocaine had been the party drug of choice in affluent circles, and marijuana and its derivatives the hugely popular – and affordable – choice among young people relishing the social freedoms of the 1960s. The R&R culture dramatically changed the scene.

The soldiers, many of them practically kids, had already been introduced to heroin as they fought a war that few of them believed in, and on their six-day leave breaks in Sydney, they wanted more of the same, plus lots of sex. A shady CIA-linked American, Bernie Houghton, opened the Bourbon and Beefsteak bar in Kings Cross, and it became the first place in Australia where heroin was readily accessible.

That had been the starting point. Now there was much jostling to control the growing multimillion-dollar market. McPherson wanted to be certain that he and his mates controlled this emerging field of enterprise. But other – and lesser – players were determined to carve out their own slices of the action. We will meet some of the challengers later, but it is important to note here that police, including Roger Rogerson, rising figures Bill Duff,

Aarne Tees and others, sided with one team or another, being as determined as their criminal mates to get their portions.

George Freeman, in around 1972, introduced another American gangster to the McPherson-led group, who they hoped would give them leverage in the highly competitive industry. Danny Stein was in his late fifties when he linked up with Freeman, who described the mobster as 'one of the nicest guys I ever met, and one of the most honest'. Freeman was also emphatic that Stein was not a criminal, but the facts state otherwise. Stein was part-owner of the Mafia-controlled Caesar's Palace gambling casino in Las Vegas. Freeman had met him during his visit to the gambling town with Joe Testa in 1968. Stein visited Australia a number of times. On one trip he bought a local racehorse – a dud, apparently – naming it 'Lansky' after Meyer Lansky, the don who had established Las Vegas as a 'legitimate' Mafia money machine. Danny Stein, wrote Freeman, hardly knew Lansky, but 'admired his success'.

Danny Stein was almost certainly the link between Freeman, McPherson and the ex-pat Australian criminal Martin Olson, who managed some of McPherson's investments in grog-running and prostitution in the Philippines capital, Manila. Police intelligence reports and evidence later given at the Woodward Royal Commission made it clear Stein's interest in Australia was to set up an international network to import and distribute drugs. Reliable evidence was produced by the federal police – but apparently never acted on – that around once a month a courier visited Olson in Manila and brought back to Australia quantities of cocaine. It was suggested that on at least some trips, Stein, Freeman or both accompanied the courier.

Before he left town for good in 1972 after being knocked back for Australian residency and threatened with deportation, Stein gave Freeman power of attorney over a bank account he had opened – the second such Mafia-linked account Freeman operated. The official rejection of Stein's immigration application to Australia was seen by Freeman as an affront to a decent man who had been demonised by police and nosy journalists.

Others not so biased viewed the decision as being consistent with the fact he had bona fide US Mafia credentials. Freeman, in September 1973, closed the bank account and transferred $56,300 ($473,976) to his mate Stein in the US. That was not the end of their financial dealings. There is evidence that Freeman continued to make regular payments to Stein; a year after the bank account was closed, Stein wrote to Freeman complaining, 'I haven't gotten it [a payment] for June yet.' The close association with Stein provides another slab of evidence that – despite their protestations – Freeman, McPherson and Smith were significant players in Australia's illegal drug trade.

8. Crims give peace a chance, all meet in same room

Peace cannot be achieved through violence, it can only be attained through understanding.
– Ralph Waldo Emerson

In 1972 members of the warring gangs arranged meetings in an attempt to bring an end to the violence. For too long the rival gangs – the McPherson-Freeman-Smith mob in the inner-western suburbs, old Paddles Anderson and his devotees in the eastern suburbs, the untouchable Abe Saffron in the 'pleasure centre' of Kings Cross, and a few others – had followed the 'eye for an eye' dictum which, as Mohandas Gandhi pointed out, ends up making the whole world blind. A few things persuaded the leaders to set up talks: the visiting Americans had expressed concern at the lack of discipline among their Australian pals, and suggested round-table chats take place to 'carve up the territory' – as the Mafia had so often tried (and failed) to do in the US – to reach agreement on which group would look after what sector of criminal activity. It was a difficult project, seeing as most of the action was now focused on the drug trade, where competition was fierce. No one was really happy about the moves to set up the talks; it was like a bit of a flurry with a whinge on top.

There had also been an unprecedented level of political mud-slinging about the Mafia coming to town, mostly as a result of keen interest from parts of the media about the new international players and their influence on the local poker-machine industry. This led some to take a closer look at allegations of Mafia influence in the NSW clubs and entertainment venues, but few people at that stage were linking the action to the emerging drugs trade; that would come later.

After three months of intensive research as a freelancer, other journalists and I at the *Sunday Telegraph* put together a story published on 16 July 1972, headed 'The night the Mafia came to Sydney', which covered the visits of Joe Testa and the lavish entertainment provided for him by the locals. Regrettably, the editor, overly concerned about possible defamation actions, had all the names removed from the piece. Crime writer Evan Whitton was later to write that the publication of the story 'led to summit conferences in July and August', a parley among the crims of various factions. The meetings were held in the home of Karl Bonnette.

The invitations for afternoon tea at Karl Bonnette's rented house at 44 William Street, Double Bay, were not printed on gold-trimmed cards; they came by word of mouth to a few who were then asked to pass on the invite to selected others. The telephone was not trusted for setting up such a gathering. Bonnette had arranged a phone connection for the house under his alias Karl Solomon (the name he'd used on the lease for the premises), but that had not stopped inquisitive state police from listening in on his telephone conversations. Those listening, however, would have heard nothing of the meeting plans.

Other crime fighters picked up some details from an informant after the event. On 3 August a federal policeman (whose identity was not revealed but who was tagged 'Sgt B' in the records) reported he had been advised by 'Sgt E' that 'for the last two weeks, three meetings have been held' and gave Bonnette's address. 'The meetings are alleged to be called to discuss the current activities re organized crime,' he wrote.

His report listed those who were known to be attending the meetings, with police-record identifiers such as their dates of birth. It included Stan Smith, George Freeman, Lennie McPherson, Paddles Anderson, Karl Bonnette, of course, Milan 'Iron Bar Miller' Petricevic and Albert Ross Sloss, the 59-year-old Labor Party State MP for the inner-city seat of King. Also mentioned

Karl Bonnette: a 'desperate, depraved criminal'

Karl Frederick Bonnette was born in Melbourne on 8 June 1935. A solid man of six foot two, his first profession was an unlikely one for a future hard man: hairdressing.

Crime beckoned and he was drawn to Sydney, where he chalked up convictions of possessing unlicensed firearms, stealing and having stolen goods in his custody. His police record says he was a gunman, standover man and a procurer of prostitutes. He first came to police notice in 1954.

He operated a massage parlour/brothel in Lebanon before authorities caught up with him and asked him to leave the country. NSW Police records describe him as a 'desperate criminal who is depraved and is strongly suspected of trafficking in drugs'. At one time he bestowed on himself the title 'The Godfather'. Other aliases he used were Karl Solomon, K. Rogers and Frederick Brock.

In his own odd way Karl Bonnette was something of a diplomat for Australia's criminal milieu: over the years he travelled abroad extensively, visiting the US, the UK, the Philippines, Germany, Hong Kong, Israel, Argentine, Venezuela, Brazil and Colombia. In each place he made contact with local criminals, working to establish an international network through which organised crime would be run on the global free-enterprise principles of a multinational corporation.

Even though he was considered one of the 'eastern suburbs' crims, he had a good relationship with Freeman and McPherson, and counted Murray Riley as one of his close partners in crime.

were the names of Arthur 'The Duke' Delaney (Freeman's shoplifting buddy) and 'a person known only as "The Fibber"', Leo 'The Liar' Callaghan.

Sgt B stated the men would typically gather at a bar until around eleven o'clock when they'd leave for Bonnette's house. A man would sit in an early-model Holden car outside the house, acting as 'cockatoo' during the meeting. He would raise the alarm if any unwanted people tried to enter.

The information had come to the federal police from an informer described as 'reliable'. Sloss, predictably, denied he had been to any of these meetings. What was happening was not the province of the federal police, and officers reported their information to NSW Consorting Squad officer Brian Ballard. After Ballard made a few inquiries, he told the feds that two other crims had also been present. One was almost certainly former cop Murray Riley.

Ballard, in turn, passed on the report to his boss, McPherson's protector, Detective-Sergeant (as he then was) Jack McNeill. The information was handed on to McNeill's loyal staffer, Detective-Sergeant Frank Charlton. In what must be one of the most inept police manoeuvres ever recorded, at eight o'clock the next morning, Charlton rapped on the door at 44 William Street and demanded Bonnette tell him whether any criminals on his list were meeting there. Bonnette, of course, was adamant they were not. Charlton and his crew promptly arrested Bonnette on a charge of receiving a stolen TV set. According to Charlton, McNeill had not mentioned Sloss's name as part of the list and Charlton did not mention it to Bonnette. The omission of MP Alby Sloss's name from the information given to Charlton clearly indicates that the senior cop was out to protect Sloss from exposure if and when the story on the meeting became public. In that, McNeill did not succeed.

Any chance the police had of gaining intelligence from some of the most important meetings in the history of organised crime in Sydney was wiped out by Charlton's ham-fisted actions. Here were people who rarely met, many of whom had had recent contact with American Mafia figures either in the US or locally, getting together for regular powwows. It is certain they were discussing something more important than that week's rugby league results. It is equally certain that one of the agenda items was the drug trade, the profits from which were running into many millions of dollars a year and increasing exponentially.

Had the William Street address been placed under covert surveillance, it is possible that more meetings would have taken place. Bugging of the premises could have provided invaluable information on just what the crims were planning, and enabled

Fred Hanson, the crooks' friend

Frederick John Hanson was born at Orange, central western NSW, on 26 May 1914, into a Roman Catholic family. He joined the NSW Police Force in September 1936, but in 1942 was released to join the RAAF, where he served as a pilot on a number of overseas postings.

Back in the force after the end of the war, he was quickly promoted to the police air wing as sergeant (third class), leapfrogging more than a thousand colleagues in an organisation that has traditionally promoted according to seniority.

The move earned him the moniker 'Slippery' (he hadn't yet met 'Slippery Sam' Askin). He rose through the ranks to become assistant commissioner in 1968 and deputy commissioner in January 1972. Hanson announced in March that same year he had been 'groomed' by present (and bent) commissioner Norm Allan to succeed him; Hanson finally moved into the commissioner's slot on 15 November.

Hanson and Askin shared the bulk of the $5000 (around *$30,299*) a week paid in bribes by just one of Sydney's thirteen illegal casinos during the mid-1970s, according to (later) allegations made by a gambling source.

As Hanson had been 'picked' by his predecessor, so, too, did Hanson offer to retire early if he could choose his successor. This would be Merv Wood's ticket to the top job.

---

law enforcement to plan effective counter-measures. But that would never be. We must be satisfied, then, with the information originally given to the federal officers: that the role of the meetings was to reorganise local criminal activities along the international corporatist lines that Karl Bonnette – and the US gangsters – had been recommending. There is no record of any further meetings of Crime Oz Inc., and it appears the participants in Karl Bonnette's pipedream simply returned to their more tribal traditions.

* * *

The hopes of brokering a peaceful future might have faded, but there was good news at the end of 1972. Fred Hanson was on his way to the top of the NSW Police Force, and he'd prove to be a great friend to crims of all creeds. As American author Elbert Hubbard so aptly puts it: 'The friend is the man who knows all about you, and still likes you.' Or likes your money.

Between Hanson's rise to power, Askin's continuing reign as premier and Jack McNeill throwing his ample weight around, major criminals had little to worry about – so long as the bribes kept flowing. The illegal casinos thrived, SP betting prospered, drugs flooded the streets of Kings Cross, Abe Saffron's sex clubs, where prostitutes openly plied their illegal trade flourished, and liquor licensing laws were rendered a joke.

The few pesky journalists writing stories about a Mafia invasion were sent to chase other stories. The honest cops in the force had given up trying to set things to rights and were quietly getting on with their jobs as best they could. Labor politicians, under Pat Hills' leadership – with too many skeletons rattling around in their own closets – just weren't game to take on Bob Askin. So ended 1972.

9. Drugs not the only racket: racing gets a fix, too

*Gambling: The sure way of getting
nothing for something.
– Wilson Mizner, American playwright*

Freeman's buddy Stan Smith had by the start of 1973 adopted a new look. His longer hair and blue-tinted sunglasses did not, however, fool the cops in Sydney's CIB who compiled the updates of the Australasian Criminal Register. That year's edition noted that since his first ACR listing in 1970 Smith had 'continued to commit crime'. Before the volume was sent to print, the authors managed to include a reference to Smith's 1973 arrest by Victorian detectives 'in relation to the possession of drugs'. As with his arrest in Sydney on drugs charges a year earlier, this latest misadventure did not apparently involve any court appearances. Smith seems to have jumped bail and come home, where he was not bothered by police, even though they would have been aware that a Victorian warrant had been issued for his arrest.

On his interstate sorties he would use one of a number of aliases: Raymond Arthur Owens, Raymond Arthur, Stanley Raymond Lewis, John Eric Kean (a popular name – Freeman had once used the name Kenneth Laurence Keane) and Ronald John Goldsmith. 'Stately Stan' and 'Stonner' were listed as nicknames in addition to 'The Man', the moniker with which McPherson had dubbed him. In that year's ACR Smith was described as having the reputation of being one of Sydney's most dangerous gunmen, an assailant, shoplifter, sexual offender and drug pusher with a record of 29 arrests for rape, conspiracy, consorting, stealing, goods in custody and assault.

While Smith became more deeply involved in selling drugs, Freeman appeared to distance himself from his close friend's activities.

Freeman began promoting himself as a 'commission agent', providing racing tips for punters and helping them lay their bets. He didn't often discuss the SP activities in public, but he was now the major controller of that end of the business. There were other tipsters and bookies at work, but nearly all of them would pay Freeman a commission to ensure the police left them alone.

I became involved in trying to expose one or two such operators in stories run in the *Sunday Telegraph* during 1973 – these were met with an interesting response from police. One published story referred to a tipster known as 'Numbers Noel' who tapped the phones of bookies, trainers and jockeys and sold tips derived from that information to punters at $50 (*$421*) a pop. Others in the same shady line of business would pay bribes – or rob safes – to obtain details of the TAB's and legal bookies' telephone-punter accounts. The safe at the TAB headquarters in Harris Street, Ultimo was blown, but the two robbers were disturbed by a nightwatchman. A month later the safe in the Pitt Street office of a bookmaker was blown and files were removed.

The most significant in this series of stories was that which detailed Gaming Squad officers' refusal to accompany me on a visit to a big SP operation in Surry Hills. The story, published on 12 August 1973, said in part:

> Police said they knew of the SP operation described to them by the *Sunday Telegraph*, but were powerless to raid. 'If we walk in the front door, all signs of gambling in the upstairs rooms are removed by the time we get there,' said Inspector Neville Grigg. Inspector Grigg said he knew who ran the operation, and that settling was done at the man's mother's house in Ridge St, Surry Hills, on Sundays.

In the week after the story ran, two senior police visited the newspaper's office, wanting to interview me. They aggressively demanded to know who my informants were (I refused), insisted Grigg had provided me with his remarks 'off the record' (not true) and should not have been used by me or attributed to him, and that I should 'take more care' with my stories that embarrassed the NSW Police Department (at which time I quite firmly asked them to leave the building).

The incident indicated the high level of protection enjoyed by the SP bookie operations in Sydney at the time. The newspaper decided not to run my follow-up story about the intimidating interview I'd been subjected to.

* * *

Twelve days after the story on the Surry Hills bookie appeared, a much larger event, one that had been months in the making, got under way. Judge Athol Moffitt had been appointed by Premier Askin – who was desperate to stem the tide of damaging revelations emerging in that election year – to hold a royal commission into crime in licensed clubs and the allegations of US Mafia involvement in the local crime scene.

Moffitt opened the hearings on 20 August 1973. The commission has been well documented elsewhere; suffice it to say that over the next year a steady parade of criminals, crooked cops and a number of honest investigators stood to give their version of events. There were daily headlines; it was a rare event to have all these 'colourful Sydney identities' examined under oath in public. Not that the oath meant very much to many of the witnesses. Lennie McPherson lied – or suffered from temporary amnesia – throughout his testimony. Freeman, who police had told the inquiry was 'McPherson's second-in-command', was sworn in on 7 November, and behaved in much the same way as his mate. For example, under examination by Garth Needham QC, Freeman said he had been associated with Smith, and knew McPherson 'fairly well'. The chat continued:

    Needham: For a number of years you and McPherson and Smith were associated in a number of ways, were you not?

Freeman: What ways do you mean?
Needham: Well, you were friends of both these people?
Freeman: I am friends of theirs, yes.
Needham: You associated in the sense that you sought their company?
Freeman: That is incorrect.
Needham: Not correct?
Freeman: Not with McPherson.
Needham: Not with McPherson?
Freeman: No.
Needham: When you were an associate of McPherson and Smith, did Murray Riley also associate with him?
Freeman: I don't know.
Needham: You do not know Murray Riley?
Freeman: No.
Needham: Never met him?
Freeman: Never met him. I know who it is you are talking about, but I have never seen him at parties.

When Freeman denied knowing Harry Wren, Judge Moffitt knew for sure he was lying; the commission had been given by the federal police a photograph of Freeman with McPherson, Duke Delaney, Iron Bar Miller and Harry Orrel Wren, well known to police since 1960 as a thief, pickpocket and false pretender. Remarkably, Freeman also denied knowing Karl Bonnette and Paddles Anderson. It was a farce. Freeman was quizzed about his association with Joe Testa – his visit with Stan Smith to Chicago and the visits Testa made to Sydney – but he gave nothing away. He was back in the box for a second round a week later, but it was equally unproductive.

One crime figure who did not accept an invitation from Judge Moffitt and his team was Murray Riley. He had made himself scarce before the inquiry got under way – as had Ray Smith, the thug Riley had been knocking around with since before he left the force. As soon as the commission was over Riley was back working for McPherson: bullying people, collecting cash payments for protection against being bullied, collecting debts from SP clients, and regularly importing small quantities of drugs with individual couriers doing the run to southeast Asia and back.

George Freeman was named in Moffitt's report as Sydney's leading off-course bookmaker; he would have been grateful for the free publicity. Moffitt's main reference to Freeman was in relation to his presence at the 1972 meeting of crooks at Double Bay. He wrote:

> In view of their notoriety as criminals, it is a better speculation that criminal purposes are involved in their associations than that these associations are for innocent social purposes. What is clear is that the reasonable chance of connection of these persons with crime and potential further crime, in relation to the registered clubs, cannot be excluded. It would be dangerous so to conclude. It should not be overlooked that the police inquiry had public notoriety in April, 1972, and thereafter, until now, there has been either that inquiry or mine in progress or debate in Parliament about the matter. It is not unusual for truly organized crime to be sensitive to such occurrences and for a while thereafter.

* * *

It was 1974 and things were as they had ever been. Nobody really seemed to be bothered that the state was run by corrupt politicians, aided and abetted by corrupt police, all of which made the likes of George Freeman untouchable.

Fred Hanson welcomed in 1974 with a big grin: his partner-in-crime Premier Bob Askin had recommended him for a Commander Order of the British Empire (CBE) in the Queen Elizabeth's New Year's honours list. Other people seeking this gong would pay Askin up to $60,000 ($437,653) each to have their names included in the shortlist sent to the Queen. In fact, Ray Kelly would receive the same honour the very next year.

Roger Rogerson also received a boost, being promoted to the Armed Hold-up Squad in May. The new role may have been dangerous work but it seemed to provide good target practice for Rogerson: in the next five years he would shoot dead three criminals on the job. He maintained a close relationship with Freeman throughout his time in the squad. The bookie would have shared information with the rogue cop; both were aware of Freeman's absolute commitment to McPherson's current arrangements with his police contacts, and at that stage Rogerson was not yet receiving McPherson's reel-to-reel tape reports.

It was a time of relative peace between the various gangs. A few low-level crims had been quietly sent off the scene, and it had been nearly a decade since the last high-profile criminal assassination. But that was about to change.

John Regan was a fiercely independent criminal who sometimes knocked about with Freeman, Smith and McPherson. Although never really a member of the team, he was able to sit and chat with the trio about goings-on in the scene.

Regan had a well-known anecdote about the time he'd made a 'citizen's arrest' in the early 1970s. He had arrived at Darlinghurst Police Station to talk to the station's senior plainclothesman, Detective-Sergeant Noel Morey, a close ally of Rogerson. After the pair had chatted for a while, Morey rushed out into the squad room and asked Detective Mal Brammer to immediately bring inside the chap in the car parked out the front.

Brammer went outside to see a 'shaky-looking chap' wedged in the rear seat between two 'rather tough-looking' individuals, before bringing him into the station. The man had apparently stolen some furniture from a flat he was renting, which was owned by Regan.

Regan had promptly arrested him. Seeing his apprehender being dealt with almost as an equal by the senior detective persuaded the thief resistance was useless; he 'fessed up and told Regan where the stolen goods had been stashed. He then bided his time in a Darlo cell awaiting his court appearance, at which he pleaded guilty. But that was mild stuff for Regan, and in the end he just got too big for his boots. A decision was made by those who sat at the top table that he had to go.

The story goes that three gunmen lay in wait for Regan in Chapel Street, Marrickville, hidden from passers-by, but with a clear view of the entrance to the Henson Park Hotel across the

John 'The Boy' Regan: not one of the lads

John Stewart Regan was born on 13 September 1945 in Sydney. Making his criminal debut at age 17, he developed into what police described as 'a most vicious and incorrigible offender with an unparalleled record of crime and violence'.

Violent rapes, vicious assaults, theft, fraud, forgery and intimidation of witnesses peppered his career, which was also marked by frequent challenges to the police. Regan headed up a one-man vigilante outfit, the 'Independent Action Group for a Better Police Force'. In his memoir Freeman described the 'group' as 'the front for Regan's blood-splattered climb to the higher rungs of the criminal ladder'.

One of Regan's victims was 'Big' Barry Leonard Flock, who had been managing two eastern-suburbs massage parlours since 1966. After he had fallen out with a friend of Regan, Flock told of receiving threats to his life. According to George Freeman's version of the story in his biography, during the evening of Sunday, 15 January 1967, he was taken into an area of undergrowth on the grounds of the Scottish Hospital in Paddington. His body was found with five bullet-wounds to the head, which had been fired at close range.

In April 1972 Fred Krahe told various crims that Regan had taken up a contract with Melbourne gangsters to wipe out members of Sydney's notorious Toe Cutter gang, Bill Maloney and Kevin Gore. Regan killed Gore's driver, Robert Charles Donnelly, in error on the morning of 4 May 1972. When Donnelly didn't return with the car, Gore went looking for him. Later that afternoon Gore was witnessed talking to Regan. He was never seen again, and his body was never found. Bill Maloney later wrote a letter to Regan's solicitor, Michael Seymour, alleging that Regan had murdered Gore and Donnelly and that 'due to all this I have reason to believe Regan will dispose of me also'. Seymour told me that the letter was intended as a warning to Regan to 'keep his distance' from Maloney. It appeared to have worked: Bill Maloney lived to tell the story.

Regan saved his biggest challenge for fellow criminals. He began collecting standover payments from the city's prostitutes, which caused serious concern among those who thought that area of commerce was reserved for them. Then he moved his 'protection racket' demands

> into more lucrative areas, including the famous 33 Club illegal casino, which was the territory of Lennie McPherson and his crowd. Details are blurry, but Regan is rumoured to have also killed an SP bookie, one of Freeman's clients. He was clearly aiming to become an independent operator, and for the crims, cops and the organisations who paid over the bribes and protection money, Regan was bad for business.

way, on the corner of busy Illawarra Road. At six o'clock every Sunday evening John Regan would collect protection money from an illegal gambling operation.

On the evening of 22 September 1974, he was right on time. But he never made it to the door of the pub. The gunmen ambushed him, fired eight .38 calibre slugs into him (coincidentally the same ammo as used by police in those days) and left him to die in the middle of the street.

George Freeman confessed he was running a big two-up game in the hotel – the same one that had seen his start in the SP business back in 1964. It was beyond doubt that this was the illegal game from which Regan was about to collect protection money. Freeman admitted to being present in the hotel that night. He claimed he was subjected to intense questioning over the murder, but refused to comment.

In his own words, 'They pulled in about 200 people for questioning in the first week alone. One hundred and ninety-nine of them said where they were. I remained silent.' He added: 'I'm convinced the police heading the case were convinced I did it and were determined to nail me for it. I said then, and I repeat today, that I was in no way responsible for Regan's death. I was able then, as I am now, to account for my movements the day Regan was killed.'

But he never did, and was never even asked to do so. The investigation came to nothing. The illegal two-up game was not busted, and either there was insufficient evidence to put Freeman in the frame, even as an accessory, or his well-worn insurance deal was dusted off and someone received a handsome top-up payment.

10. Chips are down as casinos raided: punters take a short break

> Horse racing is animated roulette.
> – *Roger Kahn, American author*

After the 1974 execution of John Regan, the main gangs had settled back to their normal level of mutual mistrust. They looked on, no doubt in anger, as Bill Maloney's Toe Cutters (urged on by Detective-Sergeant Fred Krahe), waged war on Melbourne gangs and had a few of their own members exterminated. In general, though, this was seen as an unwanted calamity brought about by independent hotheads.

There were few other problems as the 'regular' gangsters went about their business, refining their involvement in the steadily growing drug trade.

The New Year started with Bob Askin's retirement from parliament on 3 January 1975. This caused some nervousness among those whose enterprises had relied on Askin's 'benevolence'. They needn't have worried: the only change was the name of the person at the top. The Honourable Thomas Lancelot Lewis, then 53, was chosen by the Liberal Party as its new leader, and he was sworn in as Premier, a position he would hold for just one year and three weeks. Eric Willis, the man who had earlier lifted the ban on multi-slot poker machines following some gentle persuasion from Bally Australia's Jack Rooklyn, would take over the top job on 23 January 1976 and hold it for just three months and 22 days.

March 1975 saw the release of a man called Arthur 'Neddy' Smith from jail, after he'd served time for rape. Neddy (we'll refer

Neddy no ass in the crime scene

Arthur Stanley 'Neddy' Smith was born in tough inner-city Redfern on 27 November 1944. He went to Cleveland Street Boys' school until he was 14. In April 1959 he faced two stealing charges for which he was placed on a bond, and in December was found guilty of assault and discharging an air gun in public. He was sentenced to time in the Tamworth Boys' Home.

His first jail sentence in 1963 at the age of 19 was for six and a half years on charges of break-enter-steal. On appeal this was reduced to two years. Then in 1967 came a conviction of rape, for which he was sentenced to 12 years in jail. He was paroled in March 1975.

In November 1976 he was arrested by Detective-Sergeant Roger Rogerson and charged with shooting with intent to murder, assault with attempt to rob, attempted armed robbery and possession of an unlicensed pistol. Neddy would have been grateful for the evidence Rogerson gave: the unlicensed pistol matter was quashed on appeal and on the other charges the court found that no prima facie case had been established.

The Independent Commission Against Corruption (ICAC) was later told – and the commissioner accepted it as the truth – that Neddy had paid $10,000 (*$81,179*) to Rogerson and another police officer in return for their false evidence. (Rogerson denied this, as he did all other allegations of impropriety in his police career.)

Among other matters, the ICAC investigation sought to establish whether Neddy Smith had been operating under police protection from the mid-1970s to the late 1980s. ICAC head Ian Temby found the allegation to be supported, saying: 'Because of police protection Smith led a charmed existence from 1976 to 1988. Smith was a professional criminal throughout this period, yet very few charges were laid against him, and only a few minor convictions were recorded.

'There were numerous occasions upon which Smith was provided with information by Rogerson, and he and Smith were in a network which also included Openshaw and John Brown. It is in my view significant that at much the same time Hakim was being helped by other police.' He said telephone intercept material clearly demonstrated the corrupt relationships between Smith and certain police.

> Neddy agreed to become an informer for Rogerson. On reasonably good terms with Freeman and McPherson ('friendly' would be overstating it), Neddy managed to elevate himself to a well-connected position in the underworld. He became a major drug importer, but the promotion didn't get in the way of his committing the odd murder or vicious assault. We will meet him again as our story unfolds.

to him thus to avoid confusion with Stan), like Freeman, came from a fatherless home and left school early, preferring a life of crime, and like Freeman, had spent time in boys' homes during his apprenticeship years.

* * *

In mid-1975 Murray Riley, still occasionally collecting for Freeman and McPherson, teamed up with Michael Moylan (son of the founder of the famous 33 Club casino) and Bruce 'Snapper' Cornwell, a small-time cannabis importer. Ex-policeman Clive Small, in his crime exposé *Smack Express*, claims this trio brought 21 shipments of cannabis, weighing a total of more than 300 kilograms, into Australia over four months beginning in May 1975. More went to New Zealand and later in the year they imported a further tonne of weed into the country. And still McPherson and Freeman – Riley's closest criminal allies – denied they had any involvement in drugs.

* * *

In early 1976 New Zealander Terry Clark came to Sydney to set up his now-notorious Mr Asia drug racket (a story for another time and place). While he met with the major Sydney criminals – and with the Griffith drug magnate Robert Trimbole – there is no evidence that the Sydney gangs, in particular Freeman (who'd just turned 41), McPherson and Smith, did any trade with him. They would have seen Clark as a flamboyant but dangerous interloper, and they were not keen on such turbulent troublemakers. Evan Whitton revealed that Clark was given by the locals the name of a top criminal lawyer, and on their recommendation he became a client of John Aston, who had just set up practice at 54 Park Street, Sydney – and that, it seems, was about the extent of the relationship between Clark and the local lads.

* * *

The long period of conservative party control of the NSW parliament came to an end with the swearing in on 14 May 1976 of 49-year old former barrister Neville Kenneth Wran. This caused a stir among Askin's supporters out in the field. Wran took on personal responsibility for the police force, scrapping the formal cabinet portfolio – although few realised it at the time. Russell D. Grove, Clerk of the Legislative Assembly, confirmed this in a letter to me:

> Between 1976 and 1979, a Minister for Police was not represented in the official Cabinet listing as a separate portfolio. The New South Wales Police Library has concurred that this information is accurate and that former Premier Wran was undertaking responsibilities of Police Minister from 14 May 1976 and 29 February 1980.

The formal portfolio was finally restored in 1980 when Bill Crabtree, then the 65-year-old Member for suburban Kogarah (coincidentally Jack McNeill's home territory), was sworn in as Minister for Police.

Until then, Wran held budgetary and ministerial responsibility for police. One wonders what he was up to by 'concealing' the existence of his responsibility for a seriously corrupt police force. With a majority of only one in the Legislative Assembly and a hostile majority in the Upper House that could block legislation, Wran told his MPs and expectant supporters not to expect great changes to happen quickly.

And in Sydney's mean streets there was a collective sigh of relief.

* * *

By mid-1976 there was talk among politicians of legalising casino gambling, sending shudders down the spines of some illegal operators and a tingle of excitement about the possibilities up others'. The options canvassed were legalising existing casinos and closing down all illegal operations, or approving one major new casino with the possibility of others to follow outside the state capital. Any move the government made would have to include a casino commission or control board, and it was made clear its appointees would be thoroughly scrutinised to ensure they had no criminal connections. This latter point seemed lost on Stan 'The Man' Smith who had discussions with George Freeman over dinner at the popular Tai Ping Chinese restaurant about the politicians they'd have to bribe to gain control of the new casino board.

Casinos were eventually legalised in NSW, much along the lines of the recommendations made by Justice Edwin Augustus Lusher on 19 July 1977 after his lengthy inquiries into the matter. The response from the government and police regarding shutting down the illegal competition was a staggering level of inaction. For six months business continued as normal for Freeman, Bruce Hardin, Perc Galea, Tony Torok, George Walker's Goulburn Club and the other illegal casino operators (the infamous Joe Taylor had died a year earlier).

Prying journalists began asking why. The police decided to strike a blow against the adverse publicity that was building: at 2.30 in the morning of Monday, 5 December 1977 – most certainly not peak hour at the baccarat table – the Gaming Squad raided one of the more renowned casinos, Ronnie Lee's Forbes Club in Darlinghurst. The three-storey converted terrace house was almost deserted when the cops arrived: a timely warning had been issued to the club that a raid was imminent. The cops also ensured a good story appeared. The *Daily Telegraph* had been tipped off and held its edition from the press for long enough to run the story on the front page, telling its readers the raid was 'beginning the process of closing down the illegal casinos'.

It was not, of course. The raid was a sham: nobody was fined – or jailed – for having been found in breach of the *Gaming and Betting Act* 1912, as amended, which provided at that time a fine of $2000 (*$9,953*) or a year behind the inhospitable bluestone walls of Long Bay Gaol.

The next action against the illegal gamblers came 18 months later, on 2 July 1979, and was somewhat more effective. Detective Superintendent Merv Beck took charge of a group called the 21 Special Squad and started raiding the gaming houses. His team, dubbed 'Beck's Raiders', reportedly used sledgehammers to break down bolted doors to reach the gamblers. Beck later said he could have pocketed $100,000 (*$422,257*) a year by agreeing to 'run dead' on the illegal casinos operating in the Chinatown district of Sydney alone. When the bribe offers were rejected, he and his family were threatened. He said the threats emanated from police: 'men with hearts the size of a split pea' was his colourful phrase.

Beck later told the ABC's Four Corners program that politicians from both major political parties had taken bribes from SP bookmakers, and that senior police officers had discouraged him from investigating some of the big players in the SP business – of which Freeman was the biggest.

Despite the pressures, Beck's Raiders chalked up an impressive 3500 arrests in its first ten months of operation. The most successful raid took place on Saturday, 12 January 1980, on the Freeman-McPherson controlled Rozelle casino, operated by Bruce Hardin, who hid in the female toilet during the raid. He was nabbed and later convicted.

After ten months, Beck and his hand-picked team were told they had done their job, and moved on to other duties. And in no time the casinos were all back in business, with huge fortunes flowing through the tables to the operators, the crooked cops and bent politicians.

Another year would pass before there were any more major attacks on the flourishing trade.

In 1981 a new police minister, Peter Anderson – himself an ex-cop from the honest side of the force – said he wasn't happy with the illegal gambling situation. 'So I recreated a special gaming squad,' he told reporter Steve Warnock of the *Sun-Herald*. 'I got rid of the 21 Division, which had a role in that area, and put Merv

Beck back on. I gave him the brief to close the places down – and he did.' The new 'Raiders' quickly made more than a thousand arrests, and reportedly 'broke the back of illegal operators'.

But Freeman and his illegal gambling colleagues were a persistent bunch: they quickly bounced back. Following the Raiders' second phase of attacks they were left alone for many years. George Paciullo had been the Labor member for Liverpool for 15 years when he took over the police portfolio from Peter Anderson in February 1986.

Just over a year into the job, he took his first steps against the illegal gambling industry. In March 1987 in parliament he named nine operations that he described as 'hardcore' gambling establishments.

He warned that anyone visiting the casinos would be 'odds-on to get a criminal record'. He told the media, 'I'm giving everyone a warning that the pressure will be maintained, that the rules have changed. They are no longer operating under conditions where they can expect to go to people to protect them, as may have been the position in past years.

'And I will continue, together with the police, to ensure that pressures are maintained until they are out of business. No one has any protection, regardless as to whether or not they are members of political parties, of the police force, public servants or otherwise.' It was brave stuff after so many decades of corrupt inactivity, previously interrupted only for the Peter Anderson-inspired moves led by Merv Beck.

But Paciullo's approach was quickly shown to be flawed. He'd named four casinos in Kings Cross, one in Double Bay, one in Darlinghurst and three in the suburbs, and the *Sydney Morning Herald* was quick to point out that while Freeman's partner in the Double Bay establishment, Tony Torok, had been named, George had not. Another omission from Paciullo's list was the long-established Goulburn Club in the city; this was an oversight opposition leader Nick Greiner said showed the minister to be either gullible or incompetent.

The main lessee of the premises, Greiner told the parliament, was 'none other than the former secretary of the Enmore branch of the ALP, Joe Meissner'. In response Paciullo said his list of nine operators was 'never intended to be comprehensive'. He said police had difficulty closing down the casinos because of the 'elaborate security measures' the operators had installed. Maybe he had never heard of the Beck's Raiders' successful technique involving sledgehammers.

Two months later Paciullo said police were moving against two casinos and that 'action would also be taken against the Goulburn Club'.

In the previous three months, he said, 279 gambling offence charges had been laid. Still Freeman and Hardin didn't get a mention. As Nick Greiner told parliament during the debate in April 1986 to approve a legal casino:

> No one who has read the history of Sydney's illegal casinos can doubt that by placing themselves beyond the law the operators of these premises have become deeply enmeshed in the world of organized crime and political corruption. It is the closeness with which these two threads – drug trafficking and political corruption – are woven into the fabric of Sydney's illegal gambling, that causes the Opposition much concern. One has only to turn to the reports of the joint task force on drug trafficking to see the intimate relationship between the illegal casinos and the drug trade, between Murray Stewart Riley and The 33 Club, and between the Forbes Club, the Double Bay Bridge Club and the Telford Club and certain members of the Riley syndicate.
>
> I remind honourable members that those reports named Croc Palmer as the proprietor of an illegal casino at Strathfield – the same man who is now serving fourteen years gaol for the importation of $40 million (*$103 million*) worth of cannabis. His co-conspirator in that case, Dr Paltos, was an intimate associate of Sydney's gambling king, Joe Taylor, and is recorded in the '*Age* tapes' involved in discussions with George

Freeman about an illegal casino. A summary attached to those documents records that Paltos was a partner with Freeman and Stan 'The Man' Smith in a casino in Sydney's outer suburbs ... During the 1984–85 casino amnesty, ownership lists included George Freeman, who, despite his denials is one of Sydney's leading criminals.

The legal casino at Darling Harbour eventually opened, and most – but certainly not all – of the illegals closed their doors for the last time.

* * *

Returning to events in 1976: before he died illegal gambler Joe Taylor had introduced George Freeman to Patrick John Watson, a 53-year-old police inspector from the 21 Division Gaming Squad. He had some important news for the SP bookie: 'Your phone is being bugged'. Watson was described in a tapped conversation between controversial solicitor Morgan Ryan and an associate, Brian Boyd, as 'having the capacity to approve or disapprove the conduct of illegal gambling'. That Watson met Freeman with Taylor – and on such friendly terms – indicates he had given a tick of approval to both of their illegal activities.

The phone bugging was part of an extensive, and largely illegal, operation run by a number of police. The fallout later surfaced in the '*Age* tapes' affair, which began with the publication in Melbourne's *Age* newspaper of the content of tapes of tapped telephone conversations between major criminals illegally obtained by some NSW police, and particularly involving the flight from Australia in May 1981 of major drug player Robert Trimbole. Many of the allegations about this event were aired in 1985 when the NSW government appointed Justice Donald Stewart to conduct a royal commission of inquiry into the affair. Stewart also, in 1981, headed a royal commission into drug trafficking, looking specifically at the Terry Clark/Mr Asia matter.

During the bugging activity in 1976, conversations between Freeman and (by then) Inspector Jack McNeill were recorded. In later testimony an officer said there was evidence of money frequently changing hands, which gave the impression 'that McNeill was accepting money from Freeman'. Another officer described McNeill as 'a threat' (presumably to good police work) as he was heard 'tipping [criminals] off and entering into deals with them'.

The phone bugs were undoubtedly illegal, but such was the depth of corruption within the NSW Police Force that officers keen on prosecuting criminals – rather than taking bribes from them – resorted at times to desperate measures to fight their losing battles. Retired Superintendent E. E. Cannacott was to tell Justice Stewart's '*Age* tapes' inquiry that he'd been briefing on the telephone taps to Assistant Commissioner (Crime) Reginald T. Stackpool, who then briefed Commissioner Fred Hanson. After later talks between Deputy Commissioner Leonard Newman and CIB Chief Superintendent Alexander Magnus Birnie had taken place, Hanson ordered that the bugging of Freeman's telephone be stopped.

* * *

Some deaths were celebrated in grand style by the crims. The passing of Joe Taylor, gambler and illegal casino operator and founder of Thommo's Two-up School, on 17 August 1976 at the age of 68, led to a rare display of clan unity. Police Commissioner Fred Hanson was among the great throng of mourners to attend the funeral service the following Friday at St Mary's Roman Catholic Cathedral. George Freeman, who described Taylor as 'a beautiful man, in many ways he was the father I never knew,' was there, of course. A cortege stretching half a mile followed the mourning coaches to the Northern Suburbs Crematorium. A floral horseshoe, nearly two metres tall and carrying a card saying: 'Dearly loved, never forgotten, rest in peace Joe. From Thommo's', was among the three hundred wreaths. At least nobody played Sinatra's 'My Way'.

* * *

Fresh from Joe Taylor's funeral, Fred Hanson took a trip down to Griffith, in southern NSW for some duck shooting – out of the official season – with a local expert, drug kingpin Robert Trimbole. There was no report on how many birds they bagged, but Hanson did bring home a gift from the cannabis crop chief:

Darcy Dugan's last stand: against reflections in the *Mirror*
Infamous jail escapee and George Freeman's boyhood idol, Darcy Dugan, had in 1950 been sentenced to hang after he was found guilty of assault with intent to murder. The sentence was commuted to life in prison after NSW abolished the death penalty in 1955. In 1970 he was charged and convicted of assault and robbery, crimes committed while he was out of goal on licence. Dugan copped an additional sentence of 14 years, to be served concurrently with the balance of his life sentence.

In 1976 he tried to launch a defamation case against the Sydney tabloid the *Daily Mirror* for having published a description of him that he thought reflected poorly on his 'good character and reputation'. His case failed on the esoteric legal basis that a person who has been sentenced to death (even if it was later commuted) suffered attainder – a 'corruption of the blood' – that barred him from taking civil action in court. Dugan brought the matter to the High Court where, in December 1978, six of the seven judges dismissed Dugan's appeal, with only Lionel Murphy suggesting that even a person with 'corrupted blood' should have access to basic human rights. Dugan was finally released from jail in 1985, an old and tired man. He died in 1991.

an Italian-made shotgun worth around $8000 ($44,715).

Looking after a police force such as his and tending to the needs of the major criminals on his patch was surely exhausting. As early as February 1976 Hanson made it known he would be happy to retire, on the condition he could nominate his successor – champion oarsman Merv Wood. The government set up a committee, of which Hanson was a member, to resolve the question of an heir. The committee recommended, on 5 June 1976, that Merv Wood replace Hanson. On 31 December 1976 Hanson formally retired to his Terrigal home.

Only six weeks earlier, Hanson had made headlines yet again: Bill Archibald, veteran police-rounds reporter for the *Sydney Sun* afternoon tabloid, reported on 15 November that Hanson had been offered a directorship with Sir Peter Abeles' Thomas Nationwide Transport.

Abeles was widely lauded as a successful businessman but was also deeply involved in the corruption of state and federal politicians, and had earlier in 1976 persuaded retired premier Bob Askin to join his company as a director. When Archibald's story hit the streets, TNT chairman Frederick Millar stated there was no truth in the allegation about Hanson.

Archibald would have none of it: two days later he swore in a statutory declaration that Hanson had talked of his TNT directorship with senior police, and that Hanson had told him that Askin had instructed him, if asked by the media, to deny the story. The TNT posting would have undoubtedly provided a small income to the retired top cop, a vote of thanks for his loyal service to the 'brotherhood'.

For Hanson there was no glory, no grand appointments, and on the morning of Sunday, 26 October 1980 Carol Hanson found her husband, Fred, in his pyjamas, slumped over the wheel of their car in the garage of their home at Terrigal. He had committed suicide: a hose had fed toxic carbon monoxide gas from the car's exhaust into the vehicle, as confirmed by the coroner a month later. His widow, who was the beneficiary of his estate, died on 25 March 1986, leaving an estate worth $1.22 million (*$2.88 million*).

11. A shot in the dark: Freeman cops it in the neck

> It is easier to lead men to combat, stirring up their passion, than to restrain them and direct them toward the patient labors of peace.
> – André Gide, 1947 Nobel Laureate

One of George Freeman's most infamous moments took place at a midweek race meeting at Randwick racecourse on 27 July 1977. Freeman had for more than a year been providing the NSW Chief Stipendiary Magistrate Murray Farquhar with regular racing tips – said by one observer later to be '98 to 99 per cent accurate'. Normally Farquhar's clerk, Camille Abood, would place the bets, each of around $400 to $600 (*$1,990 to $2,986*), and later collect the winnings. On this fateful Wednesday, things were done differently.

Freeman's friend Dr Nick Paltos had acquired a spare ticket for the Members Stand at the racecourse and invited Freeman to join him.

Chief Magistrate Farquhar was also there. In one of journalism's great moments, the trio were spotted and photographed sitting and chatting together. Racecourse detective Frank Lynch, when alerted to Freeman's presence, ordered that he leave immediately. Freeman wrote it all off as a non-event, but the photo ensured evidence of Freeman's influence over the state's most senior magistrate would live on. Farquhar didn't help his case at the time when he refused to answer questions put to him by justice department investigators about his association with known criminals.

A fortnight after the photo opportunity at Randwick, Farquhar cemented his loyalty to Freeman by perverting justice in a case involving a big punting client of George's, Australian Rugby League boss Kevin Humphreys. Humphreys' losses had led him to steal a total of $50,000 ($279,461) from the Balmain Rugby Leagues Club, of which he was secretary-manager. The case had started more than a year earlier, after a Balmain club member laid an official complaint. At that early stage Freeman's support within the police force came into play, with unexpected outcomes. On 7 July 1976 the case had been referred to then-newly elected premier and minister responsible for police matters, Neville Wran, who'd referred it on to Commissioner Fred Hanson.

Hanson had said he would ask his assistant commissioner, Reg Stackpool, to investigate the claims. Stackpool was close to Freeman and had earlier advised Hanson to have the bugging of the bookie's phone terminated.

Fraud Squad detective-sergeant Clarence Robert Frodsham and his offsider Constable Mick Newtown were assigned to investigate the case and on 9 August submitted their first report, which clearly suggested Humphreys would be charged within the fortnight. Just days after, Reg Stackpool brought Kevin Humphreys into Hanson's office.

The commissioner then called Frodsham into the gathering, asking the investigator – in the presence of Stackpool and Humphreys – how serious a matter it was. Frodsham told them he considered the matter very serious, and was then asked to leave the office. Angry at what had taken place, Frodsham reported the incident to his superiors.

On 3 November Frodsham's final ten-page report recommended nine charges of fraudulent misappropriation be laid against Humphreys.

Copies of the file were sent to Stackpool and Hanson. Another was leaked to Humphreys' legal team. Within a couple of weeks Hanson ordered the investigating police to again attend an urgent meeting in his office. Frodsham was astonished to find that the subject of their investigation, Kevin Humphreys, again joined them.

A version of what happened was later given in evidence by then Assistant Commissioner Brian Doyle, to whom Frodsham and Newton reported after their meeting with Hanson. Frodsham told Doyle, 'This morning we were sent for to see Mr Hanson urgently. We walked in and there was Mr Humphreys sitting down with Mr Hanson, and Mr Hanson asked us would we tell him what we were doing in the case. I said I did not think we should tell the evidence in front of Mr Humphreys.' Hanson, said Frodsham, had insisted on hearing the report there and then. Humphreys said nothing while this remarkable exchange was taking place. Frodsham told Doyle that Hanson had then directed them to drop the inquiries and take no further action. Doyle said he advised Frodsham, 'Hanson is retiring in a matter of weeks ... when he retires you will no longer be bound by his direction. That is when you go and get Humphreys and whack him in the dock.' (Frodsham later disputed this quote but did not argue with the general thrust of Doyle's version of events.) On 18 January 1977, with the approval of the new commissioner, Merv Wood, Frodsham served summonses for the nine charges on Humphreys in his lawyer's office. Each of the charges, if proven, carried a maximum penalty of 15 years in jail. The first hearing was set down for 26 May 1977 but was quickly adjourned to mid-August at the request of Humphreys' lawyers. It was while these events were unfolding that Reg Stackpool took extraordinary steps to kill off a police report highly critical of George Freeman and the failure of police to move against him.

Frodsham, meanwhile, made diary entries alleging that the premier and chief magistrate were conspiring to pervert the course of justice.

The policeman later testified that a journalist had phoned him, saying, 'There's a big tip you are going to have no chance of fitting Humphreys at all. They have fixed it up.' In a subsequent royal commission Chief Justice Sir Laurence Street said that while he accepted Frodsham's evidence as truthful, he had concluded that 'the rumour can be safely and properly placed aside as having no foundation in fact'.

On the first day of the hearing, Farquhar told Magistrate Kevin Willson Jones to summarily dismiss the charges. Evidence later before Chief Justice Street stated Farquhar had said to Jones, 'The premier's contacted me. He wants Kevin Humphreys discharged.' The following day Humphreys' legal team was optimistic their client would be discharged, despite a strong case having been put by the police. After the lunch break, Jones dismissed the charges. As he celebrated the result later at the NSW Leagues Club, Kevin Humphreys told a reporter, 'It's good to be able to say thank you to so many good friends who have stuck by me.' He undoubtedly would have had George Freeman, the SP bookmaker on who he relied for a bit of credit from time to time, at the top of his list. Humphreys later said on TV that the image of his beloved sport, rugby league, suffered because he attended George Freeman's 1981 wedding, but that he 'had the right to attend a wedding of a friend of mine if I so desired.' Years later, in April 1983, in a detailed investigation by ABC Four Corners reporter Chris Masters, Kevin Jones confessed all. Humphreys was later retried and convicted on the theft charges and, thanks to a clever lawyer, got off with a bond. Freeman, whose association with Farquhar was highlighted in the same Four Corners program, was not mentioned in either of the court cases. We'll have more on Mr Farquhar later.

* * *

In 1977 assistant commissioner in the NSW Police Force, 61-year-old Reg Stackpool, sent Sergeant Anthony Lauer, then in the Criminal Intelligence Unit (CIU) into 'exile'. Lauer was given a posting to Katoomba in the Blue Mountains for producing a report highly critical of George Freeman, describing him as 'Sydney's leading criminal of the day' and suggesting the information had been brought to people's attention in the past but had not been acted on. Among the many specific claims in Lauer's report was that his close friend Bruce Hardin ran the SP operation at 252 Darling Street, Balmain, for Freeman. The CIU protocols required its reports to be sent to other appropriate squads for action. The 21 Division investigated the Lauer dossier and history repeated itself: 21 Division found no evidence of criminal activity by Freeman or any others named in the report.

* * *

Some people blame poverty for criminal activity, and while it may be a factor, clearly not all poor people become criminals and not all criminals have poor backgrounds. It's difficult to theorise about why people choose a life of crime, but for at least a few of our 'persons of interest' there was probably a cog or two missing from the main gearwheel.

This is the most likely case for the protagonist in the bizarre story of George Freeman's shooting. A number of other developments would set this in motion.

When Freeman's neophyte and loyal follower Michael Hurley received a four-year stint in Goulburn Gaol in 1977 for stealing, the older man should have treated with caution Hurley's request that he take care of things for him. Hurley had committed a robbery in a city jewellery shop with a long-standing mate, Norm Beves – who'd worked for Freeman for more than a decade – and then stole more than five thousand watches from a warehouse in Kent Street, on the city's western fringe. He said later he pleaded guilty to the second robbery but hadn't committed it; he was taking the rap for a friend he owed a favour to. Not interested, said the judge, four years' hard labour.

Freeman paid a visit to his younger mate in jail and agreed to take care of some of his business activities, and to 'look after Lena', Hurley's wife and the fearsome gunman Jacky Muller's daughter.

Freeman, still a bachelor, took the latter request too seriously, and the couple began a sexual relationship that they could not keep secret.

It was not true love, for Freeman persuaded Lena to become the madam in a brothel he had acquired in Woolloomooloo. Having heard of Abe Saffron's facilities, where the rich, famous and powerful were photographed and filmed during sex-romps, Freeman had a number of video cameras installed in his own bordello and, to a lesser extent than Saffron, managed to use the explicit footage for blackmail and bribery purposes – a useful addition to his existing indemnity arrangements.

With around a year of his jail term still to serve, Hurley learned of his mentor's treachery and his wife's infidelity, but what could he do about it? He couldn't reach Freeman from his Goulburn prison cell.

Hurley instead had a chat about his problem with Lena's father, who assured his son-in-law he would take the matter up with Freeman.

On 25 April 1979 – an Anzac Day public holiday all over Australia – Freeman dropped his son Grant, then 13, at the home of his mother, Marcia, at nearby Sans Souci and returned to his mansion at Yowie Bay to handle a busy day overseeing gambling matters on races in Sydney, Brisbane and Melbourne. His phone would run hot on big race days like this. He recalled later he'd had a winning day and 'was feeling well with the world'.

He had spent the evening with Nick Paltos and his wife of 12 years, Marie. Strained economic circumstances caused by Paltos' gambling debts had forced the couple to move from their luxurious two-storey mansion Gwandalan, in Bellevue Hill. Now they were living in the accommodation attached to a suburban surgery in Murray Street, Maroubra, a 50-minute drive from Freeman's home.

Over a roast dinner they no doubt discussed the medico's plans to resign from his post at Sydney Hospital to attend to his new private clinic at Woolloomooloo, the working-class enclave east of the city.

They almost certainly also discussed the large debt Paltos was accumulating with Freeman via his betting losses, but Paltos was a mate; there would be no violent repercussions in this case. Paltos was making some arrangements for the debt: a Sydney solicitor he had met, Ross John Karp, was happy to lend the doctor $300,000 (*$1,050,520*) out of gratitude for the medical treatment Paltos had provided to Karp's ailing father. The money would be borrowed from a family company, Karp had told him.

With appetite fully sated and in a relaxed mood, Freeman drove his Mercedes to an illegal casino in Kensington to collect his commission and then headed home to Yowie Bay. He recalled it was a calm, still autumn night. As he unlocked the front door, he felt an impact on the side of his face. Realising he'd been shot, he zigzagged back down the driveway, expecting more bullets at any moment. At his next-door neighbour's house, towels were used to stem the bleeding. The neighbour called ambulance officers and police, and, at Freeman's request, Nick Paltos, whom he knew would still be at home. Freeman recited the doctor's number from memory as the neighbour dialled.

After the ambulance delivered the survivor to Sutherland Hospital, Paltos arrived with Marcia, George's ex-wife. Freeman recalled, 'What followed was the most excruciating pain I've ever known. I was lying there half hoping I'd die so the pain would end; yet at the same time fighting to keep control. They X-rayed me again. By now I was desperate for something to kill the pain.' The .22-calibre bullet had hit him in the left side of his neck and passed up through his mouth, grazing an optic nerve and exiting near the corner of his eye. Clearly, he had had a very lucky escape.

Police spent a lot of time questioning him, trying to get a tag on the likely culprit. If Freeman told them anything, he never admitted it.

If he did know who had shot at him, he would have also known what had motivated the attack, and telling that story would have inevitably led to admitting he'd been sleeping with Lena Hurley. He spent a short time recuperating on a friend's farm, but the psychological trauma would take much longer to heal.

At 12.40 a.m. on Thursday, 7 June 1979, 43 days after the attack on Freeman, Jacky Muller turned his 1972 Austin 1800 into the driveway of his home in Quail Street, in the beachside suburb of Coogee. There, he was shot dead. The gunman had stepped from the shadow of a brick wall and fired three nine-millimetre bullets from a pistol through the driver's side window, hitting Muller in the head and neck. He died instantly. The car rolled on, crashing into a fence near the back door of the house. Police described the murder as 'a gangland execution'.

At a later coroner's hearing a policeman said under oath

that Muller had in the past been friendly with George Freeman, but that there was no evidence linking Freeman to the death. Freeman, the policeman said, was holidaying at Noosa Heads in Queensland at the time of Muller's murder.

Not everyone got their story straight: Freeman, in his memoir, wrote that on the day of Muller's murder he had been interviewed by Homicide Squad officers at Randwick police station, and then by 'dozens of detectives' at Maroubra police station, all difficult to achieve if he was holidaying at Noosa, some 1200 kilometres north. As was the case with John Regan's killing, Freeman didn't bother explain the discrepancies in his alibi in his memoir, simply saying:

> My story was always the same. 'On the advice of my solicitor I reserve the right to remain silent.' (I always accept my solicitor's advice on such matters.) I will add this about the Muller case: if I was ever charged with Muller's murder, I could certainly account for my movements at the relevant times.

In fact he had gone to the trouble of creating an alibi for himself. His good friend Nick Paltos would confirm, if he were ever asked, that his patient George Freeman had spent that whole night at Paltos' new clinic in Riley Street, Woolloomooloo, for treatment for his asthma.

That's what friends are for – particularly the ones who owe you a lot of money. But nobody ever asked Freeman, it seems, or Paltos. By that time he was well and truly one of the 'invincibles', literally able to get away with murder.

* * *

Freeman's former 'rookie bookie' turned bitter adversary, Michael Hurley, made new alliances after their falling out. The Sydney crime scene, however, has a small population: who you pick as a friend could also be a friend of your enemy. So when Hurley linked into the violent world of Arthur 'Neddy' Smith in the early 1980s after his stint at Goulburn Gaol, he also became closer to Roger Rogerson, and Roger was on friendly terms with Freeman and McPherson. Hurley also began working – stealing things –

with another of Neddy's allies, Glen Roderick Flack, who like so many in this competitive field had once aspired to be Sydney's Mister Big.

It was Flack's dangerous stupidity, evidenced by his mouthing off about being a big shot, which had ensured that McPherson and Freeman kept a close watching brief on him. In this way they were kept up to date on his activities with Neddy, Hurley and their crowd. And it was a busy team indeed.

In May 1987 Detective Chief Inspector John Patrick Toohey suggested to his superiors that a task force be set up to investigate a series of armed payroll robberies in Sydney and Newcastle being carried out, he believed, by Neddy Smith and Glen Flack. They gave him the nod, and Operation Zig Zag went into action a month later. But it was doomed to fail before it even began: Smith and Flack were told by crooked cops that they were to be put under surveillance, and the lads promptly went to ground for a while. Neddy Smith later testified to ICAC that Roger Rogerson had told him one of the police involved wanted $5000 – obviously for the forewarning of the police activity.

Rogerson, who had been thrown out of the force the year before, met with Smith, Flack and the policeman at the Returned Services League club at Doyalson, near Newcastle, on 10 June.

The work of the Zig Zag team had been compromised, and the task force was closed down after Neddy Smith and Flack were charged with an unrelated murder. Tow-truck assistant Ronnie Flavell, aged 34, had been killed in Coogee on 30 October. Neddy Smith was eventually given a life sentence for the murder; Glen Flack copped a 12-year stretch in 1988 for planning – with Neddy while he was awaiting trial for murder – to steal the Botany Council Christmas payroll.

While Neddy's departure from the scene was to cause problems for Rogerson, there was almost certainly quiet celebration between McPherson and Freeman that Smith and his arrogant mate Flack would be out of the picture for a long time.

* * *

Flack leaves his money to Mum

Eventually paroled from jail, Glen Flack at least twice a week would visit his mum, Margaret Elizabeth, in her housing department terrace cottage at 6 Broughton Street in inner-suburban Glebe.

On one such visit in April 1994 he placed a black briefcase at the rear of the top shelf in a hallway cupboard. The case contained $433,000 (*$704,126*), which he had amassed by less than honest means. He didn't mention the briefcase to his mother. Imagine her amazement, then, when a week later her house was raided by federal police, acting on a warrant to search the house for evidence of drug-related offences committed by her son.

The cops discovered the briefcase and showed her the contents. She expressed genuine amazement. The money was handed over to the National Crime Authority (NCA), but no charges resulted from the raid. Three years later Mrs Flack started an action in the Federal Court saying she wanted the money back. Judge Graham Hill rejected the NCA's argument that Mrs Flack 'did not have sufficient title' to the briefcase and its contents, and ordered it all to be returned to her.

The NCA appealed against this and in August 1998, in a two-to-one majority decision, the appeal court judges upheld Mrs Flack's right to the small fortune.

The NCA sought to appeal to the High Court, but that move was rejected, and the money – and the box – were returned to Mrs Flack. Nobody doubted that the source of the funds was from some crime committed by Glen, but as High Court Chief Justice Murray Gleeson remarked, nobody had produced any evidence to support that claim, so the occupant of the premises where the money was found had prior claim of ownership to it.

Mrs Flack never revealed whether any of the money was ever handed over to her son.

A couple of footnotes to the Hurley–Freeman saga. Lena Hurley was divorced by her husband. Freeman had Nick Paltos prescribe painkilling drugs to alleviate the continuing agony he suffered after the shooting. Paltos prescribed for his patient pethidine, a synthetic narcotic drug with morphine-like properties, and taught Freeman how to inject it intravenously. In addition to the pain from the bullet wound, he had long suffered abdominal and kidney pain, and had for all his adult life been a severe asthma sufferer.

He regularly took Valium to calm his nerves, and came to be so reliant on pethidine that he became addicted to the drug. A coroner later revealed that over time Freeman was getting supplies of pethidine from at least three doctors, none knowing of the others' prescriptions. From this time on, Freeman – who, like all crims, publicly railed against the evil of drugs – was himself so profoundly drug-dependent that he was registered with the NSW Health Department as an approved patient to be prescribed drugs of dependence, in other words, he was a registered drug addict.

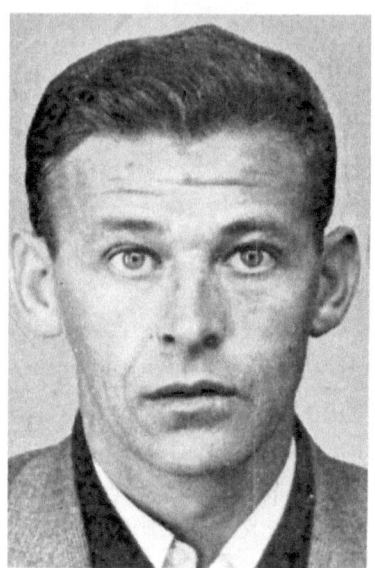

Lennie 'Mr Big' McPherson (top left) was often considered the number one crime boss in Sydney for more than three decades from the early 1950s, but in fact he shared the top job with George Freeman (top right), Stan 'The Man' Smith (bottom left) with Abe 'Mr Sin' Saffron running the sex and drug trades in Kings Cross.

Four successive NSW police commissioners from Colin Delaney (top left), 1952–62, Norm Allan (top right) 1962–72, Fred Hanson (bottom left) 1972–76 and Merv Wood, 1977–79, did little to stop the spread of organised crime or in some cases actually encouraged it.

George Freeman, Nick Paltos and Murray Farquhar's day at the races at Randwick.

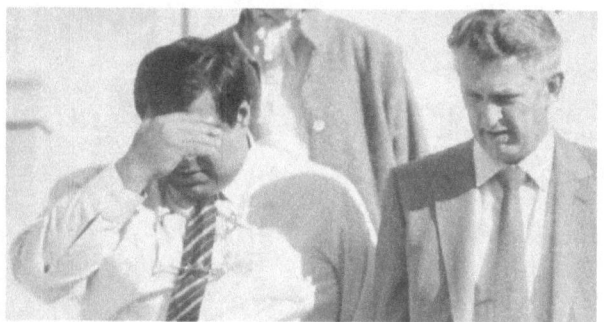

Doctor Nick Paltos, Freeman's doctor, was arrested on 15 August 1985 for involvement in a major drug importation.

Michael John Sayers, avid gambler and backer of the Fine Cotton ring-in scandal, was gunned down outside his home in the gangland warfare of the mid-1980s.

Christopher Dale Flannery became George Freeman's bodyguard. He disappeared in 1985, certainly a murder victim.

John Stewart Regan was a criminal who refused to play by the rules set by Freeman, McPherson and the bad cops. He was shot dead on his way to collect standover money from Freeman.

Michael Hurley was befriended by George Freeman, who later had an affair with Hurley's wife.

Legendary Sydney criminal Darcy Dugan became an early role model for George Freeman.

Bookmakers Bill and Robbie Waterhouse were banned from racecourses after the Fine Cotton ring-in affair. They blamed Freeman for their problems.

Karl Bonnette is described in NSW police records as 'a desperate criminal who is depraved and is strongly suspected of trafficking in drugs'.

Charles 'Paddles' Anderson, an old-fashioned criminal and corrupter of police and politicians.

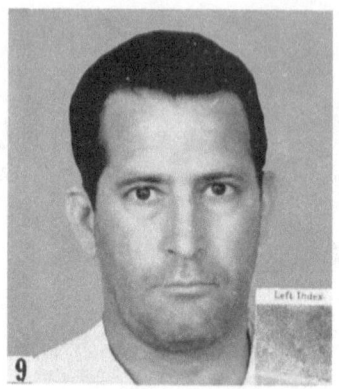

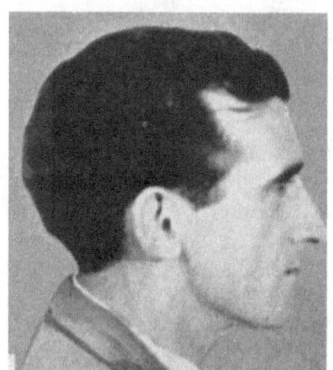

(*Clockwise from top left*) Master international shoplifter Arthur 'The Duke' Delaney welcomed George Freeman onto his team in the early 1960s. Other gang members were Richard Jarvis, Harold O'Brien, James Wilson and Cecil Lloyd.

Robert (formerly Robin) Askin encouraged police corruption during his term as New South Wales Premier (1965–75).

Judge John Foord was referred to the National Crime Authority over allegations he was lenient to clients of solicitor Morgan Ryan.

NSW Chief Magistrate Murray Farquhar engaged George Freeman as his horse-racing tipster and illegal bookie.

Chief Magistrate Clarrie Briese was involved on the periphery of the Cessna-Milner drug case saga.

Louie Sarkis El Bayeh, who was naturalised in 1951, went on to become a powerful Kings Cross-based player in Sydney crime.

Ex-boxer Terence Edward Ball was charged in 1986 with the attempted murder of Neddy Smith, but the case was later dropped.

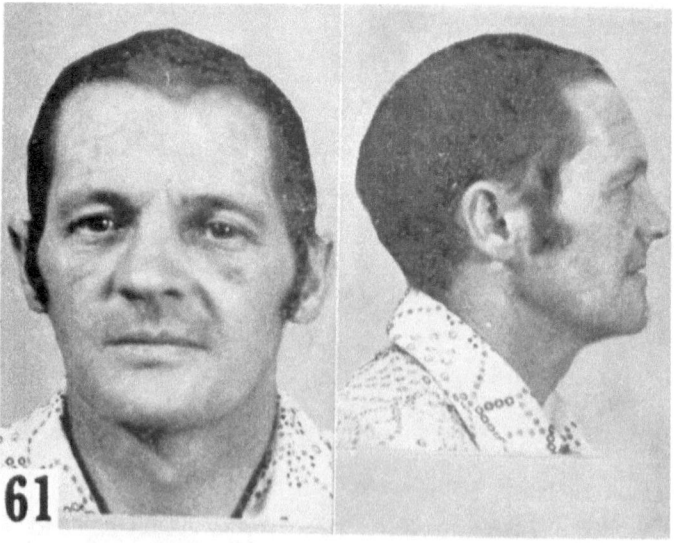

Graham 'Abo' Henry was a major heroin dealing partner with Arthur 'Neddy' Smith.

David Kelleher, who teamed up with Freeman and McPherson, made legal history by becoming the first person in Australia to be sentenced to life imprisonment under revised laws dealing with heroin importation.

Drug dealer Warren Charles Lanfranchi was shot dead by detective Roger Rogerson.

Milan Petricevic, better known as Iron Bar Miller in recognition of his combat weapon of choice, was a close associate of George Freeman.

Robert 'Jacky' Steele was gunned down in the street by McPherson. Media stories dubbed him the 'Iron Man' Steele as he survived the shooting for some time.

Murray Stewart Riley, rowing champion, ex-copper, and jail escapee, worked with Freeman before being nabbed on a major drug importation.

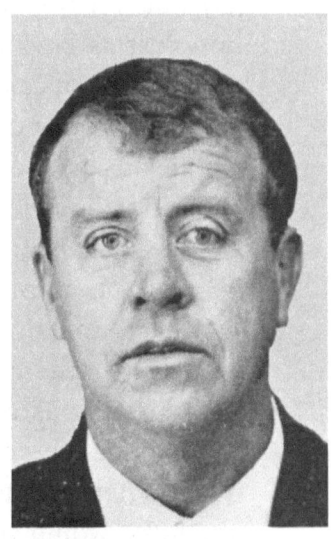

William Joseph Stevens, a violent criminal, teamed up with George Freeman, Stan 'The Man' Smith and others on a shoplifting spree to Perth.

12. A new top cop, the same old game

> The world is a dangerous place, not because of
> those who do evil, but because of those
> who look on and do nothing.
> – Albert Einstein

A police commissioner widely known to have been corrupt nominating his successor should have been unthinkable, but on 1 January 1977 Mervyn Wood took up duties as the state's top cop, just as Fred Hanson had wanted. It wasn't just corruption within the police force that allowed this travesty; dishonesty was rife at all levels of the state's administration – from prominent politicians and senior bureaucrats down. The NSW government was riddled with those who participated in, or at least condoned by their silence, such extraordinarily brazen skulduggery as Wood's appointment.

The criminals and shonky businessmen who d paid handsomely to maintain the status quo quietly welcomed Wood's appointment as a signal it would be business as usual. Some sections of the police force, and a journalist or three, opposed Wood's new role to no effect. The struggle to restore integrity to the force would prove to be lengthy. The new leader, however, would become embroiled in one controversy after another.

Those hoping that Wood – who had not worked the streets, where cops mix with crims and wads of money change hands – would run a more honest force were soon disappointed. When he learned the Criminal Intelligence Unit (CIU) was conducting an internal investigation that linked police officers to organised-crime activities, Wood ordered a raid on the unit's offices. During

Wood holds the fort

Mervyn Thomas Wood was born in the Sydney suburb of Randwick on 30 April 1917. At age 17 he applied to become a policeman, as his father, uncle and older brother had done before him. He married Joyce Shelley in 1942.

In 1940 he joined the fingerprint section, where he'd spend the next 34 years – apart from 18 months from April 1944, when he joined the RAAF to do his bit fighting in the Second World War.

While he was innovative in his police desk job, Wood's greatest interest was rowing. On signing up to the force he joined the police rowing eight, which competed in four Olympic Games and brought home three medals, including the gold in 1948. At the 1956 Melbourne games Murray Riley joined the squadron.

Riley, as we have heard, left the team within six years to become a major drug trafficker and a heavy for Freeman and McPherson.

Wood moved into police administration in 1974, becoming super-intendent of the Chatswood division, and a year later assistant commissioner under the careful tutelage of Fred Hanson. It would not, however, be an easy succession: Wood proved incapable of the ruthlessness that had protected his crooked predecessors from the media and parliament's wrath. He was not to have a long tenure, and was not offered the privilege of anointing his successor.

the raid, the team confiscated tapes and transcripts of telephone taps; among those whose phones had been bugged was George Freeman. A report later found that as a result of the raid 'the investigation which had begun into the allegations of serious corruption and police associations with organised crime ground to a halt'.

At the Stewart inquiry into the '*Age* tapes' affair, Wood denied there had been any raid. Instead, he stated that he and other officers had gone to the CIU offices to check whether a certain report on George Freeman, which had been referred to in parliament, was the same one the unit held – an insinuation that the CIU was leaking information to politicians. In his summation Justice Stewart said that despite contradictory evidence about the raid, the incident demonstrated a growing feeling in the CIU that 'senior police, including the commissioner, were corrupted by their association with organised crime figures, and would actively assist those figures by interfering with the investigations of the various units of the police force'.

Stewart also heard evidence from CIU officers that a tap on Neddy Smith's phone had picked up conversations with then Detective Sergeant Roger Rogerson. The information suggested that Rogerson tried to interfere in an investigation that resulted in Smith's October 1978 arrest on a charge of conspiring to import heroin from Thailand. Smith was later acquitted of the charge. In the taps, the officers alleged, Rogerson urged Neddy to keep his distance from heroin trade associate David Kelleher, who was getting out of line to the extent that his bad behaviour would no longer be tolerated by others in the business. Rogerson denied the allegations, falling back on the maxim that cops have to maintain contact with some criminals 'in the line of duty'.

Wood did not consider the 1977 CIU report, which contained allegations of links between police and criminals such as Lennie McPherson, George Freeman and Stan Smith, to be 'serious enough' to bring to the attention of Premier Neville Wran, who at the time held complete political responsibility for the police. When he learned of this, the premier was not happy.

* * *

Merv Wood was committed to not rocking the boat, and he issued a public statement in December 1977 stating he couldn't see any hard evidence of organised crime in the state, and that he would not force the closure of the illegal casinos because 'the loss of jobs would cause hardship at Christmas'. In one interview he elaborated:

> It's a big city and you can't drive everything underground. You're foolish to try. We've tried it with dire results. It's better to let a thing exist where you know everything about it. I remember years ago we tried to eradicate prostitution. The next thing we knew they were popping up in the better suburbs. None of these things are felonies;

they're what we call social offences, SP betting and so forth. While you don't condone them, it's better to know what they're doing than have them hidden and under the control of people we don't want to see in Sydney.

Not everyone was as generous to the crims as Wood. In August 1977 Justice Philip Woodward had been appointed Commissioner of the NSW Royal Commission into Drug Trafficking. He'd been quick to name George Freeman as a crime boss. However, royal commissions make recommendations; they cannot initiate prosecutions. Without action from the police force or government, the mass of evidence gathered in such an inquiry would not bother the crims.

* * *

The crooks usually faced difficulties when they wanted to travel. In 1977 Karl Bonnette talked with McPherson about making another trip to the US; they planned to visit some old acquaintances, and perhaps revive the Mafia's flagging interest in the Sydney scene. As a first step to obtaining a US entry visa both Bonnette and McPherson changed their names by deed poll. The changes were registered nationally and the details passed on to US immigration which, learning of the duo's interesting background, rejected their applications.

In April 1978 Freeman and Nick Paltos did make it to the US. The Australian authorities seemed not to have been aware of Freeman's itinerary – the friends travelled separately – but alerted the FBI to Paltos. The FBI's watch on the doctor led them to Freeman, who was arrested and charged as an 'excludable person'. He paid a bond of US$15,000 and voluntarily returned to Sydney.

In a subsequent raid on Freeman's home for evidence supporting a forged-passport charge, federal police discovered thousands of counterfeit TAB betting slips. News of the find was passed on their NSW colleagues, who flicked the investigation the Kogarah police station, located not far from the scene. Local cops arrested Freeman – who at that stage reportedly controlled at least 20 betting agencies across Sydney, none of which had ever been raided by police – and took him in to charge him. Before the paperwork had even begun, they got a call from Inspector Jack McNeill, instructing them to release the man, and to 'leave Freeman to me in the future'.

The drug arm of the Freeman-McPherson-Smith gang saw some serious action in 1978 after NSW Police tapped ex-cop Murray Riley's phone. Riley's conversations gave clues about a major international drug shipment he was arranging, but did not reveal his partners' names – those he had profitably collaborated with since moving into the heroin market: 'Snapper' Cornwell, Sinclair and Fellows, with Neddy Smith organising most of the local distribution.

Eventually, using new contacts, Riley had been able to order five tonnes of cannabis in Thailand, paying a large deposit out of the profits from earlier drug deals. He arranged transport from Thailand to Australia via a yacht, the *Choyro Maru*. The boat sailed to Polkington Reef, an uninhabited outcrop between the coast of Papua New Guinea and the Solomon Islands.

Aboard was a little less dope than Riley had ordered: before the *Choyro Maru* had even set sail about a tonne had been lost in a fire.

Another dealer, with whom Riley was compelled to cooperate, was also using the yacht to transport a large supply of marijuana, making a total of about 4.3 tonnes on board. In Cairns, Riley and the others involved hired another yacht, the *Anoa*, and the rest, as they say, is history.

The *Anoa* took a large portion of the drop from Polkington and headed down the coast to Coffs Harbour. It was a doomed exercise: Riley had been too free with his telephone talk and federal drug squad sleuths had been watching his moves from the time he'd gone ashore in Cairns. Riley and the others on board were caught red-handed. Riley pleaded guilty and received the maximum sentence of ten years' jail by Judge Kenneth Torrington. One drug-runner down; many more to go. And even this one would make a comeback.

Karl Bonnette, whose phone chats had initially implicated

Riley, played a bit part in the drama, but his role did not go unnoticed.

Around the time Riley had been arranging his shipment, Bonnette was being examined by Woodward's Royal Commission into Drug Trafficking. The inquiry found that over 18 months about $750,000 ($3.46 *million*) had passed through the drug pusher's bank accounts.

During two of those months he was also paid $1917 ($8,833) in dole money by the Department of Social Security, but there is no record on any action being taken against him. All the crims were well aware of the risks and consequences of getting caught in the act, so for the rest of the gang the absence of their major drug importer, Murray Riley, must have been accepted with a shoulder shrug.

* * *

Freeman, like others he mixed with, defended any attacks on his reputation, at times aggressively. In March 1979 the deputy opposition leader in the NSW parliament, Bruce McDonald, asked for an investigation into whether George Freeman had 'undue influence' over police in 21 Division. The next day Freeman was at Parliament House demanding an audience with McDonald. When news of this ricocheted around parliament, Independent MP John Hatton moved an urgency motion deploring Freeman's actions. Labor voted against the motion, and it was lost 60 votes to 34. Freeman knew where his friends were.

* * *

Murray Riley wasn't the only player to suffer a setback; his old rowing mate Merv Wood just couldn't stay out of trouble. Wood had made a grubby and inept deal with an old mate of Freeman's in an attempt to get a couple of drug dealers off lightly. The Cessna-Milner case bounced around Sydney's legal, judicial, political, media and gossip circles for years, and would eventually leave Wood's – and others' – credibility in tatters.

On 14 March 1979 American citizen Roy Bowers Cessna and an Englishman called Timothy William Lycet Milner were arrested and charged with supply and possession of Indian hemp – Buddha sticks – with a street value of $1.5 million (*$6.33 million*). They were charged under the Poisons Act, meaning they would face trial by jury.

If found guilty, they faced ten-year jail sentences – so long as the THC level of the dope was less than three per cent. Any higher a percentage and they were looking at 15 years.

However, if the value of the hoard could be reduced and the THC content shown to be low, the pair would instead face a summary charge to be heard by a magistrate. Enter Chief Magistrate Murray Farquhar and crooked solicitor Morgan Ryan and you had the makings of a deal.

Ryan and Farquhar had been seen meeting in Centennial Park, and a concerned lawman had passed on a snapshot of the get-together to Commissioner Merv Wood. But Wood was playing on the wrong team; a month after Cessna and Milner's arrests Wood also met with solicitor Ryan to discuss the case. On 10 May 1979 Ryan organised an extraordinary dinner party at his Neutral Bay home. His guests were Farquhar, Merv Wood, High Court Judge Lionel Murphy and Chief Magistrate Clarrie Briese.

Wood then discussed the matter with Superintendent Patrick Watson – the protective friend of Freeman who had previously been part of the Gaming Squad. It is not known what advice Watson gave his boss, but Wood later directed senior police prosecutor Superintendent Grant Fryer to ensure the cases were heard summarily by a magistrate.

Not just any magistrate but Chief Magistrate Murray Farquhar, who was on the verge of retirement. The new charges amended the street value of the drug haul from $1.5 million to 'some value', and indicated that an analyst's report (never seen) showed the active content to be less than three per cent.

There's more to the Cessna-Milner saga, but it has been told in detail elsewhere. Our interest lies with Farquhar, who on 24 May, the eve of his retirement as Chief Magistrate, heard the case – but not before moving proceedings to a court lacking sound-recording equipment. Farquhar passed down to Milner an

18-month sentence (of which he served six), and fined Cessna $1000 ($4,223), placing him on an eight-month good-behaviour bond.

Details of Wood's involvement emerged and his fate was sealed.

Further, on 4 May Premier Neville Wran had received an unsigned letter making wide-ranging allegations against the police commissioner.

As extraordinary as it might seem for a high-powered politician to act on an anonymous tip-off, Wran raised the matter in parliament on 5 June, stating that the allegations were being investigated by two senior police officers. He denied that there was pressure on 62-year-old Wood to resign, but Wood did just that, bitterly claiming that the allegations against him and the police were 'lowering the morale and reputation of the force'. Opposition leader John Mason told the parliament that Wood's resignation and Wran's decision to hold an inquiry were not surprising, and that he had been 'anticipating the premier to orchestrate a situation which would allow him to whitewash this whole matter of organised crime in NSW'.

Farquhar was 'retired' from the magistracy, but the legal action taken against him, Morgan Ryan and Merv Wood would take another 12 years to finalise. So, apart from a few more inquiries into what happened and why, for the rest of the Sydney crims – who had undoubtedly been watching this affair as it unfolded – it was, once again, back to business.

Incongruously, Murray Farquhar retained a plum government appointed position as chair of the NSW Drug and Alcohol Authority.

Tim Milner had served his reduced sentence and fled to Thailand by the time Mason called for Farquhar to be removed from that post, too, alleging that the former chief magistrate had used his position to free Cessna, a man convicted of international drug trafficking. Premier Wran, rarely caught out on such matters, insisted Farquhar should stay on as the Drug and Alcohol Authority chair, quoting from a report on the matter by

> **Askin leaves a wealthy widow**
>
> Bob Askin, the man the illegal SP bookies paid a good share of their winnings to, and who was credited with institutionalising organised crime and related police corruption during his reign as NSW premier, died on 9 September 1981. Most mourners attending his funeral service at St Andrews Cathedral in the heart of the city came in through the front entrance. Evan Whitton in his report in the next day's *Sun-Herald* said that George Freeman 'decently' slipped in the side door 'to pay his last respects to a fellow scoundrel'. George and his mates had certainly contributed generously to the late premier's wealth: Askin's widow, Millie, died on 26 March 1984, leaving an estate valued at $3.72 million (*$10.23 million*). Neither the crook nor his widow had discovered how to take it with them.

State Solicitor-General Gerry Sullivan, which stated, in regards to the Cessna-Milner case, 'no tracks lead to Mr Farquhar which could demonstrate complicity'.

More reports were written, and it all rumbled on far too long to satisfy any sense of justice. There is one interesting addendum here: throughout the period described and after it, Murray Farquhar was a loyal client and friend of Freeman. They talked with each other frequently and met regularly. There can be no doubt the pair would have discussed the case, as one mate to another. One of the points of interest would have been the money the drug duo had paid for such exceptionally benevolent treatment. Milner later claimed he had paid at least $50,000 (*$211,129*) so that 'things would be easier' for him and his partner. But had Cessna and Milner operated as free agents, out of the influence and control of the Freeman-McPherson-Smith group? It is highly improbable; a former senior federal government security officer told me that very few major drug deals happened in eastern Australia without the okay from that trio. Timothy Milner claimed to have been involved in three earlier Buddha stick importations before they were caught in 1979. We will take a further look at developments in this case in a later chapter.

Once again the tentacles of the major crime gang appear to

have reached deep into administrative, police, political and judicial processes to ensure that they and their friends were looked after, even if they had been caught red-handed. They, after all, got what they paid for.

13. Punting is easy when you know the winner!

When choosing between two evils, I always like to try the one I've never tried before.
– Mae West

George Freeman's passion for horses and racing over the years never faltered. He grossed vast amounts of money from his illegal SP bookmaking businesses and some of the proceeds were almost certainly put towards major drug deals. He and his mates were awash with cash, and by the end of the 1970s Freeman had found a way to make even more: fixing the outcome of races.

When a 'fix' was in place, crime-tainted money could be passed through the TAB in the form of huge bets on sure winners, and on-course bookies were on a hiding-to-none. Freeman wasn't the only man to play the game this way: drug supremo Robert Trimbole was able to buy every jockey in any given race, and offered trainers a range of chemicals that could enhance or detract from a horse's performance.

He was able to collect 'clean' money in the form of his winnings after he'd poured his dirty drug dollars into the TAB – 'the drug industry's laundromat', as crime writer David Hickie once described it. Others, including officials of the racing industry's clubs, couldn't resist the game either.

Freeman's name was always mentioned before all others' in any discussion of race fixing; rightly or wrongly he came to be perceived as the mastermind behind the schemes, the one who could determine whether a certain horse won a certain race. This was not the type of activity its perpetrators would have spoken of too openly, of course, but the flashy dresser was given to boasting about some of his more successful betting coups.

Remarkably, one horse trainer turned to Freeman when he became convinced that two of his horses had been 'nobbled'. In January 1979 racing writer Max Presnell, in an article in *The Sun* newspaper, quoted veteran trainer Dr Geoff Chapman, who did not willingly accept the excuse that the horses had suffered from a 24-hour virus.

Dr Geoff Chapman, who has a medical practice on Queensland's Gold Coast, confirmed the gist of the 1979 article. He said:

> They had inside help in stables they were nobbling. The course detectives were hopeless so eventually I asked a friend who knew George Freeman to see if he could or would find out about it. The friend came back telling me to take a good look at the foreman. The foreman owed some SP bookmaker at Coogee a hatful so they'd give him credit for each horse he got to. With this credit they would take something off the old debt and he could bet up again. He was often described as a 'nice bloke' but he couldn't train pigs to be dirty.
>
> I pulled him aside and told him that I had spoken to George Freeman (which, of course, I had not) and that Freeman had promised me that the perpetrator would disappear off the face of the earth. With that, the foreman went the colour of pale faeces.
>
> The next day he told me his mother was ill and he had to return to the bush. The virus that my horses were suffering from suddenly corrected itself. The go-slow was Timorol. Following this, they started to test lots of beaten horses.
>
> The easiest to get to were the visitors. People came and went all day, although the fence jumpers usually operated at night. All they needed was a stablehand with some sort of weakness (drug, punt or alcohol problems),

and the temptation of an easy quid would quickly manifest itself.

It might, with the clarity of hindsight, seem a bit naive of Chapman to have sought help for his horse-nobbling problems from one of Australia's leading race fixers – a man who may well have benefited from the doping activity – but invoking Freeman's name worked for a while. 'Freeman was into backing winners,' Chapman told me. 'He'd arrange for the slow-down drug Timorol to be given to the top favourites, and back the next most likely runner.' Did it all end when Freeman died? 'No way. It still goes on.'

* * *

The most notorious racing 'fix' involving Freeman was at a Wednesday meeting at Canterbury Racecourse on 5 August 1981.

Two days earlier at Randwick Racecourse a horse named Mr Digby had finished an unimpressive ninth, yet at the Wednesday meeting the horse was the subject of a betting plunge. In a remarkable reversal in form Digby romped it in, winning by nearly eight lengths and costing on-course bookies an estimated $350,000 (*$1,225,606*). The horse had been backed in from 7–2 to 11–8.

The day after the Digby race, George Freeman got married. His new bride was an orthoptist, former actress and model called Georgina Catherine McLoughlin – the granddaughter of horse trainer Charles McLoughlin, who had given Freeman a job 32 years earlier. After the nuptials at Sydney's St Stephen's Uniting Church, opposite Parliament House, Freeman, then 46, and his 24-year-old bride hosted a lavish celebration at the Hilton Hotel, attended by a who's who of Sydney's racing fraternity, a number of shifty underground figures and society elites. Freeman openly bragged to guests that his 'modest' Mr Digby win of $17,000 (*$59,529*) had been more than enough to pay for the knees-up.

It took a few days, but some serious questions were asked about the Mr Digby affair. Someone pointed out that Freeman's best man had been Graham Pash, chairman of the Sydney Turf Club – the outfit that had run the Wednesday race meeting. STC director

Don Story was also a guest, and had also backed Mr Digby for a tidy profit. Graham Pash later described his involvement in the wedding as 'one of life's great misjudgements'. (Pash continued his association with the STC, serving as a director from 1991 until he retired in 2007. He died in 2008.) The ABC documentary *The Track* later revealed that at first there was no stewards' inquiry into the race, 'despite the fact that several of the beaten jockeys seem to be working hard to stay that way'.

Under growing pressure from the media and the parliament, the Australian Jockey Club (AJC) launched an inquiry ten days after Mr Digby's win. A strange tale emerged. Mr Digby's registered owner was Peter Ernest Black, who it turned out worked with Freeman, and (according to Freeman's later version of events) who had bought the horse from George's eldest son, Grant. Black had even agreed to name the horse after Freeman's great dane guard dog, Digby. Black tried to convince the inquiry that he was the horse's bona fide owner, not simply a stand-in for George Freeman. He said, 'I own every hair of Mr Digby. I can honestly say there are definitely no outside interests in the ownership of the horse.' The horse's trainer, Harry Clarke, and the jockey, Keith Banks, were questioned, but AJC Chief Steward John Mahoney's report, released on 9 September, exonerated Clarke and said he found 'nothing irregular' in the horse's performances. But Mahoney left a question mark over Peter Black's ownership of the horse, implying that Freeman may have been the real owner. As one of Freeman's associates, Peter Black had been named as a 'person of interest' in the NSW Police Criminal Intelligence Unit report that was the subject of the 1977 raid by Commissioner Merv Wood. That report identified Freeman as a big-time illegal SP bookmaker, whose Rockdale headquarters handled the accounts of 20 SP 'agents' through a multi-line switchboard, and that Peter Black was there most race days as a casual worker.

After the Mr Digby affair, the overall picture for racing 'just didn't smell very good,' commented Arthur Harris. It proved to be another one of those stories that refused to go away.

The *Sun-Herald* of 27 September published a story on a dossier claiming to contain details of a Sydney-based 'million-dollar race-fixing gang' that involved trainers, jockeys, journalists and members of the two major racing clubs, the AJC and the STC. The mastermind behind the scheme was described as 'a Sydney crime figure'. Freeman wrote of this in his memoir, 'My friends rang up and said, "See what they've written about you? Well, it sounds like you."' Then on 15 November, more than three months after the race, the AJC reopened its Mr Digby inquiry, and as a result jockey Banks and trainer Clarke were banned from racing for 12 months. Mr Digby was barred from racing, a ban that lasted until the horse was eventually sold. The buyer was the wife of bookmaker Terry Page, a close friend of Freeman. A month later the AJC issued Freeman with a demand to show cause why he should not also be banned from all Sydney racecourses. That action was later withdrawn. For the illegal bookie and race fixer, business activities would quickly resume, and the state of racing remain tainted.

* * *

Away from the racetracks, Michael Hurley, whose trust Freeman had violated in 1977, went further than simply cutting ties with his former mentor. He unsubtly challenged the Freeman-McPherson-Smith gang by not denying in a 1980 media interview that he was the 'head honcho' of Sydney crime. Hurley had by this time set up his own gang and started importing and distributing drugs on a large scale, thumbing his nose at the gang of three and the likely jail terms waiting for those who did not fall into line with them.

In October 1980 Hurley was involved in one of the greatest robberies Sydney had ever seen. The famous Golconda d'Or diamond, weighing 130 carats and valued at around $2 million at the time, had been on display in Melbourne at Dunklings Jewellers, before being moved to Sydney and exhibited at the Town Hall. The magnificent diamond, displayed in a locked glass case, attracted great crowds. The heist was like something out of *The Pink Panther*: sixty people were crowded around the display case, admiring the gem – Michael Hurley and his brother Jeffrey among them. Suddenly, the Golconda d'Or was no longer there; it had vanished right in front of the eyes of those in the large crowd.

Within a couple of days, the Hurley brothers had been arrested.

Michael did not deny that he and his brother had been present at the display stand on the day in question. However, he argued – successfully – that because he and his brother looked so much alike, nobody would be able to make a positive identification as to which one had committed any particular action. Although, strangely, it appears that no definite evidence was offered that either Hurley had actually done anything to make the jewel vanish. Whether Hurley had his own insurance scheme in place with the cops is not known, but the case against the brothers quickly collapsed and they were found not guilty.

In a rare interview some years later, Hurley spoke to Kate McClymont of the *Sydney Morning Herald*, saying – with a laugh – that he and his brother had been at the display 'just looking around'. Asked where the diamond was, Hurley chuckled again, and said, 'I'm not saying I was an angel.' The diamond was never recovered.

***

Neddy Smith's police ally Roger Rogerson maintained a close and friendly association with Freeman, with whom he would have shared – and sought to trade – intimate knowledge of goings-on within the criminal world. Rogerson would have been well aware that any information he passed on to the bookie would quickly travel up the chain through McPherson to Jack McNeill and the other cops on Lennie's fizgig circuit. It was a useful tool, and one used to create advantageous circumstances for Rogerson and his associates.

Around the middle of 1981 Rogerson would certainly have discussed with Freeman a problem introduced by Neddy Smith – Warren Charles Lanfranchi, a young man with whom Neddy had formed a friendship in jail. Lanfranchi, then 21, had been in Long Bay Gaol since 1976 after being convicted of stealing television sets. His father, Keith, had unsuccessfully pleaded for the lad to

> **Rogerson a hot-shot from early days**
> In the mid-1970s Roger Rogerson had built on his notoriety as a tough cop with a couple of killings. He'd learned his ropes from Ray 'The Gunner' Kelly and in June 1976 was present when bank robber and alleged murderer Philip Western was holed up in a house at Avoca Beach, north of the city. Rogerson went into the house next door and called out to Western, urging him to show his face at the window so they could talk about a peace deal. Western's head appeared only to be blown away in a hail of police lead. A similar scene occurred three years later in suburban Rose Bay. Bank robber and drug addict Gordon Thomas died under police fire in a confrontation led by Rogerson.

be sent to a boys' home rather than the more corrupting environment of an adult prison. The blue-eyed kid from Camperdown doted on the drug dealer, who was 36 years his senior. Warren's brother Darrell said later, 'Warren was in awe of Smith. He said he thought he was a millionaire and that he acted like one.' Neddy Smith was released in October 1980 after he'd served the balance of his parole on a rape conviction. Lanfranchi was set free a few months later, and the pair reunited. It didn't take Smith long to train his acolyte in the intricacies of heroin distribution. Smith also introduced the youngster to Roger Rogerson, but within six months Rogerson had shot the boy dead in a laneway in inner-suburban Chippendale.

There are differing versions of what led to the killing. One held that Lanfranchi had ripped off a drug dealer working with corrupt police and now wanted to broker a peace deal with them through Rogerson by way of a large bribe. Another version was that he'd botched an armed hold-up by shooting at a policeman (the gun was said to have misfired) on his way to the job, and that he wanted to bribe Rogerson to have the armed-robbery and attempted murder charges he faced 'disappeared'. What is clear is that Neddy Smith had arranged for Lanfranchi to meet Rogerson in Chippendale's back streets on the windy afternoon of Saturday, 27 June 1981. Smith drove the younger man to the meeting, and later said Lanfranchi was going there to try to bribe the rogue cop.

Conflicting versions exist, too, regarding what happened after Rogerson and Lanfranchi had walked down Beaumont Street into Dangar Place. The area was staked out by policemen from the Armed Hold-up Squad as well as trained marksmen from the Special Weapons and Operations Squad; their presence there was arranged by senior policeman Aarne Tees, then aged 43, who had allied himself with Lennie McPherson. There were at least five people in Dangar Place itself: Lanfranchi and Rogerson, detectives Brian Harding, Graham Frazer and Rod Moore, and probably Neddy Smith. One version has Lanfranchi pulling a gun and, in response, Rogerson shooting him in the neck and then the heart.

All 18 of the police involved in the operation supported that version. Others did not. On 19 November a jury of four women and two men, having heard evidence in the inquest, ruled that Lanfranchi had died from a gunshot wound to the chest inflicted by Detective-Sergeant Roger Rogerson while he was 'trying to affect an arrest'. The jurors, however, had struck out phrases that coroner Norman Walsh had suggested, such as 'in the execution of his duty' and 'in self-defence'.

Immediately after the coroner's inquest, NSW Liberal Party Opposition Leader John Dowd raised the matter in state parliament. He moved an urgency motion to set up a judicial inquiry into Lanfranchi's killing. The motion was defeated as members voted along party lines, with Labor led by Premier Neville Wran opposing the move. The next day Rogerson telephoned Dowd to discuss the issue – in much the same way George Freeman had tried to intimidate the deputy opposition leader Bruce McDonald in March 1979. Back in the chamber Dowd moved that Rogerson's actions were a breach of parliamentary privilege. The same voting pattern knocked over that attempt to cast the light of debate under parliamentary privilege on what was an extremely controversial death.

Lanfranchi's death sent shock waves through the criminal world.

The Freeman-McPherson-Smith group would have been aware that Rogerson had a problem with the youngster. That he was shot dead by the policeman who – notionally, at least – was on their team, would up the ante as tensions heightened among rivals in the increasingly dangerous drug trade.

* * *

Dodgy deeds on the racetracks and the diamond theft may have been the big stories of those times, but Lanfranchi's killing signalled the start of gang members involved in the local drug trade facing some serious heat.

Back in Sydney after a 15-month break in a Victorian prison for drug charges, Stan Smith formed a close association with Anthony Anderson – better known as Tony 'Spaghetti' Eustace. Despite being a major heroin distributor and a familiar face around Abe Saffron's sleazy nightclubs at Kings Cross, Tony Eustace had a charm that saw him move easily in upper-class circles – among whose ranks were some who indulged in recreational drugs, a supply of which Eustace readily offered.

Eustace, however, was facing a problem. One of his marijuana suppliers, Stathopoulous, Andreas 'Andy the Greek' – anglicised to Andrew Stathis – had been arrested along with five others. The charges he faced related to a marijuana plantation near Cowra, in southern NSW, with a crop valued around at $60 million (*$253 million*). At the time of the arrests police had seized two metal boxes containing more than $86,000 (*$363,142*) in cash. The case that ensued was testament to the extraordinary reach of the gang of three, by this time the most powerful crime outfit in the country. In court police described Stathis as a 'principal' player with connections to 'a Sydney organisation', of which no further detail was provided. In October 1980 Stathis's gang was committed to stand trial early the following year, but this was deferred many times over the next two years, mainly by lawyers finding excuses for delaying the action. They were released on bail at $20,000 (*$76,679*) each. Smith had consulted his senior partners about Stathis and it was agreed that they should help him in every possible way to beat the rap. To that end Smith and Eustace swung into action. Remarkably cavalier, the pair discussed their plan in detail over the telephone, while federal police listened on under the authority of a judicial warrant. Elsewhere, without authority, NSW state police were also listening.

The first step in their plan was this: early in 1983 they would approach the newly appointed NSW Attorney-General Paul Landa to issue a 'no bill' – whereby the justice minister or attorney-general decides, for reasons rarely revealed, not to proceed with a prosecution. A similar approach to Landa's immediate predecessor, Frank Walker, in September 1982 had been rejected. As Eustace explained to Smith, 'No luck with that guy; I've tried. He's just too straight.' They initially discussed offering $20,000 (*$57,157*) for the fix, but that figure was later increased. The taped conversations revealed a great deal about how they planned to tackle the problem.

Eustace: I'll give it one more go. I'll see this guy and I'll just put it on him to do me a personal favour.

Smith: That's what I mentioned. You know, you can put that on top of what I mentioned before. It's crucial to that thing I was telling you about, you know. That's if it gets down. [*This was Smith's coded message to Eustace that the money on offer could be increased above the $20,000 they had already discussed.*]

Eustace: Well, I'll give it another try.

Eustace then rang a woman friend, noted in police records as 'Palma'. Mrs Palma Strawbridge had known Tony Eustace as an SP bookie (but was not aware, she later claimed, that he was a major heroin dealer). She was also a close friend of the former federal attorney-general and by then judge of the High Court of Australia Lionel Murphy. Palma had mentioned to Eustace that she wanted to buy a new residential unit but was about 'ten or twenty thousand' short.

Eustace: Rather than speak over the phone, I got an idea

	about something. There is a way. You'll have to do some work and you have to ask a favour from a person, from your friend.
Palma:	Ya, ya.
Eustace:	If he agrees, I can get what you need.
Palma:	Fair enough.
Eustace:	It could be the difference you need.
Palma:	Yeah, okay, why not?
Eustace:	I'll have a talk to you. Then you tell me what you think.

In a subsequent face-to-face meeting Palma told Eustace she had raised the matter with her friend Lionel Murphy. There was no tap on the judge's phone, but the police records document remarks reputedly made by Murphy, as referred to in the bugged conversations. More meetings took place. Smith said he could provide Eustace with a copy of the police brief on the case. (Freeman's contacts had assured Smith such a document was available if required.) Palma rang Eustace to tell him Murphy had just called her and that he found it 'difficult to believe that if there was any kind of an arrangement, that it wouldn't have been done', suggesting that if Paul Landa had agreed to file a 'no bill' in the case then that action should have been taken.

Palma said she'd had contact with Murphy again on 28 February. She reported to Eustace, 'He can't see there'd be much difficulty, and wanted to know how I came about this.' She continued:

Palma:	And then I told him about the units. He said, 'Don't tell me anything'. He said, 'I don't want to know'. He said, 'I get the gist of it,' and he'll get back to me.
Eustace:	He wouldn't have been very happy about that, then.
Palma:	Yeah, okay, yes, but he doesn't want to know.
Eustace:	The details of it?
Palma:	The other side, yeah. Yeah, but you know I'm always honest … He's a friend, so … I was

	thinking that, um, if he wanted, he could have half whatever, you know.
Eustace:	Yeah.
Palma:	But he doesn't want to hear it. He knew what I was talking about.
Eustace:	Yeah.
Palma:	Yeah, so basically … the only thing he could not see is … why did the other go with him at the same time? *[This was in reference to the fact that Stathis's brother, Christos, had been discharged at the committal hearings at the start of the case.]* So, anyway, he said he'd look into it for me.
Eustace:	He doesn't see any problem?
Palma:	He doesn't seem to. He said because, eh, what actually happened some years back, there was a law that, if one was dismissed, the others had to be, too, and then that was changed. It was thrown out, and it was changed, but he thinks that recently that's been reintroduced again. But he said it may not have come into order yet, um, but, er, he said, you know, he said he would look into it anyway.
Eustace:	All right. But he wasn't upset about your —?
Palma:	Well, no, not at all, no, not at all. He just, er, I told you what he is like with that and, er, he's just not interested and he didn't want to even hear it. Mm, all he's interested in is the facts and can he or can't he help, and that's it.

A short time later Palma was back on the phone to Eustace. She told him, 'I had dinner with Paul [Landa] last night.'

Eustace:	Okay. Jesus Christ.
Palma:	Uh, three of us [*herself, Landa and Murphy*]. Quite interesting. Nothing was, you know, said or anything because it's got nothing to do with him. Um, but I'll ring you later on today, and,

	uh, tell you [something] interesting, really for technical reasons. A very useful evening.
Eustace:	Hmm. Oh. So there's no joy there at all?
Palma:	Not yet, no.
Eustace:	But he is the boss, isn't he? [*This referred to Landa*].
Palma:	Ah, no, actually ...
Eustace:	He's not?
Palma:	Ah, he is but yet, ah, it's, ah, his second that would, ah, you know, that would do it. [*This refers to a prominent bureaucrat who would set up the paperwork.*]
Eustace:	Ooh.
Palma:	Okay? But I'll tell you about it in person.
Eustace:	Did you get a surprise when it happened? Is that what he was telling you about earlier in the day?
Palma:	Well, they had lunch together. I had a feeling ... that old fox ... they had lunch together, and when I got there he was still there. Yeah, yeah, yeah, it was funny.

On 9 March 1983 Palma advised Eustace that the case was being looked at for a no bill. She told him Paul Landa was the person who had joined her and Murphy at the lunch, and that Landa was 'the person who signed the papers'. On 20 March Smith and Eustace met. Smith reported the state of play regularly to Freeman and McPherson. Their continuing support for the operation was vital. On 28 March the case came before Judge John Foord in the NSW District Court. Foord had a close association with lawyer Morgan Ryan and had first met Lionel Murphy back in 1957. Foord kept Stathis's bail at $20,000 but the condition that he report regularly to police was lifted. The matter was adjourned.

Around this time Eustace was putting the finishing touches on his new restaurant, Tony's Bar and Grill. In phone calls he mentioned having two opening ceremonies – one for the 'goodies' and another for the 'baddies'. Lionel Murphy attended the first event on 13 April, and over the phone the following day Eustace boasted about the judge's presence and their conversations. George Freeman was one of the guests at the baddies' function, and Stan Smith told Eustace that Freeman would come in 'via the back entrance'. Palma invited Eustace to a party at her place to be held on 23 April, and told him Murphy had also accepted an invitation to the event. The drug pusher and the High Court judge did meet, but Eustace was later recorded as saying that Murphy 'didn't seem to want to talk'.

Paul Landa was advised by his department to reject the no-bill application, which had been lodged in May. He did so, but not until 18 August, the day before the matter was listed to go before Judge Foord. Meanwhile, on 7 June Eustace had spoken of a new 21-page application prepared by lawyers on behalf of Stathis, trying for another no bill from Landa. On 13 June Palma rang Eustace to say 'the first person' he had spoken to (presumably Landa) had 'changed his position, but he won't talk about it on the phone'. The next day Tony Eustace was visited at his Coogee Bay home by officers from a joint Victoria Police and Australian Federal Police operation called 'Operation Rock'. He was arrested and charged with conspiracy to pervert the course of justice.

Twenty-two days later Andrew Stathis quietly boarded a plane and flew to Greece on a one-way ticket, carrying a suitcase with $18.5 million (*$52.87 million*) that he had fraudulently taken from Bishopgate Insurance, a Melbourne company he had acquired early in 1983. At no stage had anyone confiscated his passport. Landa was still considering the no-bill application while Stathis was watching Sydney disappear into the distance as his flight headed northwest.

On 19 August at the NSW District Court when the star of the show failed to appear, Judge Foord issued a bench warrant for Stathis's arrest.

At deeply embarrassing moments such as this, politicians habitually call for an inquiry. Paul Landa did just that, ordering justice department head Trevor Haines to report to him why Stathis's trial had been delayed. Landa would never read the report: he died late in 1984.

There are a few footnotes to this saga.

Two days after Tony Eustace was arrested, records of illegal NSW Police phone taps were secretly handed over to Justice Stewart's royal commission, triggering a chain reaction that would lead to the '*Age* tapes' affair.

The law caught up with Andrew Stathis eventually, but not in Australia. In October 1987 – almost eight years after his initial arrest in NSW, Greek police arrested him as he boarded a ferry at the port of Piraeus. He was found in possession of a suitcase containing 23 kilograms of heroin valued at around $34 million (*around $70 million*). As a long sentence in an Athens prison appeared a certainty, Australian authorities saw no reason to extradite Greek-born Stathis back here to face his outstanding charges. He was subsequently handed a life sentence by a Greek court, and has not been heard of since.

Some, but not all, of Trevor Haines's report was released by Attorney-General Ron Mulock – nearly five years after Landa had ordered it.

On the main question of the delay in bringing Stathis to trial, Haines reported that one of the major causes had been a lack of resources among crown prosecutors and the justice department. Significantly, the parts of the report released stated there was no suggestion of misconduct by any departmental officer or the crown prosecutor, but fell short of clearing former Attorney-General Landa of blame.

Judge John Foord resigned from the NSW District Court on 19 November 1986 on medical grounds. The next day the state government announced it was referring to the National Crime Authority allegations that the judge had been particularly lenient towards the clients of one solicitor – Morgan Ryan – as well as details of a police investigation into his alleged associations with Griffith drug dealers.

Reference was made to a photograph of Foord at a party with people close to Robert Trimbole. The NCA announced in

February 1988 that it had found 'no credible evidence' that any criminal act had been committed by Foord. He died in 2008, aged 77.

Throughout this complex web of proceedings, Stan Smith double-checked every move with Freeman and McPherson, but at no stage during proceedings or the inquiry that followed were the names of the men who helped guide the whole Stathis affair made mention of: George Freeman and his mate were off scot-free.

14. The doc prescribes drugs to ease the pain of his debts

> The belief in a supernatural source of evil is not necessary:
> men alone are quite capable of every wickedness.
> – Joseph Conrad

Although Freeman's friend and family medico Dr Nick Paltos had a large number of affluent clients, including media tycoon Kerry Packer, radio's golden tonsils John Laws, police inspector Nelson Chad and Robert Trimbole, he himself was no longer a wealthy man. By the end of 1982 Dr Nick Paltos had gambled away huge sums of money, and owed massive amounts to Freeman and other bookies.

Paltos had also borrowed $300,000 (*$1,050,520 million*) from solicitor Ross Karp in 1981. The debt remained unpaid, and now the doctor was asking for a further $40,000 (*$125,790*). Karp, the son of a successful Sydney butcher, had great respect for Paltos. They had both been born on the Greek island of Kastellorizo, and the doctor had treated Karp's dying father and 'allowed him to die with dignity' in early 1981. Karp had taken the money from the family business, and the solicitor had had to sell his house to repay the firm. In an effort to reassure him that both loans would be repaid, Paltos told the solicitor, 'Don't worry, Ross. I'm working on something next year which will solve all my problems.' He was prepared to take desperate measures to ease the pressure on his bank account.

When Paltos discussed his audacious debt-reduction plan with Freeman, the bookie wouldn't have tried to deter him – Freeman's thoughts were probably firmly fixed on the cash. The plan was to import marijuana on a grand scale. Paltos would first bring in an associate of Freeman, Graham Palmer (nicknamed 'Croc' after he bit off a piece of an opponent's ear in a fistfight), who had given up life as a farmer to dabble in illegal casino operation and SP bookmaking. Palmer owned a greyhound in partnership with corrupt licensed-club operator Wally Dean, through whom he had come to know bent ex-cop Murray Riley.

Ross Karp would also play an active role in the plan, and the $40,000 he'd advanced Paltos wouldn't be used to pay off the doctor's gambling debts but go towards buying drugs and arranging transport. Another man brought into the scheme was seaman-turned drug dealer Daniel 'The Brain' Chubb, who would supervise getting a shipment of drugs from Darwin to Sydney and then look after their distribution. A committed punter, Chubb was also well known to George Freeman.

In September 1983 Paltos made an overseas trip. Investigators were later fairly convinced he had met up with his former client and friend, drug baron Robert Trimbole, who helped him arrange his own operation. Some time later a Greek ship, the *Gulf Frio*, was chartered. Its Greek captain and crew travelled to Lebanon, where Paltos had arranged for between 4.8 and 7.2 tonnes (the figure varied in versions of the story that followed) of cannabis resin to be loaded on board. The ship took its time on the 12,000-odd-kilometre voyage, arriving at Melville Island, about 100 kilometres from Darwin, on 22 February 1984. Two days earlier Stephen Brown, a local fisherman whom Chubb had hired, and an offsider had set out from Darwin in a chartered fishing boat to meet the Greek ship.

The tonnes of 'Lebanese gold' and the Greek crew were transferred to the smaller boat, and the confident team headed back to the Australian mainland. Just outside Darwin the shipment of 240 bags was loaded onto a truck headed for Sydney, where Danny Chubb awaited its arrival. With the street value of the drugs an estimated $40 million (*$110 million*), Paltos must have felt his money problems to be nearly at an end: he could settle his debts with Freeman and the others, repay Ross Karp's loans, and be left with a large bundle of cash available for punting.

Astonishingly, despite all his careful planning, Paltos had overlooked the fact that he and his team members were on the radar of numerous crime intelligence agencies. He was aware the FBI had clocked him during his 1978 visit to the US with Freeman, so he should have been far more cautious. Eavesdropping on Paltos, Croc Palmer and Ross Karp provided enough of an incentive for the federal police to maintain a watching brief on the trio and the people they contacted. Codenamed 'Operation Lavender', the investigation officially got under way in October 1985 under the leadership of Inspector Bob McDonald, and was later hailed by the feds as one of its most successful.

One conversation the AFP overheard was Paltos responding to Croc Palmer's complaints that their associate Ross Karp was 'a little rich kid', not one of them. 'No, that's wrong; you're out of order there, Croc,' Paltos had said. 'He's bored with life; he's got no kids; he doesn't give a fuck. He was looking for a high; he's found his high with me. He's an intelligent bastard, wants to beat [the] system. He gets a high out of beating the system.' But none of the three would beat the system.

As the drugs were moving out into the streets of Sydney and beyond, one of the people they became involved with was Paltos' – and Freeman's – old friend Roger Rogerson. The copper had a problem over some his unlaundered money being held in bank accounts he'd set up with help from another of Paltos' friends. Paltos believed he could do Rogerson a big favour: Ross Karp could organise the dodgy paperwork that would explain away Rogerson's dirty money.

On 19 July 1985 Paltos introduced Karp to Rogerson at a soiree at the Bayswater Brasserie in Bayswater Road, Kings Cross. The rogue cop suggested Karp provide him with a backdated contract stating that Rogerson had sold him a 1962 Continental Flying Spur Bentley car.

It was a bogus sale: neither car nor money changed hands, just a piece of paper. After the meeting Paltos and Karp rejoined Croc

Palmer in their car – oblivious to the bug the federal cops had planted under the dashboard – and the following illuminating conversation took place.

Palmer:	What did Roger want? You done something for him?
Paltos:	Fucking oath. Big. The best fucking turn, I tell you.
Karp:	He got some cash, Croc, right? ... And he opened up a couple of bodgie bank accounts.
Paltos:	[He's] the shiftiest bloke in the world, but he's a hundred per cent.
Karp:	Opened up two bodgie accounts and put a hundred thousand between the two accounts. I'm not sure of the exact split up, right?
Palmer:	Yeah.
Karp:	What's happened is, ah, Roger's gone to one of the banks to withdraw the money, right?
Palmer:	Yeah.
Karp:	In the bodgie name.
Palmer:	Yeah.
Karp:	Yeah, but they didn't know that account belonged to Roger, Nick.
Paltos:	Yes, they did.
Karp:	No. they found that out after they photographed him. Well, that's what he told me.
Paltos:	Anyway, whenever it is, they photographed them going in to take the money out.
Karp:	They recognise him, and they think now that this money is from ill-gotten.
Paltos:	Drugs. From drugs. Tell the truth.
Karp:	Well, he said drugs, right? Okay? Now he went and opened another account at a Penrith bank and redeposited the money. Right?
Palmer:	Right.
Karp:	So he's got to explain where this money's come

	from. Agreed?
Palmer:	Right.
Paltos:	He comes to me. Somehow, somehow he's got the fucking seventy fucking thousand, sixty thousand dollars he's gotta prove.
Palmer:	Right.
Paltos:	Right. That's where Rossy comes in. *[Paltos explained that Karp could help, he had withdrawn large sums to use 'for cash for our business'. He said 'another bloke' was restoring a vintage car.]*
Karp:	1962 Series 2 Bentley.
Paltos:	I've never seen two happier blokes in my life today, Ross?
Karp:	No, they could've eaten us.
Paltos:	Could've eaten. He said, 'Look mate, I don't know how to thank you: I just don't know.' I said, 'How the fuck!' He said, 'Take my badge,' didn't he? Karp: Yeah.
Paltos:	He said, 'Take me.'
Karp:	No. He said, 'Look, if you were gonna go and rob a bank,' and he'd say, 'Take the badge with you.'
(Laughter.)	
Paltos:	'Take this badge with you,' he says, 'I've got a gun, too.'
Karp:	'It might help you.'

Karp never got Rogerson's police badge. Indeed, at this stage of his career the cop was hard-pressed to retain it for his own use. His dodgy bank accounts were only one of his problems. Another – and not unrelated – issue involved accusations that Rogerson and others had earlier tried to murder an undercover drug-squad detective-sergeant, Michael Drury, who had pointed the finger at a Melbourne painter and docker, Alan David Williams (aka McClure), as a heroin supplier. In the eyes of Roger Rogerson, Williams was protected, and Drury later revealed that in September 1983 Rogerson had offered him a bribe to alter his evidence against Williams.

Early in May 1984 Alan Williams met with Rogerson and alleged hit man Chris Flannery in a York Street restaurant in Sydney, where it was agreed that the only way to get Williams off the hook would be to stop Drury going to court. A few days later Williams made arrangements for $50,000 (*$137,449*) to be paid to Rogerson. Some of this money was paid into Rogerson's secret bank accounts.

Soon after, Robert Lang, manager of the National Australia Bank branch in York Street, was introduced to Rogerson by one of his customers. According to evidence Lang gave later, the policeman then opened accounts in the names of Robert Tracey and Mike Roberts and in three deposits paid $110,000 (*$302,388*) in cash into the accounts.

On 6 June 1984 Michael Drury was standing at the kitchen window of his home in suburban Chatswood when he was felled by two shots to the head. Incredibly, he survived the attack. The NSW Police Commissioner Cec Abbott, due to retire in two months' time, immediately set up an investigation into the shooting. Abbott put Superintendent Angus McDonald, a close friend of Rogerson for the last three decades, in charge of the inquiry. Unsurprisingly, McDonald's report cleared Rogerson of any involvement.

The incoming police commissioner would change the way things were being done. The appointment of John Keith Avery on 6 August 1984 – the day before his 57th birthday – saw a new Internal Police Security Unit (IPSU) set up. Its brief was to end the 'institutionalised corruption' that had plagued the force. It was a big ask. One of the first cases referred to the unit was Rogerson's attempt to bribe Drury, and in November the cop was transferred to uniform duties. The Crown Advocate Reginald Blanch, having read the IPSU report, recommended that Rogerson be formally charged with attempting to bribe Michael Drury. It took six months for the case to come before the District Court, with barrister Chester Porter QC appearing for Rogerson. On the night of 18 June the jury had not reached a verdict, and Rogerson's bail was withdrawn and he spent the night in jail.

The next day he was back in court. Rogerson had been allowed to go for a meal during the lunchtime adjournment, when he was overheard discussing the worrying bank accounts, which he said were in the names of Tracey and Roberts. That titbit of information ensured that surveillance would be able to capture any move to withdraw money from the accounts. Back from lunch and the jury brought Rogerson the best news he'd had in a while: a not guilty verdict. But his troubles were far from over.

On 1 July 1985 Rogerson went to the bank and closed the accounts, receiving bank cheques – including interest – for $111,116 ($286,182.13). Surveillance cameras captured the whole transaction. He drove to Penrith, west of Sydney, and opened two new accounts – in the same phoney names – at the local Westpac branch and deposited the bank cheques. Just 18 days later he met with Paltos and Karp at the Bayswater Brasserie and pretended to buy a costly vintage car from Karp.

In hindsight it had something of an 'amateur hour' naivety to it – from the Paltos gang not thinking their activities would be the subject of surveillance, to a very smart cop, Rogerson, believing his deposits of large amounts of cash into bank accounts in false names would go unnoticed. And while the wheels of justice grind slowly at times, they would eventually catch up to this lot.

* * *

But not to George Freeman. In mid-1985 sympathetic police let it be known that the Paltos gang was about to be arrested by federal cops, which meant that state police couldn't interfere with the cases. Freeman decided it might be a good time to take a holiday from Sydney, in case he was implicated – it was to pay money he was owed that Paltos had embarked on his drug-importation scheme. And, as we will hear, Chris Flannery had just disappeared.

Freeman booked two tickets to London, with an overnight stopover in Hong Kong. George and his wife arrived at Gatwick Airport early Sunday morning, 28 July 1985, after a 19-hour flight. There, an immigration officer checked their papers, shook his head, telling them that their 'exclusion from the United Kingdom is for the public good'. Freeman protested, saying he hadn't been to jail since 1968 – to no avail. They were put on a flight to Hong Kong leaving at eight o'clock that night, 13 hours after they had landed, and the following day it was back to Sydney. It was the last time Freeman tried to leave Australia.

A month later Freeman felt obliged to respond to an item buzzing around the rumour mill: he emphatically denied that he was in hiding for fear of contract killers from Melbourne who were out to get him. In a later chapter, however, I reveal that there was indeed talk of a plot to murder Freeman at this time, which involved Melbourne criminals from whom he was desperate to escape.

* * *

Paltos' team members were eventually charged with conspiring to import cannabis resin and supplying the drug; those involved in the bank-account scam were charged with conspiring to pervert the course of justice. Karp, Paltos, Palmer and others were arrested by Australian Federal Police on 15 August 1985.

Ross Karp was charged over import and supply. At the time of his arrest Karp had $500,000 (*$1.29 million*) in an account at the Westpac bank in Darlinghurst. On 7 March 1986 he pleaded guilty on the supply charge and was sentenced to 14 years' jail, with a nine-year non-parole period. On 3 October 1986 he pleaded guilty on the importation charge and was sentenced to 14 years, to be served concurrently with his earlier sentence. Karp was 37 at the time. In October 1987 Karp told a Sydney magistrate that he would plead guilty to a charge of conspiring with Paltos and Rogerson to pervert the course of justice in relation to the $100,000 in Rogerson's bank account.

Nick Paltos pleaded guilty on 7 March 1986 to import and supply charges and was given 20 years and 16 years respectively, to be served concurrently, with a 13-year non-parole period. He was struck off the medical register on 18 December. In 1990 he was convicted over the bank accounts scandal, and sentenced to a further two years' jail, to begin at the end of his 13-year minimum term. That was reduced to one year and nine months on appeal. He was released on 20 December 1994. He died six days later, on

Boxing Day, of lung cancer, aged 54.

Graham 'Croc' Palmer was sentenced to 14 years' jail on the import charge and ten years – to be served concurrently – on the supply charge, with an eight-and-a-half-year non-parole period. He was released on parole from the Mannus low-security prison near Tumbarumba, close to the Victorian border, on 3 May 1990, having served less than half of his non-parole term set by the judge. Liberal Corrective Services Minister Michael Yabsley told the media that Palmer was classified as being 'on the bottom of the minimum-security pile' and that he had worked his way through the system, allowing for an automatic reduction in his sentence. Palmer was 49 at the time of his release.

Stephen John Brown was convicted on 22 August 1986 and sentenced to 18 years in jail for his key role in organising the Darwin end of the importation, with a 12-year non-parole period.

Roger Rogerson was charged in November 1985 on three counts of 'having goods in custody', the goods being his dodgy bank accounts.

In April 1986 he was charged with police misconduct in relation to the accounts. In July he was found guilty on seven of nine charges of misconduct by Judge Barrie Thorley, who said Rogerson had betrayed the community. The judge recommended he be dismissed from the NSW Police Force. Arrested in September 1987, he was charged with conspiring with Paltos and Karp to pervert the course of justice.

On 24 February 1988 he was charged with conspiring with Flannery and drug dealer Alan Williams to murder Michael Drury. Rogerson's trial on the Drury charge began in October; a 'not guilty' verdict was returned on 20 November. On 2 February 1990 Judge David Sydney Shillington found Rogerson and Paltos guilty of conspiracy over the false bank accounts. Rogerson was sentenced to eight years, with a non-parole period of six years. In December 1990 Rogerson was released after the NSW Court of Criminal Appeal acquitted him (and Paltos, though he was still serving his other sentence) of the conspiracy charges. In November 1991 the High Court of Australia heard a Crown case seeking to set aside the acquittal. On 16 June 1992, in a three–two majority, it ruled that Rogerson's original conviction would stand. In December the Court of Criminal Appeal reheard the case, with new evidence; Rogerson was convicted but had his original six-year sentence reduced to three years and nine months. On 15 December 1995 Rogerson walked from Berrima Gaol a free man – albeit with 15 months of parole to observe.

George Freeman was not mentioned in all these proceedings. In his memoir he repeated his mantra that he'd always been against drugs, and then wrote:

> That's not to say I condone Nick Paltos' crime. I don't.
> But I also don't condemn the man as a man and as my friend over a long period of time. I believe there were reasons for Nick Paltos' actions.

It was never revealed whether any of the money that came in from the sale of the drugs was ever paid to Freeman to reduce Paltos' debt.

Danny Chubb, the man who had organised the distribution of the Paltos gang's hashish haul, was shot dead, gunned down in a city street midmorning 8 November 1984. The gangland wars over drugs had begun in earnest.

15. Tall poppies mown down in killing fields

> Murder is unique in that it abolishes the party it injures, so that society has to take the place of the victim and on his behalf demand atonement or grant forgiveness; it is the one crime in which society has a direct interest.
> – W. H. Auden

When the killings started in Sydney's gangland drug wars in the mid-1980s, the two people who feared most for their safety were George Freeman and Lennie McPherson. Both enjoyed protection from a clique of heavyweight police officers, but they also had plenty of other crooks and cops who detested them for the immunity they had been able to secure through fizgigging and old-fashioned bribery. Indeed, McPherson was to feel so threatened as the war raged on that he even anointed Freeman as his negotiator. It might at times have appeared to Lennie that the blue was between his gang and the rest of the criminal world. In fact, it was far more complicated than that.

There have been many explanations for the bloodshed during those years: petty squabbles between two crims, an off-the-cuff comment taken badly, a wife belittled in company; but only those who suggest that it all arose from out-and-out greed for the spoils of the illegal drug trade are anywhere near the truth.

The tension on the streets was given heightened in early May 1984 when Murray Riley was released from jail after serving six years of his ten-year sentence for the *Anoa* drug scandal. Notionally on the Freeman-McPherson team, Riley now teamed up with Rogerson's mate Neddy Smith, who had become a major player in the heroin trade.

There were other influences at work, of course, one of which was alluded to in Judge Edwin Lusher's inquiry into NSW police administration, published in April 1981. Although his brief did not cover investigating corruption in the force, Lusher had taken a peep at the problem and suggested a new way to deal with it. In part, his report said:

> The results of effective control of corruption in the force may well cause an increase in crime temporarily. This is because the illegal systems are controlled by enforcing the law against competitors so as to leave the field clear for the favoured operator. Once the immunity is lost others will seek to enter or even capture the field. This is likely to involve struggle.

The appointment in August 1984 of John Avery as police commissioner, and his immediate declaration of war on the force's entrenched culture of corruption, saw Lusher's prediction partly borne out. The long-standing immunity enjoyed by Freeman, McPherson and Smith was under threat, and there were plenty of bovver-boys – aspiring Mr Big Enoughs – waiting in the wings to have their shot at the game. The drugs bonanza on offer to those at the top of the tree added fuel, and the establishment was not going down without a vigorous fight.

* * *

Perhaps seeing the writing on the wall, George Freeman in mid-1984 took action to defend himself. His was a twist on the old adage: when the going gets tough, the tough get bodyguards. Someone with a reputation had recently moved from Melbourne to Sydney. If there was gang warfare to be waged, Christopher Flannery figured Sin City was the place for a man of his distinctive talents to be.

It might seem unlikely that George Freeman's ego would permit him to publicly admit he had hired a minder, but in 1984 that's just what he did. Notably, though, his version of the story in his unreliable memoir has Flannery approaching him. Fanatical about his fitness, Chris Flannery had signed up at the exotic-sounding Eastern Bath House, a gymnasium and sauna facility on

Flannery makes – and takes – a big hit in Sydney

Christopher Dale Flannery's early years were almost a carbon copy of Freeman's. He was born on 15 March 1949 to Edward and Marie. Like Freeman, Christopher had an older brother and sister, and his father disappeared from the family home before his son's first birthday. Marie had divorced her husband, citing beatings and cruelty.

Flannery left school before completing third form, and took up stealing and housebreaking as a pastime, gaining his first conviction when he was 14. Like Freeman, he was initially given probation before doing a few stints in 'naughty boys' homes' for assaulting police, carrying a firearm, and having unlawful carnal knowledge.

In 1966 he served his first adult jail sentence, for a rape conviction. Out on parole four years later he was charged with attempted armed robbery, skipped bail and went to Perth, where his youthful good looks and charm landed him a job as a buyer with the David Jones department store. In May 1974 he was accused of stealing from his employer and charged with armed robbery. He had revealed to a couple of Perth crooks when and where the store's payroll arrived. They pulled a heist, shooting a security guard, and sent Flannery a bag containing all the coins they had grabbed in the haul as thanks for his help: they had no need for small change and not much time for a man they considered a small-time crook.

Flannery, given bail, fled to Sydney, and was arrested at West Ryde train station by none other than Roger Rogerson, who described the incident as 'a very violent struggle, a fight to the death, almost'. Extradited back to Perth, Flannery was acquitted of the theft charge, but sent straight to Melbourne to face the outstanding armed-robbery charge.

In October 1981 he was acquitted of the February 1980 murder of lawyer Roger Wilson – a crime said to have been committed for a fee of $25,000 (*$95,849*). A key witness had disappeared. As he walked out of court, he was arrested and charged with the murder of prostitution hoon Roger Locksley at Menai, south of Sydney, on 11 May 1979. In October 1981 he was extradited to Sydney; his wife Kathleen (who he'd married in 1978 while he was still in jail) joined him and there they remained. He faced two trials on the Locksley charge and on the direction of Judge Jack Lee the jury acquitted him in June 1984.

the 24th floor of the Boulevarde Hotel on William Street, between the CBD and Kings Cross. In those days it was well known as a meeting place for men who dabbled in illegal matters. Freeman's version is that they met at the gym every Monday, and over time Flannery smooth-talked his way into the bookie's circle.

A different source, however, assures me that it happened the other way around. That Flannery was at the gym just about every day would not have gone unnoticed by cops – both good and bad – who had the place on a regular watching roster. From such sources as allies Roger Rogerson and 20-year police veteran Bill Duff – at this time in the Homicide Squad – Freeman would have learned about the presence of a tough man looking for work. Kings Cross knockabout Frank Montague had got to know Flannery, and it was he who introduced him to Freeman.

The bookie offered the reputed heavy some $500 ($1,375) a week to act as a minder. The money – in cash, of course – was handed to Flannery in a brown envelope every Monday, when he invariably accompanied his new boss to meetings with SP bookies and others. Monday was the traditional 'settling day' after the weekend race meetings, and they'd often convene at the health club-cum-massage parlour at the old Chequers nightclub premises in Goulburn Street. Their business completed, they'd go together for lunch at a no-name Italian noshery in a Kings Cross back street, or sometimes duck down to Chinatown. If Flannery was out of the city, Freeman would personally drop the pay packet off at his home, handing it to Kathleen Flannery.

The word 'bodyguard' would not have been mentioned in those days, but the intent would have been clear: if anyone tried to take a shot at Freeman, Chris Flannery would deal with it. Until he published his memoir Freeman denied that Flannery had ever worked for him and that he had ever paid him any money. He told a court hearing that by claiming he was on the Freeman payroll, Flannery was 'just big-noting himself' and was 'trying to open doors in my name'. He added, 'Flannery never worked for me and never received a weekly salary from me.' In less than six months Flannery had become an informer – a fizgig – to Roger

Rogerson, or so the policeman later claimed. It's clear now that these associations did nothing to calm the troubled waters, and in fact ensured the whole episode ended in disaster.

* * *

The murder of a single criminal would not in itself have signalled the outbreak of a full-blown gang war. Les Cole's 1982 death, like so many others, was written off at the time as a one-off gangland killing – a score settled. Cole had moved to Sydney from Melbourne, where he was well known among the criminal elements of the Painters and Dockers Union. A big-time punter, Cole was heavily indebted to Freeman.

At 11.15 a.m. on 10 November 1982 he parked his car in his home garage at Kyle Bay, overlooking the Georges River about 20 kilometres south of the city. A concealed gunman opened fire: several shots hit Cole's shoulder and one pierced his heart. After he had collapsed, a final shot was fired into his skull behind his right ear, Mafia-style.

Police said they had known of an earlier attempt on Cole's life but that he had assured them he could sort things out by himself. He was obviously mistaken.

Two days short of the two-year anniversary of Cole's death, Daniel Chubb, then 42, met a similar fate. A short while after the pub-opening time of 10 a.m. on 8 November 1984 Chubb strolled from his mother's terrace home at 36 High Street, Millers Point, known as The Rocks, to his local, the Captain Cook Hotel. There he met one of his biggest bulk-heroin customers, Neddy Smith, and his companion, the Maltese-descended Graham 'Abo' Henry, for a couple of drinks and a chat.

It was a short meeting, and Chubb was back home before eleven o'clock. He had arranged to meet a business associate, Bruce McCauley, at home to give him some children's videos (or so McCauley later stated). He told McCauley and his mother that he was just ducking out again for a few minutes to meet somebody.

Cherrie Davies was in the kitchen at the rear of her home at 35 High Street. Just after 11 a.m., Mrs Davies heard two loud bangs that sounded to her 'like thunder'. She ran to the hallway and peeped out onto the street. There she saw Danny Chubb, a neighbour she had known for years, standing behind his green Jaguar sedan.

In a later statement Mrs Davies said Chubb was dressed in a checked coat, holding what appeared to her to be a rifle. She thought he was trying to open it. Chubb was shouting at someone she could not see.

She said it was as if he 'was going off his head'. Then she heard a louder, different-sounding report, and she stepped out into the street to investigate. Danny Chubb was lying on the road, dead.

Mrs Davies knocked on the door of number 36 and Bruce McCauley came out, looked at Chubb's body and walked away rapidly from the gruesome scene. Mrs Davies held back Chubb's mother, trying to comfort her as she cried, 'Why has he done it? Why? Why?' No one else was visible in the street.

At the police traffic branch Senior Constable Raymond Walker responded to a call over the radio network and arrived at the scene within minutes.

McCauley, a company director, later said he'd known Danny Chubb – 'a very nice guy' – for more than a decade. Chubb was an enthusiastic punter who often placed bets for McCauley at Sydney race meetings, returning winnings of up to $20,000 ($54,980) a week. After McCauley had heard the shots, he said he went outside to see Chubb's corpse lying on the road. He said he left immediately, knowing there was nothing he could do.

The police later established that Chubb had sustained four bullet wounds and one blast from a shotgun. The recovered .38-calibre bullets and cartridge cases from outside the house. The evidence was they had been fired from a Colt revolver or a .357-calibre Magnum pistol at a range of no more than two metres from the victim.

Chubb's girlfriend, Sue Hubbard, told police that Chubb was a professional punter, but that she knew nothing of his alleged connection with the drug trade. Criminals who publicly deny involvement in the drug trade don't own up to it with their girlfriends either, it seems.

It was just over nine months since Danny Chubb had escorted Paltos' haul of Lebanese hash from Darwin and distributed it in Sydney.

Detective-Sergeant Ian Kennedy told the coroner of Chubb's suspected involvement in that multimillion-dollar drug deal.

Detective-Sergeant James 'Bill' Duff made enquiries about Chubb's murder. He later told an inquiry that a pair of Homicide Squad detectives had asked him to keep in touch with Neddy Smith through Roger Rogerson, as a way of picking up underworld information about the killing. Duff first met Smith with Rogerson at the Kings Cross Aquatic Club, but denied that he became a regular provider of information to Neddy. Duff was sacked from the police force two years later after the Police Tribunal found him guilty of misconduct. Duff later ran the Iron Duke Hotel in inner-suburban Alexandria – reputedly owned by Neddy Smith and used as a regular meeting venue for Neddy's associates.

Coroner Greg Glass started his inquest into Chubb's death; however, the conversations recorded by the AFP for the Paltos case, which clearly implicated Chubb in the scheme, were not put before the court for examination. Coroner Glass was told that while Chubb had never been convicted of a crime, he had been involved in a number of multimillion-dollar drug deals, and had assets valued at more than $7 million (*$19.24 million*), including $5 million (*$13.74 million*) sitting in a Swiss bank account. He was also believed to be owed $400,000 (*$1.1 million*) for supplying heroin.

Three years after the killing, in November 1987, Coroner Greg Glass returned an open finding. He stated it was probable three people were involved – two shooters and a third driving the getaway vehicle – but that there was not enough evidence to charge anyone in the matter, and that police investigations would continue. The coroner said that while there was evidence of Chubb's success as a punter, 'a number of people believed he might have been involved in drug trafficking'.

Six months later Attorney-General John Dowd (formerly the NSW Liberal Party opposition leader) successfully sought a ruling from Judge Michael Campbell, then in his second year on the bench of the Supreme Court, that the open finding of the inquest be quashed and a new inquiry ordered. Judge Campbell reported that through no fault of Coroner Glass there had been 'an insufficiency of inquiry' into the death, which had not taken account of the federal police's phone tap material and new evidence. Jack Mater, a lawyer appearing for the Attorney-General, told the judge the new evidence, which had emerged as a result of police inquiries into an article in the *Sydney Morning Herald*, involved tapped phone conversations between Nick Paltos, Graham Palmer and Ross Karp which had been recorded by the federal police.

Police said that though they had been with Chubb shortly before his death, Neddy Smith and Graham Henry had alibis for the time of the shooting. In December 1995 Smith was committed to stand trial over Chubb's murder, but in September 1996 Magistrate Pat O'Shane ruled there was insufficient evidence to convict Smith and dismissed the charge.

Exactly one year after the first inquest into Chubb's murder, another city coroner, Derrick Windsor Hand, held the second inquiry that had been ordered by the Supreme Court. His findings were identical to those Glass handed down on 17 November 1987:

> On 8 November 1984, on a roadway outside the premises of 36 High Street, Millers Point, Daniel Chubb died from the effects of gunshot injuries to neck and chest, inflicted there and then by persons unknown.

After two inquiries and a failed murder charge, the killing of Daniel Michael Chubb remains unresolved to this day.

* * *

Three months before Danny Chubb was gunned down, Michael John Sayers was on top of the world. Reputedly a millionaire, Sayers had just funded one of horseracing's most outrageous scams: the Fine Cotton ring-in affair. He was blissfully unaware that his actions would eventually force his name to the top of someone's hit list.

On 18 August 1984 at Brisbane's Eagle Farm racecourse, a

horse thought to be called 'Fine Cotton' narrowly won an early race. It had been heavily backed with its odds plummeting from 33–1 to 7–2.

But the horse was not the inferior country gelding Fine Cotton; it was instead a classy galloper called 'Bold Personality'. Fine Cotton's intended substitute had been injured a week earlier, so a horse that bore no resemblance to Fine Cotton was chosen as the ring-in. To deal with the problem of appearance, the scammers had drenched Bold Personality with hair colouring. Trainer Hayden Haitana – who said he felt intimidated by the criminal organisers – said there was a problem with the human hair dye: 'It doesn't take to horse's hair. So they just went ahead and tried to paint its white feet brown, but the horse came out red like a Hereford bull. I couldn't believe it.' Mick Sayers had spread the word to all his mates that there was coin to be made from the bookies, and bets flowed in from all over Australia, as well as from as far afield as Papua New Guinea and Fiji. The Sayers' telegraph would have reached George Freeman, either directly or through the Rogerson-Neddy Smith network, but Freeman never let on whether he was among the big winners on the day. The betting coup reportedly cost the bookies $30 million (*$82.47 million*). Sayers had put $40,000 (*$109,959*) on the race, and a young bookie called Robbie Waterhouse had placed a $10,000 (*$27,490*) bet. In his memoir Freeman wrote, 'An investigation discovered that Robbie Waterhouse, bookmaker son of bookmaker Bill Waterhouse, had organised a nationwide betting plunge on Fine Cotton.' Robbie and his renowned father Bill were given lifetime bans from racing as a result of the inevitable inquiries, but it is a forgiving industry: the bans were lifted in 1998.

Bill Waterhouse was less forgiving. In Kevin Perkins' book *The Gambling Man*, which among other things delved into the Fine Cotton affair, Waterhouse wrote:

> Among the most amazing disclosures by Perkins was that the gangster George Freeman had caused serious trouble to Robbie and me over Fine Cotton by influencing or manipulating people of authority in the background.

These included Freeman's contacts in the media, the police, politics and even at the AJC. Perkins revealed that Freeman, with his hatred for us, took advantage of the situation to make sure Robbie and I were the fall guys.

Six months after the Fine Cotton race, on 16 February 1985, Mick Sayers and his girlfriend, Marian Ware, had a day out at the Canterbury races. The couple had met on the Gold Coast in 1981 and she moved in with him a year later. After the race meeting they went to a Greek restaurant in Liverpool Street in the city, and dined with a bookmaker friend and his wife. Then they all climbed into Sayers' red Mercedes sedan. He dropped the friends at their place before arriving home in Hewlett Street, Bronte, south of Bondi Beach, at around ten o'clock.

As Sayers stepped out of the car to open his garage door, Marian heard a barrage of gunshots. Sayers seemed confused, she later said, looking around then continuing towards the garage. More shots were fired, and he turned and shouted, 'What?' A man wearing dark clothing and a hood pulled down over his head ran past the car's headlights, vaulted over a low fence and some shrubs into the neighbouring front yard, and raised his rifle at Sayers.

Marian got out of the car and ran from the scene. She turned around to see her lover fall to the ground, the gunman standing over him and taking aim at his head. Another shot was fired, and 39-year-old Michael Sayers became the third victim of the 1980s gang warfare.

What Sayers had done to bring about his murder was the subject of many high-flown media theories, and the inevitable court case or two. One suggestion is that from his position of wealth six months earlier, he had sustained a run of losses with the SP bookies and at tables in illegal casinos, and now owed sizeable sums of money to people who were notoriously intolerant of slow payers. One of those creditors was Barry McCann, who had been accused, along with three others, of having plotted Sayers' murder two years earlier over a unpaid debt of $400,000 ($754,974).

A Mick Sayers snapshot: not a pretty picture

Michael John Sayers was born in Melbourne on 16 April 1946 and established himself in Victoria with 19 arrests for kidnapping, receiving stolen goods, car theft, armed robbery, assaulting police, offering a bribe, safe-blowing and housebreaking by the time of his entry in the 1973 supplement of the Australian Criminal Register.

In February 1969 he held up the Bank of New South Wales at bayside Melbourne suburb of Brighton, using a pistol and a sawn-off shotgun. He was quickly arrested and spent time in Pentridge Prison to atone. He was still there when the 1973 edition went to press. The entry said, 'When this offender is released he will continue to commit violent crimes.' He was on bail facing drugs and firearm charges when he was shot.

For six years Mick Sayers' murder remained unresolved, written off as another gangland killing. One man changed all that: he was given indemnity and a new name – Roger Ford – in exchange for telling all he knew about the killing to the National Crime Authority.

Ford, a heroin smuggler, poker-machine thief and general ne'er-do-well, claimed he had been Barry McCann's 'right-hand man' when, early in 1983, he took part in a scheme to recover the $400,000 Sayers allegedly owed McCann. He said he, McCann, Tom Domican, Victor Camilleri and Kevin Theobold met at the Lansdowne pub to plan how to best handle the matter. Ford said at one stage McCann turned to Domican and said, 'Well, that fucking Sayers, he has to pay one way or the other.' On the basis of Ford's testimony, the plotters – other than himself and McCann, who died in December 1987 – appeared before Judge Brian Sully in the Supreme Court in June 1991 charged with conspiring between 11 January 1983 and 16 February 1985 to murder Sayers. All three pleaded not guilty and provided alibis for the time of the killing.

That people planning a murder over a debt that existed in 1983 would wait two years to carry out their plot seems unlikely.

Barry McCann: no dope when it came to the drug trade
Barry Raymond McCann was born on 28 July 1943. He was an inner-city kid but did not come from an impoverished background or a broken family like so many others in this story. His father owned the Lansdowne Hotel on City Road, in the inner suburb of Chippendale, which under Barry's management would later become a major meeting place for the criminals he called friends.

McCann owned a number of illegal casinos, including one in Wollongong, and had various connections to the underworld. He was associated with drug running ex-cop Murray Riley, and among his close mates were drug baron Robert Trimbole's son Craig, and 'colourful Sydney identity' Tom Domican.

By the mid-1980s McCann was a wealthy man: he owned a few racehorses – through his interest in racing coming to know George Freeman well – and had paid $450,000 (*$1.59 million*) in cash for a property at rural Denman in the Hunter Valley.

While McCann created the impression his wealth came mainly from gambling, subsequent police inquiries put it beyond doubt that he had become a major player in the importation and distribution of heroin, cocaine and marijuana.

What was even more extraordinary was that such an improbable tale should have made its way to court. That it resulted in people being charged with murder raised some serious questions about the NCA and the judicial processes of the time – questions that remain unanswered.

Camilleri's lawyer, Bernard Gross QC, introduced a sensational element into the case when he told the court that Mike Sayers had also owed George Freeman $83,000 (*$213,768*), and that Christopher Flannery had 'threatened Sayers with a weapon at his Bronte home' over the debt. In another earlier case involving Domican it was revealed by a National Crime Authority officer that Flannery's wife, Kathleen, had told police that her husband refused to take on a contract to kill Mike Sayers, which had been offered to him by George Freeman. According to her statement, Freeman told Flannery he would provide him with a Valiant car and a false beard for the job. Flannery then met Stan Smith's close mate, heroin trafficker Tony Eustace at the Royal Oak Hotel in Double Bay to discuss the matter, before ringing Freeman to say he would not take on the Sayers job.

Somebody did, of course, and somebody else paid for it to happen.

The court system found it was not the McCann group conspirators: the charges against them were dismissed and Sayers' murder remains unresolved to this day.

* * *

A killing or three did not interrupt the drug trade. Neddy Smith told the Police Tribunal that in March 1985 Roger Rogerson and Bill Duff were hatching a plan to import heroin worth $40 million (*$103 million*) from Thailand through Papua New Guinea, using Smith as their distributor. Through a legal federal police tap on Duff's phone in April, it was learned that Rogerson and Duff were taking flying lessons, and that Sydney identity Dr Geoffrey Edelstein had provided the duo with the clear bills of health necessary for their pilots' certificates. The plot unravelled when its details, and those pertaining to a partner in the deal, Murray Riley, were exposed during a commission of inquiry headed by Judge Theo Bredmeyer in the PNG Supreme Court.

The hitch in the drug deal was a temporary problem. The drug importers would have to make other plans. There was to be no hitch, no let-up for some time, however, in the drug-war killings and a few other lines of business the crooks involved themselves in.

16. NCA targets Freeman – and misses

> To do evil that good may come of it is for
> bunglers in politics as well as morals.
> – *William Penn, English philosopher*

Note: this chapter does not follow the chronology of the rest of the book.

Between tending to his boss's insecurities and being constantly on the lookout for the 'main chance' – an opportunity to improve his bank balance – Christopher Flannery had not endeared himself to many of Sydney's criminal community. He'd formed a friendship with Bruce Hardin, who operated a casino in the inner-western suburb of Rozelle on behalf of its owners, George Freeman and Lennie McPherson. Freeman and his associate Tony Torok had taken over the prestigious – and illegal – casino, the Double Bay Bridge Club, which Hardin visited frequently, and Freeman had also made arrangements for Hardin to front an SP bookie shop for him in Balmain. Flannery provided collection services for these venues, as he did for all Freeman's illegal gambling outfits.

One firm friendship Flannery had made was with the ageing but still powerful Charles 'Paddles' Anderson. Neither Freeman nor McPherson had ever developed a close relationship with the patriarch of Sydney's criminals, and Flannery's acceptance by Anderson would doubtless have caused pangs of jealousy among the sensitive egos of the crime bosses. Anderson had good advice for the young newcomer to the scene, including who he should be wary of. High on that list was Roger Rogerson. Flannery would fatefully ignore this advice.

Flannery's other ally was Michael Sayers, the big-time punter and drug-trade player, whose hit Flannery would pass up. Also in Flannery's inner circle was Ian McLean, his wife's cousin. McLean was often with Flannery when he had meetings with George Freeman at the Eastern Bath House at the Boulevarde Hotel. McLean's former de facto partner, Goldie – who used the McLean surname – was close to Chris's wife, Kathleen. There were a number of others, some with criminal records up and down the Australian east coast, but the most influential was Peter James Cross, a former Victorian high school teacher who had become increasingly involved in the drug trade.

While Chris Flannery had an interesting circle of friends and close business associations with powerful people like George Freeman and Roger Rogerson, he also had enemies, and more than one was looking to kill him.

On Sunday, 27 January 1985 Flannery had been out and about with his wife and ten-year-old daughter, Christine, when they pulled into the driveway of their home in Turrella Street, Arncliffe at around 5.50 p.m. Christine had run to the doorway and Kathleen and Chris were walking up the path when a early-model dark-green Mazda coupe screeched to a halt directly opposite. A man disguised in a clown's wig and Groucho goggles leaned through his open car window and fired a volley of shots at the family from a .223-calibre Colt self-loading assault rifle (it was later described as an Armalite rifle) before speeding off. Kathleen and her daughter escaped injury, but Chris Flannery was wounded in his right ear, right hand and suffered superficial wounds to the left side of his body.

In the late afternoon the day after the shooting, Irish-born Thomas Christian Domican reported to police that his 1978 green Mazda coupe had been stolen some time between nine o'clock on the night of 25 January and two in the afternoon of 28 January, the day he was making the report. The ever-helpful but rarely truthful Kings Cross identity Louie Sarkis El Bayeh, who had migrated from Lebanon 34 years earlier, was later to testify that on the day of the shooting a shot was fired into Domican's front door, and that Domican had told him he thought Flannery was responsible.

What followed must now rate as some of the worst bungled criminal investigations and prosecutions in Australia's history. A year before the shooting at Arncliffe, a new crime-fighting body, the National Crime Authority (NCA) had been set up by the federal government.

It had taken agonised debate in Canberra – honourable members on both sides of the parliamentary chambers had associations with those who might be targeted by the new body – but on 1 July 1984 the NCA came into being.

The royal commissions of the 1970s had all pointed to the ineffectiveness of the police force in dealing with gangsters' activities, and the NCA was established in line with recommendations from the reports of Costigan, Stewart and Williams. To initiate an investigation the NCA needed a 'reference' from either a state or the federal government, depending on whether matters extended across state borders. Initially, it was given a limited tenure – shackled with a 'sunset clause' that, as Commonwealth Director of Public Prosecutions Michael Rozenes QC later commented, 'had the unfortunate, and no doubt unintended, effect of forcing the Authority to get some early "runs" on the board before its very existence came up for review, even if a fair proportion of them were "extras".' The NCA certainly had its critics, including the federal parliamentary committee charged with keeping a watchful eye on it. Their first report, tabled in November 1985, complained that the committee was 'unable to fulfil its statutory duty to the parliament because it did not have – and was not able to obtain from the National Crime Authority – sufficient information of substance to serve as a basis for the monitoring and review role required of it.' The report added that unless the law under which the NCA operated was amended the committee was toothless. Unless the proposed amendments were adopted, the committee warned:

> There is no point in retaining a parliamentary committee to act as a watchdog over the National Crime Authority.

> Indeed, in the absence of the necessary amendment, the retention of the committee would be a charade, as it provides the appearance but not the substance of the Authority's accountability to parliament.

After its second birthday, the NCA sought and obtained a commonwealth reference – ominously titled 'Curtains' – to investigate organised-crime activities in NSW, and placed George Freeman and his associates at the top of its list of those whose activities it planned to look into. Within days, on 4 April 1986, the NSW government came to the party and provided its reference, allowing to the NCA to investigate the Sydney-based criminal milieu. Those who clustered around Chris Flannery, as mentioned previously, were named as targets of the NCA's investigation.

A particular investigator involved from the outset – who has requested anonymity – was part of a small group who began surveillance on Freeman, which included tapping his telephone conversations, a facility legally available to NCA operatives. The team quickly amassed considerable information on his criminal activities, ranging from money laundering to extortion. Both Freeman and McPherson were found to have invested large sums of ill-gotten money in real estate in Australia and elsewhere, hidden from view by having ownership recorded in the names of their offspring. The evidence the team gathered provided clear grounds for criminal and proceeds-of-crime cases to be made against Australia's top two criminals. But, remarkably, the powers that be at the NCA, driven by the push for good press and big results, thought extortion was too pale, too small fry, and redirected the organisation's focus.

While Freeman notionally remained a target, he was put on the back burner as the NCA decided to pursue someone who would give them their best chance of securing positive headlines and even some political support. Tom Domican was linked to the Right-wing faction of the NSW ALP, through an association with party powerbroker Graham Richardson. Richardson has never denied that he had a friendly association with Lennie McPherson, his drug-connected mate Danny Casey, Joe Meissner and Domican. While once close, Domican and 'Richo' had a bad falling out in the 1980s, a fact that would be known to any federal MPs who might have had some say in advising the NCA on who they could pursue for a more productive outcome.

Three years after the Curtains reference got under way, at the start of May 1989, the NCA launched a related operation first known as 'Icon' and then 'Sugar'.

From here on, the story takes a fantastical turn, but this account is based on internal NCA documents, to which I have been privy. All interviews referred to were carried out with a 'non-dissemination/non-prosecution' clause to provide indemnity to the informants and ensure that their statements would not fall into the hands of other law enforcement agencies. One investigator's report states that Kathleen Flannery was interviewed on that basis on 28 June 1989:

> ... mainly to obtain information about George Freeman, and the areas of her criminal activity were not canvassed. However she did indicate having unspecific knowledge of an attempt on Freeman's life and following or causing Freeman to be followed.

That NCA agent recommended 'that consideration be given to continuing investigations into the activities and information concerning Kathleen Flannery and associated persons with the view of criminal prosecutions'. But that was not to be.

Peter Cross, Flannery's old mate the major cocaine importer, officially approached the NCA seeking indemnity from prosecution on drug-related charges he faced in Victoria. He became an NCA informant against his co-accused Melbourne team before December 1985 and on 17 October 1986 gave the organisation a lengthy signed statement that became the basis for later probing by NCA investigators. An internal report revealing this said in part:

> The statement mentioned the criminal activities of Cross' involvement in the importation of cocaine into Australia, indicating other principal offenders namely Christopher and Kathleen Flannery and Maureen Childs. Freeman

was not mentioned in this statement other than to indicate that Chris Flannery worked for Freeman.

That report was an evaluation of material that had been stored in the safe of Judge Donald Stewart, who had been the first chairman of the NCA. It noted that the material did not relate to George Freeman, who was supposed to be the real target of the NCA probe. It must be stressed here that in this and other NCA documents informants' allegations and many conclusions reached by NCA staff do not constitute proof of criminal activity by anyone mentioned: they are merely accusations.

Cross went on to claim that Chris Flannery and Mick Sayers had arranged for Ian McLean to go to Italy, link up with drug baron Robert Trimbole and organise the importation of drugs into Australia. When McLean became NCA's protected informant, he corroborated this allegation, saying he spent three weeks in Italy and saw Trimbole several times 'but not on a daily basis'. On his return flight to Melbourne McLean checked in a package containing car parts, in which was hidden a large amount of heroin. Mick Sayers and two acquaintances met him at the airport, saw the package passed through customs and took it back with them to Sydney. A fortnight later McLean flew to Sydney and at a meeting with Sayers and Chris Flannery was paid $9000 (*$25,720*) for (as he told it) 'looking after Robert Trimbole in Italy'.

Cross claimed that once he'd arrived in Sydney Chris Flannery told him of a robbery he'd committed, from which he'd netted a quantity of opals. On 9 May 1985 Flannery disappeared. Not long after that a friend of the Flannery couple, Maureen Childs, and Ian McLean took the haul of stolen opals to the Philippines, trying to sell them to Australian-born criminal Dennis 'Fatty' Smith, who ran the Aussie Bar in Manila. The mission failed and the duo came back, handing the haul to Kathleen.

Cross's most extraordinary claim was that he had conspired with Kathleen Flannery, notorious Melbourne criminal Amos Atkinson and Ian McLean to murder George Freeman, who Kathleen believed was responsible for her husband's murder. The date set for killing Freeman was 26 July 1985. McLean, under the

NCA's indemnity from prosecution, spoke freely of his role in the alleged murder plot. He said he'd accepted a loaded revolver from Kathleen on the morning of the 26th (Cross said that McLean had loaded the weapon himself) but denied having any intention to use it. He claimed he'd telephoned George Freeman anonymously to warn him of the plot. Clearly, the action never went ahead: George Freeman had taken McLean's warning seriously and hopped on a plane to London – where he was refused entry, as has been detailed earlier.

When these dramatic claims were sent to the organisation's chiefs in October 1986 they would throw the NCA into turmoil, for in that month Kathleen Flannery had also become an informant and was now placed in protective custody by the NCA. She was to help the NCA pursue Tom Domican, by way of testifying against him for the attempted murder of the Flannery clan back in January 1985. It had taken Kathleen nearly two years to come forward with a statement identifying Domican as the man in the green Mazda. Obviously, after having dodged some 30 or 40 bullets, the woman suffered from considerable shock. In May 1985 Kathleen had told police she could not identify the gunman, but later she said the shooter was Tom Domican. She had been too scared earlier to name him, she said, and she was also distrustful of police. Flannery remained in various forms of protection until June 1990, by which time the NCA had racked up a bill of $64,000 ($112,543) in sums paid to or on behalf of Kathleen.

When Peter Cross arrived on the scene saying Kathleen was involved in a conspiracy to murder the man who was still ostensibly the main target of Operation Sugar, the NCA had to make some serious decisions. Pursuing the politically expedient Domican meant they required Kathleen's help. The NCA chief investigator in Victoria, Carl Mengler, had been charged with looking into Cross's allegations.

Whether Mengler took legal advice or just flipped a coin is not known, but the conclusion he reached was that Kathleen Flannery would not be further investigated for the conspiracy to murder allegation.

On 29 January 1987 Mengler wrote a minute to Mark Le Grand, a Brisbane barrister who at that time was the general counsel assisting the NCA, based in Melbourne. The inquiry into Peter Cross's allegations was closely aligned with the Curtains investigation, which involved George Freeman and Kathleen Flannery. Mengler wrote that he now wanted that part of the inquiry suspended. He pointed out that Kathleen was a vital witness who could provided evidence against Domican, and recommended to the chairman and members of the NCA to consider 'relieving the investigators of their task pending a future decision on the continuation of the inquiry'.

In September 1988 Domican was charged with shooting at the Flannerys with intent to murder; added to this was a back-up charge of shooting with intent to do grievous bodily harm. He predictably pleaded not guilty, but after a lengthy hearing the jury was not convinced of his innocence. The sentence was 14 years. He appealed against both the sentence and the conviction, the grounds of which relied on the 'unreliability' of Kathleen Flannery's evidence.

Despite the appeal still being before the courts, the NCA publicly pronounced the Domican conviction a great success. George Freeman, the NCA's original target, was not mentioned in their gloating. On 5 September 1990, however, a different story started to unfold inside the NCA. A new acting team leader wrote a memo to his superiors, discussing the way forward with Cross's allegations of the conspiracy to kill Freeman, which had been corroborated by McLean. Here's some of that document:

> The Authority is in an invidious position whatever decision it makes. Should the Authority adopt Investigator [name withheld]'s recommendation and prosecutions result there would very likely be criticism for the delay in investigating and prosecuting matters especially those relating to Kathleen Flannery. In addition there would be criticism for the Authority relying on her as a witness in its prosecution of Domican and then prosecuting her when they had the Cross information at

the time she became a protected witness. Despite these drawbacks the Authority may well have no alternative save to implement Investigator [name withheld]'s recommendation, which recommendation I support.

Three months later an NCA legal adviser issued an even grimmer warning of the problems the authority had brought on itself:

> The enquiry has reached a point at which a decision must be made as to the extent of the Authority's future involvement in it. The matter is, as you are aware, not limited to McLean and may have implications for the conduct of previous Authority investigations. While preliminary enquiries appear to support the allegations of an attempt to murder Freeman made by Cross and McLean, considerable further investigation is required to determine the totality of evidence, the extent to which it corroborates or contradicts the informants and the sufficiency of evidence to support prosecution without their evidence. I note also that there are some discrepancies between the evidence of Cross and McLean which will require a further debriefing of Cross.
>
> Before the question of Cross' use as a witness in a prosecution of Kathleen Flannery and others for the attempted murder of Freeman can be resolved, it is submitted that the matter of the (then) Authority's failure to make his evidence in that respect available in the prosecution of Domican must first be addressed.

The chronology of events outlined in the report, its author went on to say, 'indicates that the Authority, at the time it charged and proceeded to secure the conviction of Domican, was in possession of information severely damaging to the credit of Flannery, a vital prosecution witness.' Possible repercussions for the NCA, the report said, were an appeal by Domican against his conviction and 'an abuse of process argument by Flannery and other defendants on the basis of delay, particularly in view of the fact that Freeman, an important potential witness, is now dead.' (George Freeman died in March 1990.) It continued:

> Both these consequences would involve the Authority in a re-examination of the conduct of the Domican investigation and prosecution. Arguably, therefore, that re-examination should be conducted without delay, lest the present Authority, in its further investigation of the matters contained in McLean's statements, be subsequently seen to have concealed or disregarded potentially embarrassing material.

Most tellingly of all, the memo recommended that the NCA should 'initiate enquiries to ascertain the reasons for the termination of investigations into the Cross allegations in January 1987' (on the advice of Carl Mengler) and to examine 'the failure of the Authority to make available those allegations which concern Kathleen Flannery in the prosecution of Domican'. Those enquiries should commence with a review of the relevant files and identification of the Authority officers concerned with this aspect of the Curtains Reference.

* * *

Had the NCA been more open with their star witness, Kathleen Flannery may now, all these years later, have some kinder things to say about that experience.

'I can tell you, the NCA was not on my side,' she told me. 'Some [NCA officers] felt we needed a break, others set me up.' Kathleen Flannery said Peter Cross was a cocaine dealer who got caught, and 'would say anything' to stay out of jail.

'Carl Mengler told me when Cross was arrested that there were telephone taps of me talking to one of Cross's offsiders, a man called Tom, but Mengler made it clear that I was not involved, the tapes did not implicate me in any plot [to murder Freeman].

'Ian McLean is my cousin. He was taken into witness protection in 1986 and even to this day his mother doesn't know where he is. They [the NCA] have told her if he dies, she will be notified.' McLean came to Sydney after Chris Flannery died, and Kathleen quickly learned he was dealing in drugs with a person she knew. 'They used Chris's name to get credit of around $40,000. When I found this out I had a very big argument with him and never saw him again. I never learned the precise reason for his arrest or who his were accomplices at the time.'

After the drug dealers made their allegations to the NCA, Kathleen Flannery was approached by NSW Police. 'I had a call to see two officers in regard to the allegation by McLean and Cross that I had conspired to kill Freeman,' she told me. 'I went to meet them with my lawyer and it turned out they were close to [detective] Aarne Tees, and they tried to intimidate me. I just laughed at them.

'On the word of two junkies, believe me if I was going to kill someone, as if I would have told them!' After this experience Mrs Flannery moved interstate, changed her name and went about rebuilding her damaged life.

* * *

Even without access to this scathing assessment of the whole sorry saga, Domican's legal team saw their appeal to the High Court succeed in May 1992. While not suggesting that Kathleen Flannery's testimony was incorrect, the judges quashed the conviction on a technicality, and ordered a new trial. In summary, they said:

> Whatever the defence and however the case is conducted, where evidence as to identification represents any significant part of the proof of guilt of an offence, the judge must warn the jury as to the dangers of convicting on such evidence where its reliability is disputed.

Eventually, the director of public prosecutions decided not to take the matter further. For Tom Domican it was the conclusion of one of many confrontations with the law. For the NCA, however, it was the beginning of the end. Change moves slowly through law and politics, and in 2002 the Australian Crime Commission replaced the National Crime Authority. Finally, it was 'curtains' for the NCA.

17. Building a new deal in extortion

> If Mr Gyles were to continue inquiries into organised crime in the building industry, it would take him 10 years and a thousand investigators.
> – Kirk Walker, former scaffolding contractor, in testimony to the NSW Building Royal Commission, 1991

With all the money to be made from race fixing, betting commissions, illegal casinos and the booming drug trade in the mid-1980s, it may have surprised people when Freeman and McPherson got involved in standover and extortion activities in the building trade. But when the volume of tax-free cash that flowed to the crooks became known, their motivation was clear. It came into public view much later, when Roger V. Gyles QC, a barrister of 45 years standing, was appointed in 1990 by the NSW government to conduct a royal commission into the building industry. The inquiry was intended to be a union-bashing stunt, bolstering Nick Greiner's Liberal government in the dying days of his leadership. There is, however, a fine axiom that all politicians should observe: never ask a question – or launch a public inquiry – unless you already know the response. The Gyles inquiry, as well as exposing dubious behaviour on part of individuals in the industry's unions, also unearthed evidence of building companies' corrupt practices, and the fact that some of them had hired McPherson, Freeman and other thugs to use menacing standover tactics with their workers.

A shady private detective, Tim Bristow, had got McPherson involved early in 1985 – to intimidate and stand over, as may be required – by introducing him to Richard Knebel, owner of a home-building firm that was under takeover pressure. Knebel undoubtedly knew of McPherson's reputation and quickly arranged to pass his stock in the dwindling family company to the bigger firm. Buoyed by that success, Bristow took McPherson to a building site at Campbelltown, where the workers were agitating for a better deal. 'This is Lennie McPherson,' Bristow said at a workers' meeting. 'He'll have a chat with you.' The unions thought that very intimidating behaviour indeed. McPherson said he'd had a friendly chat with them, but added, 'That is all that happened and those poor bludgers left the job the next day because they were frightened of me.' Bristow and McPherson shared a $9000 (*$23,180*) fee paid by Civil and Civic for this activity.

When demolisher and earthmover Paul Henry Menere ran up a debt of $350,000 (*$901,434*) with the big scaffolding company GKN Kwikform, a man called 'Bronco' phoned to discuss the problem. Menere thought the man was McPherson's offsider, Branko Balic, and started to worry.

When he then heard through a horseracing contact that George Freeman wanted to see him, he really got scared. He went to the Chequers Health Club where, he said, he'd met Freeman, McPherson, Branko Balic, Bruce Hardin and ex-boxer David Bruce Ballard, known professionally as 'Charkey Ramon', who was later named in parliament as 'a notorious standover merchant with convictions for assault, assaulting police and giving false testimony'.

After a 'bit of a chat' with Freeman and his pals, Menere realised Branko Balic was not the heavy GKN had arranged to talk to him about his debt. That man was later identified by Menere as John 'Bronco' Ratcliffe. Menere explained to the inquiry that when he had made the mistaken identity clear to Freeman, the SP bookie and his team got up and left, apparently satisfied that their pal Branko Balic was not about to be called into witness box. Menere told Gyles he'd gone to the club another time, escorted by Charkey Ramon, to see George Freeman to discuss the sale of two horses. Menere couldn't be certain, but he told Commissioner Gyles he may have the mentioned the problems he was having with GKN.

The GKN scaffolding business became heavily involved in running extortion rackets. An executive of the firm, Edward McFadden, told the Gyles inquiry that $46,500 (*$119,761*) had been paid to Bruce Hardin's company for them to replace GKN scaffolding that had been stolen.

Hardin was to source the scaffolding by stealing it from other sites, but it appeared not to have happened that way. Around $21,000 (*$54,086*) of the money was split between McFadden, another GKN executive Michael John Smith and 'security consultant' Bronco Ratcliffe. The balance went to Lennie McPherson and Bruce Hardin. Michael Smith told Gyles he would not apologise for using underworld figures to solve his company's problem of chronic theft. Under questioning, Smith admitted he had a criminal record dating back to 1957. Bruce Hardin had been the one to arrange Smith's first meeting with McPherson.

In April 1991 the Gyles commission issued a summons requiring Bruce Hardin to take his turn in the witness stand. But his then de facto partner, Carolyn Bain, said she had not passed the summons on to Hardin 'because every time I say something bad to him, he bites my head off'.

Bronco Ratcliffe, then 52, denied to Gyles that he knew the details of GKN's payments to his partner, Hardin – which totalled about $800,000 (*$2.06 million*) over a year: 'He would pay money out, which I don't know who he was paying money to, because I didn't ask. If he said I paid 20 grand there or 50 grand here or something, I wasn't going to ask him any questions.' Authorities took six months to track down Bruce Hardin and haul him before the Gyles inquiry. On the evening of 30 September 1991 he was arrested by commission investigators and brought that night before a magistrate at Ipswich, west of Brisbane, more than 900 kilometres north of where the Gyles summons said he should be. The magistrate didn't hesitate to conclude that he should be extradited south. He and his escorts flew back to Sydney the next morning, a Tuesday, and in a special late-afternoon session that day the reluctant witness appeared before Gyles, but it took half an hour of squabbling and the threat of being found in contempt of court before Hardin finally agreed to take the oath. The 46-year-old man Lennie McPherson said he had 'known since babyhood and looked on as a son' spent that night in the cells.

Hardin had been charged with failing to comply with the summons, and was denied bail.

The next day he gave headline-making evidence. Hardin said he had loaned former Liberal federal MP John Abel $50,000 (*$85,217*) because he was 'short of money'. Hardin had also helped Abel – who'd represented the NSW seat of Evans from 1975–77 – to invest in a casino resort called 'Radisson Royal Palms' in Port Vila, Vanuatu's capital.

Abel was later confirmed to own the casino, but it appears there were no repercussions other than a few unwanted headlines for the former conservative politician.

Hardin told the inquiry that in the year from November 1989 a little more than $300,000 (*$527,545*) had gone into his business account.

Expenses drawn from the account paid for 'a lot of surveillance people,' he said, 'and we had to pay various people. George Freeman received a fair bit of money.' Asked what Freeman was paid for, Hardin replied, 'The company [GKN] wanted him to look after them and make sure there were no problems in the building industry, so he received some money. They just asked George to make sure no organised gangs were pinching their scaffolding.'

At no stage throughout the Gyles inquiry did any of the witnesses offer any real evidence of surveillance being carried out or that scaffolding was even being stolen. What they all alluded to was a massive extortion racket, with McPherson and Freeman at its helm, and criminals like Hardin doing the running around. After a few days' adjournment, during which time Hardin was released on bail, Gyles was intent on finding out where all the money had gone. He told Hardin, 'I just wish to make it clear to you that, as I have already indicated, knowing what I know about your background and what I know about ordinary principles, that you know very well what happened to this money, not to the last dollar, but I would vouch, for the last thousand dollars. And

I am going to ensure that I find out. Whether I find out today or next week, or if I get the assistance of some other bodies with compulsory powers to assist me, you can be assured I will.' In the end he was only partially successful.

Freeman, said Hardin, was called in by the GKN executive 'to help with industrial disputes', for which Freeman received 'large amounts of money'. After saying he didn't get on very well with Freeman, and had only worked with him to make money, he told Gyles, 'George knows everybody in Sydney. He wouldn't use any violence or anything like that. The way George operated was "I can fix anything. I can fix industrial disputes and anything." He virtually said he was Superman. I just think George thought he was entitled to the money. I mean, George would charge $5000 (*$12,877*) to speak to you.' Hardin spoke freely about Freeman but was more restrained when he referred to McPherson; Hardin claimed McPherson had not been paid any money as part of the arrangements, but appeared to immediately contradict that when he said that on one occasion McPherson had 'visited' [read 'intimidated'] a man called Brian Baker, of Alpine Scaffolding, who Hardin had accused of stealing GKN's scaffolding. After McPherson's visit – for which he was paid $20,000 (*$51,510*) – Hardin met with Baker to demand $500,000 (*$1,29 million*), of which, he told Gyles, he collected around $100,000 (*$257,552*). Most of that had been 'snaffled up' by Freeman, the man Baker had naively turned to for help to 'fix this matter'. The pair met at Chequers, where Freeman, McPherson and one or more of their thuggish back-up men spent some hours every Monday afternoon.

Another builder, bricklaying contractor Robin Warren Bass from Lavington, in southern NSW, had used George Freeman to help him when he believed the unions were forcing him out of business. He mentioned his problems to a horse trainer, Paul Sutherland, who had told him, 'Look, you can't beat these bastards. I'll give you a phone number.' He gave him George Freeman's number, which led to a meeting at the Chequers club. With Freeman was John Brady and Charkey Ramon. Brady, who

Bass thought was from a building union, said that for $20,000 he could do something for him. Bass and Brady met later and the former handed over cash and cheques equalling the bribe amount. Brady told him he would soon be getting plenty of work, but that Bass would 'have to pay a percentage'.

When nothing had happened six weeks later, Bass got on the phone again to Freeman, who assured him it had been fixed. 'I have got nothing to do with it. I will get in contact with him and get him to contact you straight away,' Bass said Freeman had told him. After a few more phone calls, Bass met with Bronco, Charkey Ramon and John Brady, who told him $10,000 had 'gone to a union official' and the rest of the amount covered expenses, and that 'they' wanted him out of the industry.

* * *

The witnesses kept appearing, often reluctantly, at the inquiry, which lasted over a year. But as witness Kirk Walker (who had previously worked with GKN and described himself as 'an associate of former GKN executive Mike Smith, whose words are used at the start of this chapter) said, the underworld had taken control of the building industry and was 'exploiting the managerial weaknesses' of building companies. 'My personal opinion is that the horse has bolted. It is capitalism gone to the extreme,' he said.

The money extorted in the Freeman-McPherson racket, which ran from around 1985 most probably until Freeman's death seven months before the inquiry began, only scratched the surface of the rorting. Gyles found in GKN's scaffolding business alone, eleven projects where initial estimated costs of $6.7 million (*around $17.26 million*) had blown out to $32.8 million (*$84.48 million*) by the time the final bills arrived. Companies had hundreds of thousands of dollars worth of gear stolen from them, but the inquiry concentrated mainly on the GKN group's use of criminals to try to curb the thefts.

As the inquiry was winding to a close, on 9 October 1991 *Sydney Morning Herald* journalist Malcolm Brown remarked:

There has been exploitation from the highest levels – from

well manicured, silver-suited businessmen (on one occasion cheerfully whacking on $2.25 million (*$5.79 million*) a piece to cover unsuccessful tenderers' fees and hiding the imposition from their clients) to the most humble builder's labourers going 'all out' on a trumped-up safety issue. It raises the question whether, if they have happened in this industry, similar wrongful activities would be revealed in other industries.

A few people faced charges over the Gyles inquiry revelations, but not Freeman, of course; by the time police acted on the royal commission evidence, Freeman was offering winning odds to those approaching the pearly gates. Bruce Hardin was charged with conspiring with George to demand money with menaces, and a handful of building industry types and a union official or three took their turn in court.

A lot of wrist-slapping penalties were imposed before Sydney settled down again to its corrupt old ways.

Most startling, however, is the thought that the federal crime watchdog could have moved on the major extortionists, Freeman and McPherson, years before. The NCA's listening activities in the mid-1980s, via taps on Freeman's phone, grew to include McPherson and others who were to star in the Gyles inquiry. The authority compiled damning evidence of major extortions run by the crime bosses, and also had evidence they poured their ill-gotten gains into the property market. As previously mentioned, many properties were in the names of McPherson and Freeman's family members.

But the NCA, under pressure to 'perform or be sacked' by the federal government, told the investigators that the extortion racket – possibly amounting to a multimillion-dollar sum – was a minor infringement, and would not be pursued. The NCA was after material that would lead to big headlines, and a few rough-necked standover men running rackets in the building industry simply didn't cut it.

18. The slaughter goes on

> A shocking crime was committed on the unscrupulous initiative of few individuals, with the blessing of more, and amid the passive acquiescence of all.
> – *Publius Cornelius Tacitus, Roman historian*

In 1985 a man's death led to a meeting of crims from all factions, but this one was not a murder. Frederick Charles 'Paddles' Anderson died on 2 January, aged 70, after spending most of his life involved in standover thuggery, bribery and corruption. These pastimes had brought him many admirers, and a few hundred of them gathered at the St Mary the Virgin Church at Waverley to say their last farewells.

Immaculately dressed and sombre-faced, George Freeman and Lennie McPherson might have discussed other deaths in their much-photographed tête-à-tête in the churchyard. At this stage only Chubb had fallen victim to the drug-war killings: Mick Sayers' murder would take place in a bit over a month's time. In this troubled era McPherson's and Freeman's perceived vulnerability guided their deeds. They were now rarely seen in public – and never alone, always with a 'minder'.

This meant, paradoxically, that they relied more on phone calls to maintain their regular contact – but they were always aware that those conversations might well have a wider audience listening at the receiving end of a wire tap.

But at the funeral there was a general mood of camaraderie among the mourners; all those who were prepared to talk to the media stressed what a wonderful man Paddles had been. 'He was a man of great compassion,' said illegal casino operator Ronnie

Lee. There was too much blame and injustice going on, blackening the names of people like Paddles and George Freeman and others who were there on the day, he added.

Unlike Paddles' send-off, the funeral of Tony 'Spaghetti' Eustace was a low-key affair: few crims wanted to be seen at the interment of a victim of the gangland war.

Tony Eustace was a heroin dealer with flair; he was equally at ease chatting with a High Court judge or a state attorney-general as knocking about with Stan Smith, George Freeman and their drug-running doctor mate Nick Paltos. Eustace, who sometimes used the alias 'Tony Anderson' and had been awarded the unflattering but rhyming moniker 'Useless', was as much at home in high-class eastern-suburbs nosheries as he was in Saffron's sleaze-pit strip joints in Kings Cross selling drugs to hookers, or in the outer-western suburbs supplying pills and powders to the bored kids of working-class toilers.

At about 12:30 p.m. on Tuesday, 23 April 1985 – the eve of the sixth anniversary of the shot fired at George Freeman and just 66 days after Mick Sayers' murder – Tony Eustace sat down to a sumptuous lunch at the upmarket Prontos restaurant in Double Bay. One of his companions was Kevin Hannah, a friend to Freeman and McPherson and owner of an about-to-go-broke fast-food business called Jilly's Roadside Diners. The chain of five outlets was later revealed by the Independent Commission Against Corruption (ICAC) to be part of a heroin-distribution network. The third man at the Prontos table was Chris Flannery, who was also the first to leave the restaurant.

At around seven o'clock that evening Eustace drove his gold-coloured Mercedes to Gertrude Street, Arncliffe, a short stroll from the Airport Hilton Hotel and across oil-slicked Cooks River from the Sydney International Airport. Half the street was parkland; the remainder was a grab bag of light industry, builders' yards, panel beaters' works and a car-hire firm.

Three men in a brown Chrysler Valiant sedan parked facing the Mercedes. A passing jogger and two men doing football drills in nearby Cahill Park heard shots, hurried to the scene and found

Eustace thrashing about on the road beside his car, blood gushing from six gunshot wounds in his back. He was rushed to St George Hospital, where detectives Sergeant Doug Knight and Senior Constable Wayne Gordon of the Homicide Squad tried to get him to identify his attackers. It was a brief conversation: Eustace told Knight to 'fuck off' moments before he died on the operating table. He was 43.

At the time Eustace was on bail from a Victorian court, where he faced a charge of conspiring to import cannabis with a street value of around $8 million (*$20.60 million*). During committal hearings the Melbourne magistrate was told it would be a groundbreaking trial: the first in Australia to use evidence obtained through legal police telephone taps. Five others charged along with Eustace, including Victorian policeman William 'Dingy' Harris, were later convicted.

A brown Valiant car was found abandoned in the airport car park by federal police two days later. Its owners were not traceable; police said it had been bought a couple of weeks earlier by someone using a fictitious name. When the witnesses were separately shown police photographs, two of them identified the driver of the car as having similar features to Tom Domican's mate and self-proclaimed world karate champion, Transylvanian-born Ladisla 'Joe' Meissner.

Mysteriously, Meissner, then aged 42, never appeared at the subsequent coronial inquiry into Eustace's death. Through his solicitor he had promised to appear as requested, but failed to do so. His lawyer then contacted inquest staff saying his client would give evidence on the morning of Tuesday, 1 March. But by then it would be too late: Coroner Greg Glass had already officially closed the hearing. In what could be seen as usurping the coroner's powers, police said they had made enquiries and were satisfied about Meissner's movements at the time of the murder. Neither the coroner nor the public were given any further detail, but nothing came of Meissner's deliberate absence from the inquest.

After the inquiry had concluded, Chris Flannery told police

he'd had an appointment to meet Eustace at the Airport Hilton Hotel at six o'clock on the evening of his death, but that Eustace had not kept the appointment. Flannery's interview with police was on Wednesday, 8 May 1985. The following day Flannery himself vanished, never to be seen again. Flannery's widow Kathleen later told police that George Freeman had said that George had supplied the gun – a .45-calibre pistol, she claimed – used to murder Eustace. Further, she named Tony Torok as the one who had bought the brown Valiant, and that Nick Paltos (who hadn't yet been arrested on the drugs charge) had given Freeman an injection to provide him with an alibi. The murder weapon, she said, had been thrown into Sydney Harbour from Pier One.

Kathleen Flannery said her husband had earlier told her that Freeman organised Eustace's murder to 'protect his position' in the underworld. She said Eustace had been murdered after another criminal reported to Freeman a conversation in which Eustace had commented, 'What happens if George goes?' It was at this time that Mrs Flannery levelled the first of many accusations about Freeman having organised her husband's murder. She said a policeman told her that Freeman and two others had held a meeting at which they decided to murder Chris Flannery. Kathleen Flannery never provided detail of these remarkable allegations. In the coroner's inquest into the Eustace murder, she said, 'It was a power struggle. These fellows wanted to take over Sydney. They would kill anyone who got in the way. My husband was a threat.' All of this was vigorously denied by Freeman, of course. And police told the coroner they could find no evidence to support Kathleen Flannery's accusations. Police also said they had searched the waters around Pier One for 15 hours and found no trace of a weapon. Coroner Glass suggested Flannery 'could have played a part' in Eustace's murder. Kathleen Flannery denied in her evidence that her husband was a hit man and that he had killed Eustace. 'It is easy to blame someone who's dead,' she said.

Notably, Freeman told the court that in the two and a half years since Eustace's murder, he had never been interviewed by the NSW Police or the National Crime Authority about Kathleen

Flannery's allegations. In his memoir, however, he directly contradicted this, stating that he'd in fact been interviewed by both organisations over the matter.

On 1 March 1988 Coroner Greg Glass delivered the inquest's findings: Tony Eustace, he said, had died of gunshot wounds inflicted by unknown persons. In plain language, it was deemed to be another gangland killing. But that was not the end of the matter by a long shot.

Three years earlier, on 7 May 1985 – two weeks after Eustace's murder – federal police had taped a phone conversation between Freeman, Nick Paltos and Graham 'Croc' Palmer. The eavesdropping was part of Operation Lavender, which eventually provided evidence that saw the trio convicted of drug importation and supply.

In one conversation, recorded two days before Flannery disappeared, Freeman said to Paltos, 'Gonna have to knock someone off ... wanna know about blood, how long blood lasts and all this and how can we scrub it off.' Paltos and Palmer were then taped trying to work out who Freeman had been referring to. Palmer suggested it might be Tom Domican. 'No,' said Paltos, 'I think it's Flannery.' A bugged conversation between Paltos and Palmer was even more damning. Though their words are at times garbled, there is a reference to what sounds like 'Buseless', Tony Eustace was referred to by some as 'Useless'.

Paltos:	It's a funny thing you know ... about him knowing it, and I'll tell you who shot Buseless. I got to be honest with you.
Palmer:	Freeman?
Paltos:	Yeah, he did, Freeman, he shot him all right. That's why he's been so crook.
Palmer:	Yeah.
Paltos:	He owned up to it today and I said, I thought I said. He got me out the back and he said ...
Palmer:	Where, did ya see him today?
Paltos:	At the practice, he rang me up last night and said he's gonna possibly see ya.

Palmer: What did he say?

Paltos: Tell ya everything slowly right … so don't ask.

The conversation then turns to other matters. Paltos' mention that Freeman had seen him 'at the practice' was clearly a reference to his medical surgery at Maroubra. A NSW Police task force referred to the bugged conversations in a report it prepared for the National Crime Authority. It read in part, 'If accepted, then Freeman has openly admitted to Dr Paltos that he murdered Eustace.' The revelation has added significance when it is recalled that Paltos was Freeman's doctor, a trusted friend of many years' standing, his confidante.

But none of this material, with its clear implications, was placed before the coroner as he weighed the evidence he had heard about the fate of Tony Eustace. The *Sydney Morning Herald*'s Andrew Keenan took up the story and pressed Police Commissioner John Avery for an explanation. The top cop ducked for cover. First, a spokesman for Avery said the commissioner felt that any comments were 'in the domain of the investigating police and/or the coroner'. When the question of why the material had not been shown to Greg Glass was put to the police generally, rather than the commissioner's office, the spokesman said that 'because the matter is being looked at by the National Crime Authority, it is inappropriate for them to comment'.

The NCA, pointed out the reporter, took over the gang-murder enquiries in 1986 but had completed its work and sent its report to Commissioner Avery by the time Greg Glass's inquiry had commenced.

The *Herald* also pressed John Avery on the apparent failure of police to interview Freeman (referred to as 'the underworld figure' by the paper to avoid defamation problems) after they'd been made aware of two separate allegations 'concerning his knowledge of it'.

Within 24 hours, the minister for police, George Paciullo, had predictably ordered an 'immediate investigation' into the *Herald*'s claims.

Then the newspaper published parts of another earlier bugged conversation, this time between Paltos and Ross Karp, in which they discussed Danny Chubb.

Karp: Right, but let's say, for instance, let's work it completely backwards and say, all right, say they started looking at Danny and Danny was still alive, right, and we didn't know it.

Paltos: Oh, it was my shot that Danny's dead, you know.

Karp: Yeah, that's right.

Paltos: Yeah, really, Ross, he would have brought us all undone.

Karp: Oh, look at the way he used to talk on the phone.

Paltos: Yeah.

Karp: We'd visit him, they'd be looking at his joint, watching the cars coming and going. You'd come undone from things that aren't really, you know, anything vital.

This material had not been submitted to the coronial inquiry into Chubb's murder. So Greg Glass never got to probe the veracity of Paltos' allegation that Freeman killed Eustace or that it was possibly Paltos who had shot Danny Chubb. Acting Police Commissioner Angus MacRae Graham (Avery was interstate on police business) ordered an immediate investigation into the revelations, and Attorney-General Ron Mulock said he'd seek a second inquest into the Eustace case.

And just to round out the growing list of 'immediate enquiries', the federal police on 11 March said they would investigate whether publication by the *Herald* of parts of the intercepted conversations breached the Telecommunications (Interception) Act.

Nothing came of the probe into the *Herald*'s publication of the phone bug material, but a second inquest was eventually held into Eustace's murder. As with the earlier second inquest into Danny Chubb's killing, coroner Derrick Windsor Hand took action on the Supreme Court order made in March 1988 to hold the new inquiry. It turned out not to be a productive exercise: as with the

Chubb case, Hand's finding in the second Eustace inquest, held on 27 June 1988, was identical to the first – yet another opportunity to invoke the 'gangland killing by unknown persons' clause, which overrode the strong hearsay evidence that had pointed the finger at George Freeman.

* * *

Within a week or two of Eustace's murder, Lennie McPherson had been trying to get the warring sides to come to peace talks. He was getting rattled, scared. He'd had enough. The crims were split into two antagonistic factions, each with its own supportive coterie of crooked cops.

In April 1985 a few key players met at the home of Kings Cross identity Louis Bayeh, who then lived at Ermington in the western suburbs. Bayeh was host to McPherson, Flannery, Neddy Smith, Rogerson – by then suspended from the force – and detective sergeants Bill Duff and Aarne Tees.

Neddy Smith later gave details of the meeting at a hearing of ICAC. Asked whether police had taken part in the discussions, Neddy replied, 'They led the discussion.' He said one purpose of the meeting was to discuss how the gang war was going, and the other aim was to 'pull it up'.

Barry Toomey QC assisting ICAC Commissioner Ian Temby, asked, 'When you say to try to pull it up, you meant to stop the gang wars?'

Smith:	Yes.
Toomey:	Was that because [people] were being killed?
Smith:	No one was making any money.
Toomey:	No business was being done?
Smith:	No.
Toomey:	The gang wars were stopping criminal activity?
Smith:	Yes.
Toomey:	Because everyone was too busy staying alive?
Smith:	That is right.

Neddy told the barrister that one side included Barry McCann, Joe Meissner, Tom Domican and quite a few others, while he (Smith) was on the other side with Graham Henry and Chris

Flannery. Danny Chubb had been on the McCann team.

Toomey: What about McPherson?
Smith: He was on both sides.
Toomey: What about the police, did they take any part?
Smith: There were two groups of them, one on each side.

Smith said he had attended two other meetings with the same people.

Bill Duff's role was to provide them with information about the other side, to pass on what the surveillance police watching the McCann group were reporting.

On 15 April McPherson had made an early-morning phone call to Duff:

McPherson: Listen, mate, if you see that, ah, Melbourne fellow [referring to Flannery] will you tell him to give George a ring?
Duff: All right, mate, good as gold.

A major criminal was getting a senior policeman to contact a man with a reputation as a gun for hire to arrange a meeting with another major criminal. Duff later explained that he thought this was 'appropriate behaviour' for a detective sergeant.

There would be no peace. Not yet. More killings would follow and at the top of the list was the one we were being told was the hit man, Christopher Dale Flannery.

19. The hit man becomes the target

The infectiousness of crime is like that of the plague.
– Napoleon Bonaparte

As American statesman, lawyer and orator Daniel Webster observed, every unpunished murder takes away something from the security of every person's life. If this is true, then Sydney in the 1980s would have done irreparable damage to humankind's sense of security.

A populace cannot continue to believe its environment to be safe if the slaughter of four people in less than three years is written off as 'gangland violence', and no one is brought to justice.

Corruption in that period was widespread and ingrained – worse still, it was accepted as the status quo. It was now public knowledge that George Freeman was allegedly complicit in two murders and yet had not been seriously questioned by police, nor had any alibi of his been seriously checked out. It seemed better to keep one's head down, mind one's own business, show interest in only the tip of the iceberg of the scandals that kept breaking. The media, in general, was not prepared to take on the fight, and the interests of good journalism often fell by the wayside.

So it was with Chris Flannery. After he'd arrived in Sydney the media labelled him a hit man, 'Mr Rent-a-Kill', and attributed 'more than a dozen' unsolved murders to him without suggesting who the victims were or where these bodies were piled up. Interestingly, it appears that it was George Freeman who created the 'rent-a-kill' moniker, and the media followed his lead, quite possibly urged on by one or two policemen who had taken sides in the gang wars. Having enlisted a well-known 'gun for hire' would have seemed a sound defensive ploy.

The 'Mr Rent-a-Kill' sobriquet first appeared in the *Sydney Morning Herald* when it published extracts of George Freeman's autobiography on 30 April 1988, almost three years after Flannery disappeared. Freeman introduces his readers to Flannery:

> They called him Mr Rent-a-Kill – and not because he worked for a well-known pest exterminator. Christopher Dale Flannery exterminated people. It's not something I readily admit, but Flannery scared me. Anyone who wasn't scared by him didn't know the man. Flannery simply killed for money. Personalities didn't come into it. If the money was there, he'd do it. He worked on a sliding scale. For $10,000 ($25,755) he'd kill someone – anyone. Then for lesser amounts he'd belt people up. Iron, bars, baseball bats, even cricket stumps, were part of his tools of trade.

This is the same George Freeman who had hired Flannery as a bodyguard; the same man Nick Paltos referred to as Flannery's murderer in the bugged conversation with Croc Palmer. The media picked up on the reference immediately, and from then on there was rarely a mention of Flannery that did not include the 'hit man' or 'Mr Renta-Kill' tag. Another line from Freeman's musings puts Flannery at odds with the very public nature of Sydney's gangland murders: 'Flannery's trademark,' he wrote, 'was bodies that never got found.' This is not an attempt to whitewash the sullied reputation of Christopher Dale Flannery. Far from it: he was a standover man and a convicted armed robber with a history of violently threatening people. The circumstances surrounding his acquittals on the two murder charges clearly raise suspicion that witnesses were pressured, or even disappeared. But there is no proof of that, just as there is no proof of his involvement in these Sydney attacks. On the evidence it appears Flannery was given the 'Mr Rent-a-Kill' label after his death to try to absolve the sins of others.

Between Flannery's 1981 arrival in Sydney and his disappearance on 9 May 1985, there had been three gangland murders: Danny Chubb, Mick Sayers and Tony Eustace. Flannery – along with several others – had been mentioned in a police brief on Chubb's killing but was not otherwise linked to his death. The inquest into Sayers' murder was told that Flannery had refused to take up a contract to kill the drug-dealing punter that had been offered to him by George Freeman. Others faced charges (and were eventually acquitted) over that killing. Flannery was interviewed by police over Eustace's murder – and disappeared the next day.

Then there was the failed attempt on the life of undercover drug cop Drury on 6 June 1984. A witness, Alan Williams, later admitted in court that he had conspired with Roger Rogerson and Flannery to bribe Drury to drop drug charges against him. Working undercover, Drury had been negotiating a $100,000 ($274,898) heroin deal with Williams in Melbourne. On a nod from Drury, police raided the street corner meeting and arrested the drug dealer. Williams was desperate.

My sources have confirmed that Williams, Rogerson and Flannery met over lunch at a restaurant in York Street in the city, where Williams handed over $50,000, of which Flannery was given $10,000. The balance was to be Rogerson's share plus the proposed bribe for the undercover cop. Drury later accused Rogerson (though not Flannery) of having tried to bribe him.

On the night of the shooting Rogerson had asked Flannery to join him at the Arncliffe Scots Club, a sporting and social venue in Burrows Street, next to the local railway station and a kilometre and a half from the Flannery home in Turrella Street. Neither needed a better alibi for the attempted murder of Drury, but both were charged – along with Williams – with conspiring to murder the policeman. Williams eventually admitted he'd tried to bribe Drury, using Rogerson as a go-between, 'to make sure Drury did not make court'.

Flannery had long since vanished before a jury found Rogerson not guilty of the charge on 20 November 1989. Drury, by then a detective sergeant, stood stunned as the verdict was read out, and had to be helped from the court by a supportive senior policeman. Judge Colin Allen had warned the jury about convicting Rogerson on Alan Williams' uncorroborated evidence, as that witness had during the trial admitted to lying and seeking immunity from police in return for a 'better deal' on the drugs charges he still faced. Flannery undoubtedly would have also been acquitted on the charge of shooting Drury; Rogerson had established an unshakeable alibi for them both.

* * *

In May 1985 Flannery rented an apartment in the 30-storey Connaught building at 185 Liverpool Street, overlooking Hyde Park. He, his wife and daughter had been moving frequently; Flannery believed their lives were in danger. He had kept the new location a secret. Then on May 8 he went to police headquarters, just up the road, to give a statement about Eustace's death – that he'd had a six o'clock appointment to meet Eustace at a hotel close to where he'd been shot. From that moment on his place of residence was no longer a secret. During that evening, at home with Kathleen, Flannery made a phone call to George Freeman in response to a message he – or someone who knew the drill – had left on Flannery's beeper asking him to contact 'Mercedes', Freeman's codename.

He made an appointment to meet Freeman at the bookie's Yowie Bay mansion the next morning, 9 May. The Connaught building security staff saw him leave the apartment at 8.15 a.m. His car parked in the basement wouldn't start – he thought the battery must be flat – so he returned to the flat with the car keys and asked Kathleen to call the roadside assistance to get it fixed. He'd hail a cab downstairs to get to Freeman's, he said. He'd have to ring Freeman as he approached Yowie Bay to ensure the guard dogs, which he feared, were secured when he arrived. Kathleen never saw her husband again.

After Kathleen Flannery had reported her husband missing at around 4.30 p.m., police descended on Freeman's mansion and made a thorough forensic search of his house and boat. They did not record finding anything incriminating, but it is interesting to note that Freeman, in his memoir, specifically mentioned the police searched for bloodstains on the carpet. Recall that in a bugged phone conversation with Nick Paltos, recorded two days before Flannery disappeared, Freeman had referred to 'knocking someone off' and said, 'Wanna know about blood, how long blood lasts and all this and how can we scrub it off.' When a mechanic came to fix Flannery's car, they reported to Kathleen that it started without a problem. They suggested somebody may have removed a battery lead and later, after Flannery had left the area, replaced it.

* * *

Of the many theories, fantasies and deliberate red herrings that arose out of Flannery's disappearance, only two stand out as being possibly close to the mark.

A taxi driver, Colin Sefton, from Woollahra, stated he had picked up a fare from outside the Connaught building just after eight that morning and drove the man to the airport. The cabbie had tried to talk with his passenger, but he seemed 'fidgety and restless', and mostly just looked out the cab window. At the airport Sefton pulled up at the TAA domestic airline terminal, and as the passenger was finding the money for the fare, Sefton noticed a 'good wad' of cash in the man's leather handbag. The passenger paid the fare plus a tip $1.50 and walked briskly into the terminal.

There's a problem with this story. Sefton – who retired soon after these events took place – never gave evidence as to how he knew that his fare was Chris Flannery. And the 'good wad' of cash is in conflict with Kathleen Flannery's recollection that her husband had only taken $50 to cover the cab fare. And why the TAA terminal? By any reasonable test of credulity, the Sefton story fails. Sefton, who had never seen or heard of Flannery before 9 May, stated his fare 'was in the habit of renting cars from the airport at this time'. If Flannery was in his cab, he almost certainly would have gone to Yowie Bay, not to an airline terminal, to rent a car to drive the last 20-kilometre leg of the journey to his destination.

The other story – equally speculative – takes its threads from a number of sources. It runs like this: Detective Aarne Tees, who had played an active role in the gang warfare, and one or more others had tampered with Flannery's car to ensure it would not start. Earlier they had left the pager message for him to ring Freeman – they would have certainly known the password Freeman used in his communications with his bodyguard. The result would be predictable: Flannery, unable to start the car, would come out of the building and look for a cab.

'Friendly' police known to Flannery would pull up and offer him a lift.

He would have no hesitation in accepting the offer.

In the mid-1990s when these events were partly forgotten history, Louis Bayeh had reached a stage in his life when he decided it was time to tell the truth, or at least his own colourful version of it. To this end he gave a lengthy sworn testimony to the Police Royal Commission.

Recall it was at Bayeh's home that members of the warring factions of crims and cops met to try to broker peace.

Much of what Bayeh told that inquiry was vigorously denied by the people he named, which did not prove that any of them were telling the truth either. Among Bayeh's stories were recollections of conversations he had had with his trusted friend Lennie McPherson. In one such chat McPherson had said he had offered Detective Aarne Tees $20,000 (*around $53,000*) during the gang wars to have Tom Domican killed, and McPherson allegedly said that Tees had replied that he 'would do something about it'. Another conversation had McPherson telling Bayeh about Flannery's disappearance. Lennie said he knew police had broken into the basement of the Connaught and disconnected the battery of Flannery's car so it would not start. As Flannery was waiting for a taxi, they grabbed him, put him in a police car, and shot him. Predictably, in front of the Police Royal Commission McPherson denied he'd ever said this.

Gary Crooke QC, who was assisting the commissioner, suggested to McPherson that he had told Bayeh that 'two policemen plus another two waited for Flannery outside the building where he was living, they had picked him up from across the road and one of the policemen, whom you named, shot Chris Flannery.' In response McPherson snapped that Bayeh was a liar, and that he'd say virtually anything to justify his presence at the inquiry. One of the policemen named in the Bayeh statement was Aarne Tees.

Other threads of this story, which I have picked up from contacts within the police and from other sources, support this view. Some go even further, saying that after Flannery was shot, the police car was driven to a boat berthed in the Georges River alongside Henry Lawson Drive at Georges Hall, a 45-minute drive from the city. There the body was placed in a half-cabin cruiser boat owned by one of those in the car. Less than 30 kilometres downstream was open ocean off Botany Bay, where a weighted body could be safely dumped. There could well be parts of the river that would also have served the purpose. The boat alleged to be involved was never examined by police. Freeman's boat was examined in great detail, obviously with no remarkable findings.

Back at Georges Hall, it's only a short stroll across Coleman Park to the western perimeter of Bankstown Airport.

Neddy Smith, who had a half-share in a cabin cruiser and a speedboat (he didn't reveal who his partner was), was later to testify that the one person Flannery trusted was Roger Rogerson. 'There was no way that Flannery would go missing or be murdered unless Rogerson had either given permission or done the job himself,' he said. During the inquest into Flannery's death in 1993, Neddy told the coroner that the day after Flannery disappeared, he and Graham Henry had met with Rogerson at Bankstown Airport; they stood out on the tarmac – a security measure only seriously paranoid people take. Rogerson assured Neddy there was nothing at play he should concern himself about, adding, 'Chris had to go, mate. He was becoming a danger to us all.' Neddy said he had agreed, 'Everything was all right. We could now get back to leading normal lives and making money once more.' Neddy did not elaborate on whether Rogerson had a boat moored locally, or why they were at that particular place that day.

But all of this, of course, is conjecture. Unless one or two more people break down and tell the truth before their final boat rides, we will never really know what happened to Christopher Dale Flannery. As an anonymous blogger wrote of the event years later, 'When a notorious criminal is murdered, everyone's got the rolled-gold story on who did it. Most of them are lying.' In a later trial Rogerson, accused of taking part in a drug swap with a protected witness, offered the court an alibi. He said at the time the alleged exchange took place, he was aboard his own boat on the Georges River with a young lad called Peter, 'the son of missing hit man Christopher Flannery', who was 'in a bad way' after his father had 'gone missing'.

In the same court hearing a man (whose name was suppressed) who lived in Georges Hall said he had been out boating previously with Rogerson. They had made a date to go out again with Flannery's son in the first week of May 1985, he said. But after reading a newspaper article about Flannery's disappearance, he changed his mind.

'My wife and I had a bit of an argument over this because Roger had gained a bit of notoriety over the Lanfranchi case,' the witness said.

'After some discussion, we decided we would tell Roger we wouldn't be going on the picnic and also we would like to disassociate ourselves a little bit. As much as I respected Roger, the publicity and everything he was getting wasn't the type of publicity I wanted to be involved in.' Kathleen Flannery later said she'd received a visit from Roger Rogerson a week after her husband disappeared. She said he offered her $50,000 (*$137,450*) as a 'condolence gift' from 'George and the mates' to help her while she recovered from her loss. She understood him to be referring to Freeman and McPherson, among others. She indelicately told him to 'shove it'. She saw it as a clear indication that her husband was not simply 'missing' but was, to Rogerson's knowledge, dead.

* * *

Remarkably, it took until June 1997 – more than 12 years after Flannery's death – for the Sydney coroner to reach a conclusion on what had happened to Freeman's former bodyguard. The expedient excuse for delays of this magnitude is generally that 'police enquiries are still in train', but there was never any public explanation of the inordinate delay in this case. By then, one of the 'stars' of the coronial show, Roger Rogerson, had finally been drummed out of the force.

Greg Glass had presided over 130 sitting days listening to Flannery's friends (the very few of them) and foes (plenty of those) tell mostly tall tales about the man many thought was 'out of control' and needed 'dealing with'.

The coroner felt certain that Flannery had been killed, and by someone he'd trusted or felt at ease with. Glass recalled that Kathleen had stated her husband would have 'resisted violently' if he had been attacked or threatened. Seeming to support the second hypothesis mentioned above, and to dismiss the cab driver's story, he said:

> I am therefore comfortably satisfied that Flannery was betrayed, deceived, possibly lured into a motor vehicle, by someone, or by some persons, whom he trusted and was then killed, with the remains being disposed of in a manner unknown.

Glass said that among the most prominent of possible suspects was Tom Domican. He had a motive having feuded with Flannery, but there was no direct evidence that he caused his death or even knew where he was living at the time. A number of policemen (including Aarne Tees) were also cleared of being implicated in the murder, but Glass said that police involvement in the death could not be ruled out. He stressed, however, that 'rumour, suspicion, hearsay, speculation and hypothesis can never be a basis for the commencement of any criminal proceedings.' The inquest was hampered by a number of witnesses suffering an affliction common among criminal types. Dr Nick Paltos, Graham 'Croc' Palmer, Branko Balic, Victor Camilleri, Bruce Hardin and George Savvas all had no memory of the events in question. The amnesia also spread to Tom Domican, and former cops John Openshaw, Bill El-Azzi and, of course, Roger Rogerson. Georgina Freeman assured Greg Glass that her husband had not been involved, although she conceded that she'd 'never really asked' her husband anything about the issue.

Glass said he suspected that George Freeman might have been 'connected with Flannery's fate', and while Freeman had insisted the phone call he'd allegedly made to Flannery was a 'set-up' – although he provided no detail of the claim – the coroner added that the evidence did not allow him to reach a view that Freeman had had a direct role in Flannery's death.

Glass saved his biggest bombshell until last, though, concluding that on the evidence he had 'a strong suspicion that Roger Rogerson was involved in Flannery's disappearance and his death, or at least knew what happened to him. Rogerson had the motive and opportunity to cause harm to Flannery'. However, there was not enough hard evidence to make a prima facie case against Rogerson. When asked by a reporter who he thought had killed Flannery, Roger Rogerson replied:

> I think he's there with Harold Holt. I think they're still swimming. They'd be about under the Antarctic now. I don't know. There're all sorts of suggestions. Flannery became a pest. We've had a lot of pests from Melbourne that've come up here and they haven't quite fitted in with the milieu and they tend to sort of disappear. People on the other side of the line decided they'd had enough of him – and bingo! But, again, I wasn't involved in that, either. I was at home in bed that night. I've got a perfect alibi.

Tom Domican was subsequently charged with Flannery's murder but the case was dismissed in August 1987 by Magistrate Bert Wilson when the prosecution's Robert Lord QC, admitted he did not have enough evidence to convince the court that a prima facie case had been established. As mentioned earlier, Domican was convicted of the attempted murder of Flannery, his wife and daughter after the shooting at their Arncliffe house in January 1985. The conviction was later quashed in an appeal to the High Court.

There was an addendum to Greg Glass's enquiries. New information came to light, in the form of Louis Bayeh's evidence given to the royal commission into the police. On the basis of that remarkable story, Glass announced on 10 November 1995 that he would reopen his inquiry for three more days of hearings in December. Finally, on 7 December McPherson, then aged 74, took the stand before Greg Glass.

He'd been brought from Cessnock Gaol, where he was serving time for a bashing conviction – they did get him in the end. But McPherson did what he had always done during such public appearances: suffered from temporary but total amnesia about the events in question.

He denied he'd been concerned that he was part of a 'fading generation', threatened by people like Flannery and Domican. He also denied that he had offered policeman Aarne Tees $20,000 to have Domican killed. McPherson's appearance added nothing of substance to the eight thousand-plus pages of testimony Greg Glass had gathered, and Glass did not alter the substance of his findings, other than to add his view that McPherson was 'an argumentative, cantankerous and belligerent' witness.

Speculation rattled around the town for a long time about what had really happened, who had really killed Mr Rent-a-Kill. Freeman's name was always high on the list, as was McPherson's. Barry McCann's name popped up as a highly likely suspect, he having fallen out with Flannery after he had once abused and hit McCann's wife at the Lansdowne Hotel. Kathleen Flannery later said that her husband and McCann had argued and that Mrs McCann threatened Flannery with a broken glass, but he got in first and in a swinging punch, broke her jaw.

Many believed Rogerson could have revealed what had happened, as coroner Greg Glass had suggested. One story, from a criminal knockabout I spoke to, had Flannery at the Mandarin Club in Pitt Street on the evening of 9 May, being farewelled at the front door by club boss Denis Wong. Then he reportedly got into the back seat of a car, a burly cop on either side of him, one of whom shot him dead before the car had driven around the corner. There was a reported sighting of Flannery in Melbourne four months after his disappearance. Another version had Neddy Smith and some police shooting Flannery in a car as it headed north on the Newcastle freeway, the body then taken to Caves Beach near Swansea, where it was weighted down and buried in the mud-flats at low tide.

So who did kill Chris Flannery? I'd probably cop a writ if I put the name to it ... Maybe one day he'll do the improbable, and tell the truth.

With the reputed hit man no longer on the scene, optimists might have hoped an end to the bloodshed had been reached. But there were more killings to come.

* * *

Following the Flannery story to its conclusion so many years after his disappearance has got us somewhat ahead of ourselves in the unfolding story of George Freeman, who, early in 1986, copped a blast from Judge Don Stewart. The judge had called Freeman into the witness box during the inquiry he held into the '*Age* tapes' affair. He concluded that Freeman had been 'deliberately untruthful' and that his witness was involved in illegal SP bookmaking, race fixing and illegal casinos, and had an 'improper relationship' with some police, particularly Inspector Jack McNeill and his offsider Frank Charlton. These activities were all quite harmless as far as Freeman was concerned, because nobody within the police force, politics or the various judicial and legal arms of the state seemed remotely interested in doing anything about them. That had been the scene for around three decades, and it was not about to change.

* * *

Neville Wran, the man who spent four years with parliamentary responsibility for the corrupt NSW Police Force without officially awarding himself the ministry portfolio, retired as the state's premier on 4 July 1986. It was, purely coincidentally, 11 years to the day since Juanita Nielsen's murder. Barrie John Unsworth, then aged 52, took over as premier – but with no responsibility for police matters. When Wran was proposed as the new chairman of

CSIRO five months later, the move came under fierce attack in the senate. He was accused of having given 'the mantle of protection' to corruption in NSW for many years. Liberal Party senator Peter Baume supported by a more moderate Liberal, Chris Puplick, accused Wran of 'allowing appointments to the state judiciary now known to have been tainted, and protecting those people as well as failing to investigate matters crying out for attention until forced to do so'.

Baume's motion for an urgency debate 'on the unfitness of Mr Neville Wran for appointments to high federal office because of his protection of corruption and because of tainted appointments made while he was Minister for Police, Premier of NSW, and federal president of the Australian Labor Party' was lost when Democrat party members voted with Labor. Of passing interest: like most observers of the NSW political scene, clearly the two Liberal senators who hailed from that state also thought that Wran was Minister for Police. Their attack made no difference: Wran was appointed to the position.

* * *

Tony Lauer had been brought back from exile in 1986 by Police Commissioner John Avery as part of the latter's anti-corruption drive, launched two years earlier. Lauer, by then a chief superintendent, was put in charge of a new state investigative group and, among other moves, quickly set up a task force, code-named Omega, to re-examine the attempted murder of undercover sergeant Michael Drury. Rogerson and Bill Duff came under renewed scrutiny. Duff did not deny he had talked with another officer about his plans with Rogerson to import drugs from Papua New Guinea, but denied he had fed sensitive police information to Rogerson's informant Neddy Smith.

In the upshot, after a hearing by the Police Tribunal on misconduct charges, Duff was dismissed from the force in March 1986 for having an improper (read 'corrupt') relationship with crime figures, particularly Neddy Smith. That decision prompted shadow Attorney-General John Dowd to tell state parliament there was 'something wrong with a police administration that allowed Rogerson to remain on the force.' He said Rogerson was 'carrying on the tradition of Freddy Krahe and Ray Kelly'.

Dowd's statement was generally seen to be ill-informed; Rogerson had already faced a two-day interview with Internal Affairs at the end of March, and then went on a popular TV current affairs show to protest his innocence, during which he outed Neddy Smith as a paid informer.

He told show host Ray Martin that in all his career he had never taken a bribe or, he thought, a free lunch. It was a bravura performance, and notably it went to air on April Fool's day. On Wednesday, 2 April 1986 outside his Iron Duke Hotel at Waterloo, Neddy Smith was knocked over by a car, resulting in a broken leg and fractured ribs. Ex-boxer Terence Edward Ball was charged with Neddy's attempted murder, was released on $100,000 (*$236,178*) bail on 30 April. A year later the charge was dismissed when Neddy swore to the court that Ball had not been the driver of the car that had rammed into him, which was at odds with a signed confession Ball had given to police.

Meanwhile, back in the fight against police corruption, 53-year-old Superintendent Eric Strong, who had notched up 30 years in the force, told the Police Tribunal that holding bank accounts in false names and having an 'improper' relationship with Neddy Smith formed the basis of police misconduct charges levelled against Rogerson. Strong said the solicitor for public prosecutions had been briefed the previous November of possible criminal charges arising from the bank accounts, but that no summons had been served. Strong said he had also received submissions a week earlier that Rogerson might be charged with conspiring with Paltos and Karp over the bank accounts.

Seven of nine misconduct charges against Rogerson were upheld by the tribunal, which recommended that he be dismissed from the force. He was 45. His appeal against the decision was dismissed, and on 11 April the rogue cop followed Duff out the door. He'd served more than 28 years in the force. In what might have appeared as an attempt to soften the blow of the inevitable corruption headlines, Police Minister George Paciullo announced that a total of 138 police were under investigation for corruption, representing just 1.3 per cent of the entire 10,500-strong force.

* * *

Rogerson's fellow conspirators in dodgy banking matters, Nick Paltos and Croc Palmer, had been in jail for just a month when the doctor was assaulted by the Croc. Paltos apparently sustained no serious injury, no bites to body parts. They had argued over a remarkable plan by Paltos to import drugs worth $12 million, all organised from his prison cell. An undercover cop had discussed the plan with Paltos at length; the doctor was charged, but the charges were subsequently dropped. It appears in NSW people are not convicted of having fantasies.

* * *

Another policeman friendly to Freeman and his associates was given his marching orders after being found guilty on 4 November on three misconduct charges. The Police Tribunal found that Detective-Sergeant John Openshaw had an 'improper' association with Neddy Smith, that he'd gone against police regulations by giving McPherson's drug-running mate David Kelleher information about his impending arrest, and that he had lied about these things to an internal security officer.

The departure of these heavyweight cops posed a problem or two for Freeman and McPherson: the entire indemnity agreement would be in danger of collapsing if trusty alternatives were not available at senior levels. Moreover, there was the ongoing gang warfare that urgently needed to be brought to a close. The crime bosses noticed that their relationships with state police began to get more difficult from this time on. In addition, federal police and the National Crime Authority – august bodies over which they had little or no corrupting influence – were becoming increasingly active in tackling major organised-crime activities. Only the previous November the totally invincible Abe Saffron, who ran the vice, illegal booze and drugs scene at Kings Cross, had been arrested over tax evasion and was on a sure path to a jail sentence. The empires, built up over more than three decades, would last a while yet, but there would have been signs that they were beginning to crumble. Despite their denials, they were slowly becoming members of a fading generation as younger crooks took over their traditional territories. But that second ambit claim on the insurance policy was not about to happen: the killings would continue.

20. McCann clan blown apart

> Peace is not an absence of war, it is a virtue,
> a state of mind, a disposition for
> benevolence, confidence, justice.
> – *Spinoza, Dutch philosopher*

For more than two years after Chris Flannery had been removed from the Sydney scene there was peace, but it was a phoney truce. The body count didn't rise but the intent was still there. The lull came to an end on 6 August 1987, when heroin dealer Barry John 'Sugar' Croft died from a single bullet wound to the head. He was having a quiet drink at the Cauliflower Hotel on busy Botany Road, Alexandria when he was called to the phone at about 6.35 p.m. He must have known the caller for he didn't hesitate, downing his drink and leaving immediately.

He drove his Ford Fairlane towards Barry McCann's Lansdowne Hotel in Chippendale. Police said later he often drank at McCann's pub, as did many heavies involved in the drug scene.

On this night he'd passed the hotel, driving south down City Road, and was probably looking for a parking spot near Myrtle Street. A small blue sedan with two men inside pulled up alongside Croft's bigger car and two shots were fired, the first smashing the Fairlane's windscreen, the second smashing into Croft's head. He was 49.

Croft had been a major heroin supplier to illegal casino operator, publican and punter client of George Freeman, Barry McCann, who had set up his own drug-distribution network in 1981, often using his Lansdowne Hotel as a storage depot. McCann had also set up a direct link with a Bangkok bulk-heroin supplier referred to as 'Chinese David'.

Roger Rogerson later denied he had told Neddy Smith that it would be best to 'get rid of Croft', as Neddy alleged. Police said two heavies wanted to cut Croft out of the supply chain and deal directly with McCann, and that there may also have been stolen drugs and missing money involved, but they could not put together a strong enough case for a coroner to recommend they be charged. So, with tiresome predictability, Coroner Kevin Waller determined that Barry Croft had been the victim of a gangland killing.

The next one was quick to follow. The policeman who investigated the murder was Detective-Senior Sergeant Brian Harding, then 42, who had been in Dangar Place when Rogerson had shot Lanfranchi.

Barry McCann's drug network had expanded rapidly, which meant taking on more runners – and creating more enemies. Tom Domican had long been close to the hotel-owning drug dealer. Domican's associate, Marrickville council alderman George Savvas, had joined the team in the early 1980s, attracted by the huge sums of money to be made in the drug business. A kilogram of heroin could be bought in Bangkok for around $40,000 ($114,314); after cutting, it would bring in more than a million dollars when sold on the streets of Sydney and Melbourne. Victor Camilleri and karate king Joe Meissner had always been part of McCann's inner circle. A 41-year-old who had migrated from Malta two decades earlier, Camilleri had been shot at, but not fatally, in April 1985. It was probably a case of mistaken identity, with the bullets meant for Domican. Former boxer Roy Lawrence Thurgar, who worked as a bouncer at McCann's gambling clubs, was also identified as a member of the team. Others moved around the fringe, and Kevin Theobold was one their major suppliers of bulk imported drugs, mainly heroin and cocaine from Thailand.

These tough criminals would sit with their leader, McCann, plotting their next haul or discussing distribution networks, and when they wanted a distraction McCann would talk of all the people he wanted to have murdered. As we've heard, a former gang member turned informer revealed that Michael Sayers had been on McCann's hit list at the time he was killed, in February 1985. So, too, had been Chris Flannery – with whom McCann had fought at the Lansdowne one night – as well as Flannery's wife, Kathleen, and Neddy Smith.

But the would-be mass murderer had the guns turned on him. On the night of Saturday, 26 December 1987 Savvas and others had been McCann's guests at a Boxing Day barbecue at his pub. The following night, just after nine o'clock, McCann was seen pacing back and forth under a lamp at Mahoney Park, Marrickville, obviously waiting to meet someone. Two hours later he was dead, lying face down on the ground with more than thirty bullet-holes in his body, fired from two revolvers. He was 44.

On the evidence of the protected former gang member, George Savvas was convicted in August 1988 of conspiring with McCann and others to import heroin valued at $200 million (*$515.11 million*). He was acquitted on the charge of being an accessory before the fact in McCann's murder. In handing down a 25-year sentence, Justice David Hunt said, 'The amount of money involved in this horrible [heroin] trade was staggeringly large. The prisoner's principal consideration in this awful crime against humanity was greed.' Savvas lost an appeal against the conviction. On 25 May 1997 he committed suicide in Maitland Gaol, aged 48.

No one has been convicted of McCann's murder. Neddy Smith later faced a charge of murdering Croft, but it was dismissed at committal hearings in August 1996 by Magistrate Pat O'Shane. Other charges against Smith that were ultimately dismissed included the murders of Danny Chubb in 1984, Barry McCann and a South Australian drug dealer Bruce Sandery in April 1988. Despite this, the media didn't describe Neddy Smith as a hit man, nor did they apply to him a moniker like 'Mr Rent-a-Kill'.

* * *

To ensure we get the balance right, it's important to understand that not all activity in the scene was carried out with the same degree of violence. Less vicious but highly intimidating moves were also made.

A strange example comes from when a relative of George Freeman's wife got married in 1987.

Young cadet journalist Kate McClymont, working on the social columns for the *Sydney Morning Herald*, covered the wedding. In her report she mischievously referred to Georgina Freeman's dress being 'heavily sequinned' as though it were a 'suit of armour'. Mr Freeman was not amused.

The phone calls started. George Freeman had got McClymont's number and started ringing in the wee small hours, identifying himself and saying things such as 'George is not happy', and, 'You should watch what you write'. The young reporter discussed the threatening calls with her editor and they agreed to report the matter to the police.

As a result a call tracer – a phone bug – was placed on the reporter's line at the exchange at Edgecliff. The phone calls immediately stopped.

Such were Freeman's contacts within the force that he was notified as soon as the bug went on the line, and was smart enough to stop the outrageous – and extremely petty – behaviour.

The episode certainly had no long-term ill effects on Kate McClymont; she went on to become one of Sydney's most adept and courageous crime reporters.

* * *

Over the years more names were added to the gang warfare victims' list: Roy Thurgar, Jackie Cooper, Ray McClune and Harvey Jones; drug dealer Lewton Shu; heroin addict, prostitute and girlfriend of the late Warren Lanfranchi, Sallie-Anne Huckstepp … and certainly others who didn't rate a mention in the shell-shocked media, weary of using the cliché 'it was yet another gangland killing'.

Every killing increased the paranoia of those who remained alive, particularly Freeman and McPherson, who had decided to become as invisible as possible after Flannery's murder. They may have been off the radar for a while, but their crime empire was as strong as ever. The SP gambling thrived, the drugs flowed and the money just kept rolling in.

21. Crims play law games: win more time for crime

> It is a sin to believe evil of others,
> but it is seldom a mistake.
> – *H. L. Mencken, American writer*

Left to its own devices, the law proceeds slowly. When the process is tampered with by crooked cops and lawyers who would fight for years to prove the innocence of the Devil, it can take much longer.

George Freeman, who had busied himself in 1986 recording his unreliable memoir for our collective misguidance, might have been excused for believing at times that his friends' troubles had vanished rather than being simply tied up in the legal process.

Dr Nick Paltos was a case in point. It was February 1984 when his hired boat met the Greek ship carrying Lebanese hash north of Darwin. More than two years had passed before Paltos pleaded guilty to the drugs charges and copped his 20-year sentence. Another four years elapsed before the conviction of conspiring with Rogerson over the false bank accounts was added to his record.

Another 'victim' of the law's slow progress was Freeman's friend Fayez 'Frank' Hakim, who had a unique relationship with a number of police that had earned him the nickname 'Mr Fix-it'. He had been particularly helpful in sorting out problems between police and illegal gambling operations – both casinos and SP bookmaking – dating back to 1971. In that year he had become a Justice of the Peace. He also had a delicatessen close to what was then the NSW Police Academy in Redfern, and police were among his biggest customers. Being a JP, he would often sign warrants enabling police to raid illegal premises.

For a reasonable fee, he would also telephone the illegal operator to give them advance notice of the raid.

His close associates were Freeman and McPherson, and he worked closely with Croc Palmer, Nick Paltos and Leslie Jones – probably the biggest operator of illegal gaming machines on the east coast. Hakim, like Freeman and McPherson, had visited Mafia mobsters on trips to the United States. And, like the others, he became involved in the drug trade.

When Hakim was called to give evidence at an official inquiry into a prisoner early-release scheme (a corrupt scam in which he played a significant role), it was Dr Nick Paltos who sent a letter to the inquiry commissioner saying Hakim was too ill to attend.

In 1985 Hakim was charged after police found heroin in his possession, but it was more than a year before he faced trial, receiving a six-and-a-half-year sentence. In 1988 a judge ruled that Hakim was too unwell to face further unresolved proceedings: cases involving Croc Palmer and Les Jones. Despite the claims of ill health, Hakim lived to the ripe old age of 75. He died in January 2005.

* * *

The law took a great deal of time – and a number of attempts – to determine whether using the word 'evil' to describe Roger Rogerson was justified.

To recap: in September 1987 Rogerson was arrested and charged with conspiring with Paltos and Karp, and more than a year later, in November 1988, Rogerson was committed to stand trial for conspiring with them to pervert the course of justice. Their trial didn't get under way until January 1990. It ran for three months, and all three were found guilty. Rogerson was given a jail sentence of eight years, with a non-parole period of six years. Rogerson lodged an appeal. In December 1990 the NSW Court of Criminal Appeal acquitted Rogerson and the others on the conspiracy charge. In June 1992 the High Court of Australia overturned the acquittal decision. Within days, the acquittal no longer valid, Rogerson was granted conditional bail pending a rehearing of the case, initially set down for October. In December 1992 he was again convicted on the conspiracy charge, but with his sentence reduced to the minimum term of four years. It had taken more than seven years from the initial event – and five years from the time of his arrest on the matter – to reach this conclusion.

In December 1995 he was released after serving three years, with a 15-month parole granted by the Offenders Review Board.

* * *

Any delays in the delivery of justice, however, were put in the shade by the seemingly never-ending debate and the political and legalistic obfuscation over the Cessna-Milner affair. It began, as we have seen, with the phone taps that led to the March 1979 arrest of two drug dealers, Roy Cessna and Timothy Milner. By April 1980 interest in the story had waned.

Premier Neville Wran had quoted a report into the matter, 'No tracks lead to Mr Farquhar,' the retired chief magistrate, a close friend and confidante of George Freeman. Wran was responding to a call by Liberal Party Opposition Leader John Mason to remove Farquhar as chair of the NSW Drug and Alcohol Authority, the position of chief adviser to the government on drug matters. Farquhar had picked up the choice position after retiring from the magistracy immediately after hearing the Cessna-Milner case. Mason told parliament it was obvious that Farquhar had allowed his position as chief magistrate to be used to free Cessna, a man involved in trafficking millions of dollars' worth of drugs. Mason said he had also provided material from his 63-page dossier to Police Commissioner James Travers Lees, who had succeeded Merv Wood in October 1979. Lees said later he could not understand the reasons for the decision made by Wood and Farquhar to reduce the charges.

Farquhar labelled Mason's allegations as lies, and Police Minister Bill Crabtree told honourable members a few days later that the matters raised by Mason had been 'thoroughly investigated': 'The Commissioner has told Mr Mason that his suspicions alone could not be regarded as admissible evidence in a court of law.' The report Wran had quoted from was prepared by Solicitor-General Gerry Sullivan, but Wran steadfastly refused to table the entire report.

And there the matter rested for a few years. It bobbed up again in February 1984 when a report by Solicitor-General Mary Gaudron was cited in parliament by Attorney-General Paul Landa, which stated the case would not be reopened unless further new evidence came to light.

Then a month later came a breakthrough: then state political reporter for the *Sydney Morning Herald*, Mike Steketee, got his hands on a copy of the Sullivan report – the one Wran had refused to table. It reads:

> The investigation causes me to conclude that there was pressure put on Sergeant Wayne Evans [the police prosecutor in the case], Sergeant Smith, Inspector Lawrence [head of the Drug Squad], and Superintendent Fryer, directly or indirectly by the then Commissioner [Merv Wood]. Mr Wood appears to have acted in the way he did to please his own solicitors, in my opinion, and did so by directing his subordinates to perform a role which they continued to regard as improper. It becomes even more reprehensible when the defendants were trafficking in narcotics.

But Sullivan raised doubts about whether a case could be made out for conspiracy to defeat the cause of justice, suggesting that the only parties would have been Wood and solicitor Morgan Ryan. 'We could show a connection between them,' Sullivan said, 'but that falls short of establishing a conspiracy between them.' One difficulty, Mary Gaudron pointed out, was that some of the material that might be produced in evidence may have been illegally obtained by NSW Police telephone taps (on Morgan Ryan's phone, among others). These were later examined by Justice Donald Stewart (during the '*Age* tapes' inquiry), who suggested that 'a court when confronted with evidence which was unlawfully obtained has a discretion to admit or exclude the evidence.' There was another lull in proceedings (some may think of it as a coma) that lasted until July 1987 when the *Sydney Morning Herald* reported that 'sufficient evidence has been uncovered to justify a criminal charge against the former NSW Police Commissioner, Mr Mervyn Wood, in relation to his involvement in the Cessna-Milner affair'. The paper reminded its readers that Wood had been instrumental in ensuring the Cessna-Milner case be dealt with by a magistrate, rather than going to trial.

Merv Wood, Olympic sculler, crooked commissioner, had resigned in June 1979, but had remained untouched over the controversial case for more than a decade. Eventually he was charged, on 19 August 1987, on two counts of acting with intent to pervert the course of justice. Wood and his legal team looked for some 'wiggle room', any way of avoiding justice. Wood's lawyer, Greg James QC, put it to a magistrate in May 1988 that there was no evidence his client had done anything wrong nine years earlier. The matter should be dismissed, said James, because of the long delays in bringing the matter before the courts. Magistrate David Armarti would have none of it; he rejected the application.

At the committal hearing on 5 June the prosecutor, Roger Gyles QC, introduced two additional charges against Wood relating to misconduct by a person who holds public office. Wood's new lawyer, Clive Steim, asked Magistrate Armarti that his client be excused from attending court due to his age – he was then 70 – and because Wood wanted to avoid the 'barrage of press' waiting to confront him outside the court each day. The magistrate shook his head, ruling that Wood must attend the hearings. But neither Wood nor his lawyer were at the next hearing on 24 August: a strike by court staff had apparently meant they did not get the notice. That did not stop Magistrate Armarti from finding a prima facie case that Wood had done the things he stood accused of, saying that in his view a jury would convict on the 'totality of evidence' that had been presented to him. At the following hearing Wood was ordered to stand trial on the charges, starting on 4 March 1991.

In state parliament the new opposition leader, Nick Greiner, challenged the Labor government to either lay charges against Morgan Ryan and Murray Farquhar over the case, or explain why it would not do so. He said any new terms of reference for Don Stewart's inquiry should allow proper investigation into the 'substantial evidence that Murray Farquhar, Morgan Ryan and the former Police Commissioner, Merv Wood, perverted the course of justice.' The new Attorney-General, Terry Sheehan, agreed this to be the case. Greiner said he approved the summons served on Wood that directed him to appear in court on a charge of intent to pervert the course of justice. The Cessna-Milner case had been, he said, 'a blot on justice in this State and on the Government's administration of justice for eight long years.' He added:

> The whole thing has been a classic NSW Labor Party cover-up. On each occasion the instinctive reaction has been to cover up and say there's nothing new, there's nothing we can do, we've had a look at it. The truth is that within a matter of days of this case being heard by Mr Farquhar, the dogs were barking. Within a matter of days, anyone interested knew that something was fishy about the Cessna-Milner case. It is a real indictment of justice in NSW that it has taken eight years and will ultimately take nine or ten before the matter is resolved.

To add to the pressure on the government, the opposition produced a photograph of Morgan Ryan and Murray Farquhar sitting together in Centennial Park, taken days before the magistrate began hearing the Cessna-Milner case. The snapshot had been sent on to the police commissioner. It was later revealed that Cessna had also been present at that meeting.

Days before Wood's hearing began in the District Court, Judge John Sinclair, who was within a month of celebrating his fourteenth year on the bench, ruled that the trial would not go ahead. He said:

> On the evidence before me, during the period from August 1979 until November 1986 the Crown did not exhibit any interest in prosecuting these charges. The

total delay of almost eleven years since these events occurred is extremely long. The reasons ... for the delay since August 1979 and February 1987 have not been explained by the Crown; there is no evidence before me to suggest any fresh evidence has come to light since August 1979 and there is no basis for suggesting any conduct on the part of the accused responsible for the delay.

The judge said he had accepted medical evidence that there had been a general decline in Mr Wood's health in recent years, and that 'probably his most distressing symptom is that his memory has declined'.

Mr Wood, by then aged 74, vigorously denied he had memory problems. He had retired to a simple life at his Maroubra home with his wife of 43 years, Betty.

In May 1996 Don Stewart's inquiry found that Farquhar, Wood, Ryan and his offsider solicitor Bruce Miles were involved in a conspiracy to pervert the course of justice in the case, although the finding was not published until November that year. It had now become impossible for the government to ignore the scandal, but police minister George Paciullo tried: on 12 November he told parliament that the management committee of the State Drug Crime Commission would take part in investigations into the Cessna-Milner case. That was going on for 18 years after the initial arrests of Cessna and Milner. Merv Wood had got off scot-free, but what of Farquhar and Morgan Ryan? Morgan Ryan had been issued with a summons to appear in court on 23 March 1987 to answer a charge that he gave false evidence to the Stewart inquiry about illegal phone tapping (which had helped uncover the conspiracy alleged in the Cessna-Milner affair). It did not get very far; Director of Public Prosecutions Ian Temby announced in mid-January that he had decided to drop the charge. Among the reasons he gave were that the case was old, and concerned an offence that allegedly had started ten years earlier; that even if Ryan was convicted, he would face only a light penalty. So as far as the Cessna-Milner case went, the prime mover of the conspiracy, Morgan Ryan, was also off the hook. And while Murray Farquhar faced some extraordinary legal battles in the years ahead, as we will see, he was never even charged over the affair.

In the circumstances it would seem fair to vary H. L. Menken's quotation at the head of this chapter to something like: 'It is not a sin to believe evil of others, and is seldom a mistake, when seriously corrupted political, legal and law enforcement administration makes their sins palpably evident.'

22. Illegal bookie suffers amnesia, writes life story

> An autobiography usually reveals nothing bad
> about its writer except his memory.
> – *Franklin P. Jones, American businessman*

Criminals live – we have been led to believe – by what the Mafia call *omerta*: the code of silence. The code forbids the crims from betraying fellow baddies to the authorities. The penalty for breaking the code is death. Clearly, the code has not been enforced among Australian villains or Lennie McPherson and George Freeman – both accomplished informers, fizgigs to police of their choosing – would not have survived much past the 1950s. Many others could be added to the list.

The strictest of Mafia dons apply the code to the population at large: anyone who helps the authorities is an enemy and should suffer the penalty. But the main focus of the code, obviously, is to ensure that criminals don't rat on each other.

Criminals supposedly writing about their life experiences – and those of their colleagues – would, if they told the truth, be in clear breach of even the watered-down local understanding of *omerta*. There were plenty of crims being killed in this period, but none because they were guilty of breaching the code of silence. Their deaths, as we have seen, came as a result of unbridled greed for the huge fortunes generated by the drug trade.

McPherson valiantly pretended until the day he died that he had never broken with *omerta*, Oz-style, despite the fact he was known within the milieu as 'Lennie the Squealer', such was his reputation.

His fizgigging for Ray Kelly and Jack McNeill – to whom he supplied a tape-recorded monthly report on what all the crims he didn't like were up to, and a selected few other crooked cops – was infamous.

Weeks before he died, McPherson rejected probing from a couple of honest young cops who had thought in his dotage Mr Big might start telling the truth to people outside his circle. He would have certainly never written an autobiography, although when a journalist friendly to McPherson told him I was writing a book on his life, Lennie quipped: 'I hope he doesn't say anything bad about me.' Arthur 'Neddy' Smith did, however, write a book, but long before he put pen to paper he had talked enough to fill quite a sizeable volume.

Smith's murderous ways had landed him in jail for a very long time, and his advancing Parkinson's disease symptoms made him realise he would probably never walk free. So, eventually, with his police protector Roger Rogerson thrown out of the force and doing time, Neddy Smith contacted ICAC and had a long talk with investigators there. The resulting reports were titled 'Investigation into the relationship between Police and Criminals', and its first report, released in February 1994, ran to 294 pages. While the investigation ranged far and wide, almost all its work originated with the stories Neddy had told them, as ICAC had established to its satisfaction that he was a credible witness. Unlike other prisoners who came forward from time to time seeking indemnity for telling their stories, Smith had nothing to gain from his massive breach of the *omerta* code of silence.

* * *

George Freeman undoubtedly saw his life flash before him on the night he was shot, 2 April 1979. He claimed that he first started talking into a tape recorder as he lay in the hospital bed, overloaded with painkilling drugs, recovering from the attack. He wanted to 'set the record straight' after all the years of being branded a criminal: 'Give a dog a bad name and it stays with it for life; give a man a "reputation" and he takes it with him to the grave' are the opening words in the preface of *George Freeman, an autobiography*. It took a lot of talking over a long time; the self-published 256-page attempt to put right the damage to his reputation finally hit the streets nine years after he began it, launched with a big 'media event' on 4 May 1988.

The venue was Peter Antonopoluos's Le Sands restaurant at Brighton-le-Sands, where a life-sized ice carving of a racehorse bearing the name 'Mr Digby' dominated the room, an impressive memorial to the 1981 race-fixing scandal. It somehow distracted attention from the line-up of old criminals, a few of their supportive thugs, 'colourful racing identities', sporting personalities and even a Penthouse 'pet', who jostled with the star of the show, George Freeman, to be the focus of the inquisitive media.

Freeman's earliest crime hero, Darcy Dugan, was there, showing all of his 67 years and having difficulty feeding himself without assistance, due to the ravages of a recent stroke. Lennie McPherson, a year younger, occasionally put what passed for a smile on his stern and rugged face. The heavyweight 'support team' included Branko Balic, Tony Torok and Jimmy Goodman. This was the trio who had been accused of involvement in Tony Eustace's murder, but the coroner could find no evidence to support the claim. Balic, Torok and Freeman had also been cleared of charges that they assaulted and maliciously wounded one Frank Hing – described in parliament as 'an influential member of a Chinese Triad' – at the Empress coffee shop in Kings Cross in August 1984. McPherson made the point that smart criminals eternally escaped the long arm of the law.

TV personality Debbie Newsome gave the 54-year-old Freeman a kiss, and announced she would soon 'tell all' in her new job on a television chat show – but not, presumably, about her host and some of his guests. She had come to the launch with Freeman's close friend, former bookmaker and illegal casino operator Bruce Galea.

Julie Mulherin had featured as a 'pet' in Penthouse magazine two years earlier, and was there as a close friend of George's son Grant, the erstwhile 'owner' of Mr Digby. Its ice replica was now melting in the heat generated by the crowd of exciting and excited personalities.

Julie, who was helping sell copies of the book, said to one reporter that what she'd read of it was 'boring'.

Georgina Freeman described her husband's book as 'a bit biased, but good', while her mother, Gloria McLoughlin, said she couldn't put it down – even though her surname had been misspelt 'McLaughlin' throughout.

A prominent lawyer for the crims, Chris Murphy, dampened the spirits a tad when he suggested that those present were 'yesterday's men' who formed 'a sort of RSL of crime'. But that didn't stop the gathered crowd from buying up their copies and elbowing their way to get to George, Lennie and Darcy for their autographs.

The launch and the extract printed in the *Herald* three weeks later were surely the high points of Freeman's new-found literary career.

People curious about how much the criminal would reveal and how honest he would be, no doubt acquired their copy, as did the library at the NSW Police College at Goulburn.

It is not my view that the book is useful to researchers looking at the history of the criminal milieu, or to the aspiring upholders of law and order going through their training at the police college. I have used paragraphs from the book to provide direct access to Freeman's thoughts on some subjects – at least how he thought at the time he was putting the pages together. But included in there is a huge range of omissions and downright lies, rendering the book useless as a serious commentary on crime in the city in which Freeman grew up.

He repeats his denial that he was involved in drugs, entirely ignoring his own addiction to the narcotic morphine substitute, pethidine.

He denies he ever employed Chris Flannery, despite the overwhelming evidence he did so. He blamed journalists and politicians for his tarnished reputation as a criminal. Although agreeing he was no angel, Freeman had not come to grips with his major role in a period when savage gang warfare was fought over the booming drug trade, and politicians, police, magistrates and judges were corrupted to enable him and his powerful cohorts to almost – as McPherson put it – eternally escape the long arm of the law. Official figures for heroin-related deaths in Australia were at 550 in 1995 and rising steeply, but nowhere in the book, of course, is there any mention of the hundreds of people who died taking the addictive drugs that Freeman's friends pushed to all levels of society, to all age groups.

Quotes from the book illustrate some of its shortcomings in the way of truth:

> As I have said, drugs are not my scene. I've always been against all drugs, and all drug sellers.
>
> That's not to say I condone Nick Paltos' crime. I don't. But I also don't condemn the man as a man and as my friend over a long period of time. I believe there were reasons for Nick Paltos' actions *[importing drugs]*.
>
> You don't have to be Einstein to know there is a big difference between hard drugs, like heroin and cocaine, and hashish …
>
> Hashish, as far as I can make out, isn't going to turn somebody into a hopeless wreck, someone who has to sell his or her body just to get another fix. Nor would it mean injections with a needle, and the risk of AIDS and every other killer disease under the sun.
>
> The passport charge was one I was found not guilty of. *[In 1968 he was found guilty and fined $200 for uttering a forged passport application.]*

There are, however, pathetic defences of the US Mafia figures he'd befriended: Dan Testa, Sandy Waterman, Danny Stein, none of them guilty of anything, said George. Again, an abundance of proof shows otherwise. There is no mention of Bela Hejja, who worked for Freeman collecting from slow-paying punters, who told the story of the routine finger amputations. There are quite a few names missing that any comprehensive story of Freeman's life would have included.

Murray Riley, who worked with Freeman and McPherson, doesn't rate a mention. Neither does the drug-runner David Kelleher, who was very close to McPherson and Neddy Smith. Nor does Neddy for that matter. Abe Saffron is overlooked, but he and George were not all that close. Neither Michael Hurley nor his former wife Lena rate a paragraph despite Freeman's close association with both of them, one way or another – although Lena's father, Jacky Muller rates seven – enough for Freeman to try to convince his readers that he didn't kill Muller.

By far the most remarkable omission is the name 'Roger Rogerson'.

A number of other 'bad' cops get a serve, but there is not a word on the one who used George as a fizgig and did shady business with Freeman's close friend Nick Paltos. Maybe Freeman's book wasn't in breach of the code of silence: he paid out on those he didn't like, whitewashed the tarnished reputations of others, and didn't mention the ones who were the integral parts of his crime empire.

Freeman wasn't the only crim to write what we were asked to believe were true life stories, but it seems he started the trend. Others, with less to say but equally amnesiac, have sought their own place in the limelight. Roger Rogerson's 'autobiography' is one of the most recent.

And the murderous Melbourne mobsters have had a few forest plantations razed as they compete to tell stories of the deaths they have had a hand in. There's an apt quotation that acts as a general critique of probably all of them: 'An autobiography usually reveals nothing bad about its writer except his memory.'

23. Death of a drug addict

> There have been murderers and tyrants, and for a
> time they can seem invincible. But in the end
> they always fall. Think of it always.
> – André Malraux, French novelist and statesman

A new decade, some believe, should bring new hopes, freedoms, loves; dreams; see needs fulfilled, and thoughts spared for those who didn't make it this far. Not many of Sydney's crims were mourning the deaths of those who'd been gunned down in cold blood over the 1980s: trouble makers all, and best forgotten. And the problem with another item on the New Year's wish list – dreams – is that all too often they become nightmares.

By 1 January 1990 George Freeman was surely having his share of those. His book, the great 'excuse' for his misspent life launched just seven months earlier, had already fizzled into the public's distant memory. In increasing numbers his friends found themselves in prison cells. And he was now totally dependent on pethidine just to get him through the day.

The drug habit had started when he was shot, to ease the pain of a dreadful wound, and to help with the psychological trauma of that near-death experience. He came to believe that the drug helped with the kidney and stomach pains he'd suffered for years. Had he known of it, he may well have been haunted by the Tennessee Williams line, 'Time rushes towards us with its hospital tray of infinitely varied narcotics, even while it is preparing us for its inevitably fatal operation,' for he knew he was not a well man. No longer could he turn to his long-time friend, Dr Nick Paltos, for a sympathetic ear; Paltos was not set for release from jail for nearly another five years.

Lennie McPherson may have been Freeman's mentor and protector for around four decades but he was not the type of warm-hearted pal you would turn to when you needed to have a whinge about the gathering pains of old age. With such a history, nor were they likely to sit around in a backyard barbecue swapping yarns – 'And do you remember the time when we got Danny Chubb knocked?' – or recalling the sheer ineptitude of their early years as criminals.

In 1988, when he was under enormous pressure from the inquest into Tony Eustace's death, the disappearance of Chris Flannery and Kathleen Flannery's accusations of Freeman's involvement, George underwent a psychiatric examination. The report would have only upped his stress levels, had he got to see it. He was a physical wreck, with asthma, kidney pain and constant stomach troubles, had high blood pressure, smoked heavily and took Valium regularly to calm his nerves, the report said. He was getting pethidine from a number of doctors. Even then, he told his examiners he wanted no autopsy to be carried out on his cadaver when he died. Clearly, he never wanted anybody to discover that his body, particularly his shoulders and thighs, were a pin-cushion of injection scars from the pethidine – and possibly other drugs he'd used – possibly from as early as the mid-1970s, even before he was shot in 1979.

Having been through a bad night, Freeman was taken by ambulance to nearby Sutherland Hospital on the morning of Tuesday, 20 March 1990. He arrived there at about 6.45 a.m., and fifteen minutes later he was dead. He was 55. Initial reports reaching the media suggested he had died of heart failure after a massive asthma attack. Friends and family were content to leave it at that, but over time a different story altogether was revealed.

State Coroner Kevin Waller, although mindful of Freeman's request that there be no autopsy on his remains, did not find it binding. There were rumours circulating of foul play: that somebody had got to him in the hospital and 'finished him off' somehow. Police were making quiet enquiries. The coroner ordered a post-mortem partly to help dispel the rumours.

In blunt terms, Waller found Freeman had died of an overdose of pethidine he'd injected into his body. In officialese: 'The initial cause of death ... was found to be associated with pethidine poisoning,' and that although asthma 'led to his death [it was] exacerbated by the self-administration of pethidine.' His death was directly caused by the combined effects of asthma, high pethidine levels and 'adrenal insufficiency', the coroner reported. He had almost certainly injected pethidine at his home shortly before he died.

Pethidine, a morphine-like drug, frequently produces 'marked euphoria' that lasts for about an hour after it is administered. Studies show pethidine addicts typically inject the drug twelve to fifteen times a day. Withdrawal symptoms shown by some addicts are similar to those addicted to morphine. An Australian study says pethidine is a drug of addiction and can be habit-forming if taken in large amounts for a prolonged period. Large doses can impair breathing, hazardous indeed to a chronic asthmatic like Freeman.

Coroner Kevin Waller talked to doctors who had supplied drugs to Freeman, and said, 'In effect, Mr Freeman was a registered pethidine addict and ... it may or may not be that all his pethidine was legally supplied. Certainly, much of it was.' Once addicted, Freeman would have increasingly built up a tolerance to the drug, resulting in more injections being needed to produce what he felt as the same result.

Georgina Freeman told Waller, 'George kept very much to himself in relation to the medications that he took as he was on so many. I believe he had been obtaining pethidine under prescription from doctors for many years. There was [sic] often needles in the house ... [but] I never saw him inject himself, as he disliked me seeing it.' An extensive report by Ned Lydon in the *Sydney Morning Herald* on 3 August 1991 suggested doctors who had treated Freeman were concerned about his pethidine use. Dr Tass James, who shared a surgery with Nick Paltos for a time, reported to the coroner that he first saw Freeman in January 1985, and he was 'the most severe asthmatic I have treated in fifteen years'. By

March 1986 James said he was concerned enough by Freeman's use of the drug that he notified the health department, an act that enabled Freeman to have pethidine prescribed for him only on certain conditions. The doctor tried to wean him off the drug and in January 1988 tried him on a methadone program similar to the treatment offered to heroin addicts. It didn't work; his kidney pain got worse and an allergy to aspirin-based drugs kept driving him back to pethidine. By December 1988, Dr James said, 'He began to deteriorate more rapidly'. Another doctor said he gave Freeman scripts for Valium injections 'and occasionally left him an ampoule of pethidine in case of an emergency. He was a very persuasive man.' There was evidence that one or two more doctors had been supplying pethidine to the 'persuasive' Freeman. An empty pethidine ampoule was found near his bed after he died.

The funeral on Saturday, 24 March 1990, at St Stephen's Uniting Church – where he had exchanged marriage vows with Georgina nearly nine years earlier – attracted some 350 people: punters, bookies racing identities, lawyers, entertainers and a few folk who were plainly just curious. Chubby club performer and friend to the crooks Norman Erskine sang, 'That's What Friends Are For' and 'I'll Be Loving You', bringing tears to Georgina's eyes under her black-veiled hat. Freeman friend Paul Beirne reflected on Freeman's reputation: 'The only thing George never got the blame for was the Newcastle earthquake.' But his welcome at the Golden Gates would have been warm, Beirne assured the mourners. George would have been eagerly met by Saint Peter, saying: 'Come on in mate. God wants to know your tips for the Golden Slipper.' The cards attached to the wreaths that lined the church vestibule were removed to ensure the media couldn't see who had sent them. Paranoia was never far away from this cluster of misfits. Lennie McPherson, proving yet again that he couldn't lie straight in bed, said that since they had first met Freeman had 'led a pretty clean life'. They had met in jail in 1956, and without discussing how he had achieved it, added:

And we've never been back [to jail] since. He knew a lot

of things but people don't seem to get the idea that the reason George is not being arrested is that he is simply not doing anything … isn't it a fact that you get arrested when you do something wrong? Both Freeman and I get blamed for things we had never done. Everyone that was murdered, I killed them. Every hold-up that was done, I done it. Even the Commissioner of Police said I couldn't possibly do those many things; that he would have to be twenty people in the same day. It was the same thing with Freeman. And would he have all the friends he's got if he had that reputation.

No one at the funeral made the point that Freeman had broken the law every week of his adult life – and had got away with it.

It seems appropriate here to quote American philosopher Elbert Hubbard, who succinctly defines death as 'to stop sinning suddenly'.

Freeman had, at last, stopped sinning. In life he had contributed extravagantly to the social environment in ways that saw his home town become dubbed 'Sin City'. The massive levels of corruption, the political cover-ups, the police involvement in crime, the murders written off as 'gangland killings', the magistrates and judges who took a nod and a wink from crooked cops and lawyers and let the favoured crims run their own race without intrusion of the law, the fixing of races, the rorting and extortion and standover thuggery, all added up to making Sydney a very dangerous place to live.

Crime writer Evan Whitton penned an obituary for Freeman in the *Sydney Morning Herald*, headlined 'Freeman: he was Big Crime's artful dodger'. Whitton noted that 'Freeman was a Mr Big Enough of organised crime in Sydney for 25 years; it may seem a fair criticism of NSW Police that the best they could manage against him in that period was a couple of fines for illegal betting.' Freeman was dead, but he left a lasting reek, a miasma that didn't leave town after the funeral, but lingered on.

Epilogue: unfinished business: Freeman's bequest lives on

> An evil life is a kind of death.
> – Ovid, Roman poet

George Freeman tried to control how he'd be viewed in posterity, to revise his history. He wanted no autopsy performed on his corpse, knowing it would reveal his addiction to drugs. He left no last will and testament to provide inquisitive reporters with sets of figures that would make headlines on his evil ways having earned him a great fortune.

Freeman and McPherson would have discussed how their worldly belongings should be dispersed among their families to conceal the real value of their estates. McPherson had arrangements in place before he died, but Freeman beat him to the mark. Freeman looks to have dealt with the matter in the following way. The value of his entire estate was listed as $301,008 (*$529,318.25*), an extremely modest amount, of which his widow, Georgina, became administrator. When Freeman auctioned his Yowie Bay property, 'Dallas', in 1987, it went for $1.46 million (*$3.18 million*). Freeman said he'd made a 'nice profit on the deal' and moved to a slightly smaller waterfront home in Ellesmere Road, in nearby Gymea Bay, worth $400,000 (*$870,436*). But title deeds later showed that George Freeman owned neither Dallas nor the new property; this real estate was in the name of Greig David Freeman. Greig David Freeman is George Freeman's second son by his first marriage (although his name appears as 'Greg' in Freeman senior's memoir).

Reporter Kate McClymont did a bit of digging for the *Sydney Morning Herald*, and found that despite George claiming ownership of Yowie Bay after he'd bought it from gambler Bruce Galea in 1978 for $220,000 (*$1,013,70*), land title records showed that in fact Greig David Freeman had bought the land from Dr Nick Paltos for $65,000 (*$227,613*) in 1981 – the same year in which Paltos had borrowed $300,000 (*$1,050,520*) from solicitor Ross Karp.

To add to the confusion, in August 1988 records show that Greig David Freeman sold a half-share in the Ellesmere Road property for $200,000 (*$405,926*), and that George and Georgina splashed out $310,000 (*$629,186*) for a 10.5-hectare rural property, 'Jyndarra Lodge', at High Range, near Bowral in the NSW Southern Highlands. That property was subsequently sold. To end up with an estate valued at just over $300,000 must have taken some inventive book-keeping indeed.

* * *

If George Freeman's last years on earth saw him suffer some financial and tactical complications, these paled to insignificance when compared to the extraordinary manœuvres pulled by his old friend Murray Farquhar. The one-time chief stipendiary magistrate of NSW almost certainly would have first discussed his moves with his trusted advisor and the master of the game, Freeman. Here, then, is the bizarre plot hatched by Farquhar.

In the central bank in the Philippines capital, Manila, sat 550 tonnes of gold bars, valued in 1990 at around seven billion dollars (*around $12.31 billion*) (or so Farquhar believed). This was the prize Farquhar and his co-plotters were aiming for. The plan was absurdly simple but it was also just plain absurd. The plotters would use up-front money to finance Filipino rebels to overthrow the government of President Corazon Aquino. The gold, so the plan went, would be stolen during the chaos following the attempted coup.

The seed was planted when Farquhar, then 72, and his co-conspirator, Irish-born Gerald Kron, aged 60, heard a story that former Filipino president Ferdinand Marcos had stashed the gold bullion in the bank before he was deposed, and there it remained. It was never there, of course, and poorly researched facts were just some of the shortcomings of their plan. It was never revealed whether George Freeman gave an approving nod before he died as his mate outlined the plan, or simply shook his head in disbelief, but it's doubtful anyone could have deterred Farquhar.

They needed phoney passports, IDs to get them past the security guards at the Manila bank, transport and protection for their haul, and a disposal plan for after they had shifted the gold to a safe place. And they would need to raise funds for their initial out-of-pocket expenses An acquaintance, 62-year-old Donald Lawton, a construction supervisor of Cobar Place, North Ryde, was roped in to organise passports for Farquhar and Gerald Kron. Other travel documents would also be needed. Farquhar's job included raising the $35,000 ($61,547) required to pay for the passports. Kron's daughter Joanna became involved when she secretly took her husband's birth certificate and other identifying documents without his knowledge to get a passport in his name.

On 23 April 1990 Farquhar left Sydney for Dubai, where he planned to raise some of the money. He was unsuccessful and faxed Kron an authorisation to withdraw $6000 ($10,550) from his (Farquhar's) bank account in Sydney. The former magistrate, back in Australia, then bought five paintings – including one by William Dobell, so Farquhar was told – from a man he'd met in the street. The ex-magistrate expressed shock when he discovered they were genuine: they had been stolen earlier from wealthy Melbourne businessman Samuel Smorgon. He later tried – but failed – to sell them to fund the Manila project.

While fundraising for the heist, Farquhar and Kron talked to a pair of food wholesalers who turned out to be crooked ex-cops. Farquhar claimed they conned him out of more than $23,000 ($40,445), and had hit Kron for $5000 ($8,702). Despite hitting these speed bumps, Farqhuar and Kron persisted with their plan. They organised a ship to take the gold from the Philippines to Europe or Asia. The vessel was none less than the *Spritely*, an ex-Australian navy minesweeper armed with Exocet and surface-to-air missiles, crewed by 20 or more mercenary commandoes.

They set the date for the start of the coup d'état: Friday, 1 June 1990. Soon after that date Farquhar and Kron flew to Manila in the hope of collecting the gold. Details of just how they planned to trigger the action never emerged, but it all went horribly wrong. Someone had alerted police. Police in the Philippines had also been notified, and the hapless Dad's Army duo were detained and returned to Sydney.

Nearly all the conversations between Farquhar and Kron – and the crooked ex-cops – had been secretly recorded. They and a few other participants were arrested, but remarkably only faced charges of trying to obtain false passports. Their planning a coup in a foreign land was mentioned often in the court hearings, but nobody seemed to take it seriously enough to lay charges in connection with it. Some observers thought it was just an elaborate hoax: there was never really a plan to get the gold, just a scam to raise the working capital for the scheme from unsuspecting participants.

In March 1991 Farquhar and others were committed for trial, but two years later, still waiting for the action in court, he suffered a stroke.

He was optimistic he'd make a recovery. Two months later Farquhar applied to have the charges dropped, citing his continuing ill health.

Judge William Knight, unimpressed, set the trial date for 18 October which, he said, should give Farquhar enough time to recover. But the law doesn't move fast, as we have seen. The trial finally got under way in the District Court in November 1993. Prosecutor John Agius said the plan to topple Corazon Aquino allegedly involved the Catholic Archbishop of Manila, Cardinal Jaime Sin. 'But,' the lawyer said, 'it may be we will never know whether the gold was really in the bank or whether there was a plot to overthrow Mrs Aquino.' Agius was spot on. Halfway through the trial, on 3 December 1993, Farquhar died of a massive heart attack at the Prince of Wales Hospital. He was 75.

***

Another of Freeman's mates was somewhat luckier, despite having his own scrapes with the law. Murray Stewart Riley decided in 1990 to change his name by deed poll to Murray Lee Stewart. He went to London and tried to set up a fraud worth $100 million (*$175.85 million*), was arrested and jailed. In January 1993 he escaped from Aldington Prison in Kent and vanished – but not completely; I have been assured that Riley is alive and well, albeit with a facelift or two, and living on the Gold Coast in Queensland.

***

Lennie McPherson hit the headlines a few times after his mate Freeman had died. The most serious of these related to a charge for organising an assault in April 1991 on businessman Darren Burt, with whom Lennie's sons were having some business difficulties. Facing a stern judge, Robert Court, over the matter three years later on 16 December 1994, McPherson said if he was sent to jail, he would die there.

Noting that concern, the judge said that was obviously a risk, but 'the simple and obvious answer to that complaint is that anyone who does not want to die in jail should not engage in criminal activity'. With a thump of the gavel, Judge Court sent him away for a maximum of four years, and a non-parole period of two and a half years, having regard for the 'special circumstances of his health'.

McPherson didn't make it out again: just after seven o'clock on the evening of 25 August 1996, the 75-year-old phoned his wife, Marlene, then collapsed and died of a heart attack.

***

Michael Hurley, in 2004, got into some big-time drug importing, an activity with which some Qantas baggage handlers at Sydney Airport gave a helpful hand. Around 200 kilograms of cocaine from South America got past customs officials and their sniffer dogs. The drugs were estimated to have had a street value of around $30 million (*$37.51 million*). One of Hurley's associates was former first-grade rugby league footballer Les Mara, aged 51 at the time of the deal. Hurley was arrested in February two years later and Mara in early December. They were awaiting trial and facing possible life sentences when 61-year-old Hurley died of a rare cancer on 23 January 2007. His coffin was carried from the St James Catholic Church in Glebe to the strains of Frank Sinatra's 'I Did It My Way'.

* * *

Freeman's closest friend and ally from the time they knocked about on the streets of Annandale as kids, Stan 'the Man' Smith, stayed in the drugs game until he found God in 2003. A source told the *Herald* that Smith went to bible classes on Tuesday nights, was a regular at the Evangelical Bible Church at Putney and took up letterboxing religious tracts around the suburbs. Smith died on 17 January 2010, aged 74.

* * *

Freeman's friend and supporter, ex-police commissioner Merv Wood, pottered around at home for more than a quarter of a century after he resigned in June 1979. He died on 23 August 2006, aged 89.

* * *

When Roger Rogerson was released from jail in December 1995, he went into business, becoming director of two companies in the scaffolding industry. Corporate law, however, prohibits anyone who has been convicted of fraud or dishonesty charges – as had Roger – from being involved in the management of a company. The legal process took a while (as always) but in October 2001 he pleaded guilty, was put on a two-year good behaviour bond and barred from being involved in running a company for five years. So he went into a different line of business: he wrote a book and launched himself onto the speakers' circuit, doing 'entertaining' gigs in pubs and other venues where there is no requirement to swear to tell the truth, the whole truth and nothing but the truth.

* * *

A few more crims were gunned down at the start of the 1990s, but the ferocity of the gang wars was a thing of the past. The drug dealers had become more orderly and sophisticated, the politicians less so – earning the scorn of voters – and the seriously crooked cops waned in numbers and influence. The age that saw Freeman, McPherson and Stan Smith reign as Sydney's criminal triumvirate had come and gone. It would never be a 'clean and tidy' city, but if a major capital must have crime, surely it's better to exist discreetly in corporate boardrooms rather than flaunting itself on a racetrack with a chief magistrate and society doctor in tow for all the world to see.

Freeman was much more than a 'colourful' illegal SP bookie: he was a standover thug who ordered the brutal punishment of his laggardly customers and extorted huge sums of money from vulnerable victims.

He was a major corrupter of police and politicians and was directly involved in murders. He sat at the top table in the criminal world, beyond doubt a 'Mr Big Enough' of Sydney crime for three decades.

* * *

In April 2010 Freeman's widow, Georgina, then around 53, appeared in a 'tell-all' feature in *The Australian Women's Weekly* magazine. She had formed a close relationship with John Ibrahim, the new major operator in Kings Cross, who ran nightclubs in that sleazy precinct once ruled by Abe Saffron. Georgina's two sons, Adam and David, had earlier become associated with Ibrahim, who many years previously had been a debt collector for George Freeman and was now something of a 'father figure' to the dead bookie's two sons. In the magazine story Georgina is quoted as saying, 'I always thought he [Ibrahim] was gorgeous. I think John once said to me: "I always had a crush on you when I was young." John was so good looking. He's generous like George, he's funny like George, I guess he's a playboy like George was.' The widow also acknowledged she had been dubbed the 'Queen of the Cross', clearly showing a greater affection for the area and its major players than had never been demonstrated by her late husband.

* * *

The stench of corruption lingers. In August 1990 a Saulwick opinion poll published in the *Sydney Morning Herald* showed 72 per cent of respondents believe there was a serious corruption problem in NSW government organisations, while 19 per cent thought there was no point in trying to stamp it out. Just 6 per cent felt there was so little corruption that it wasn't worth worrying about. The performance of the corruption-fighting ICAC had 41 per cent saying it was doing a 'fair' job, and 38 per cent suggesting its performance rating was 'good' or 'very good'.

* * *

By the turn of the century the ranks of the major established criminal groups had been thinned out considerably: a few had died of natural causes, some from drug overdoses, many violently gunned down, their murderers never brought to justice. And the departure from the scene of many of the corrupt police of that volatile era might lead readers to the view that Sydney's major crime and corruption problems have been fairly well resolved.

That clearly is not the case. The events of this period can be seen as one of the 'waves' of criminal activity referred to at the start: the survivors of that tsunami slinked off into dark crevices to carry on their illicit behaviour in a more discreet manner, less visible but never totally inactive. The successors to the Mr Bigs of the previous half a century gained their positions by brute force, for few of the sons and heirs of the departed thugs have made much of an impression in the milieu, having been little more than spoiled little rich kids playing on the periphery of the vile world their fathers created. New groups have emerged; they are running the drugs, extortion, illegal gambling; they are fighting with others emerging on to the scene; they are paying bribes to cops and politicians.

At Sin City's headquarters, Kings Cross, the nights prickle with a greater violence than ever; on a recent visit I was abused by a phalanx of thuggish 'doormen' outside a strip club over my polite rejection of an aggressive invitation to step inside to 'play with the girls'. In nearby doorways drug-soaked young men and women sell their bodies to finance their next fix. A fresh-looking police duo patrol up and down.

A fight breaks out and a young man is left unconscious on the footpath, no one helping him as his attacker dissolves into the crowds of gawkers. Drugs continue to devastate so many lives, despite proud public boasts by customs and federal police when they seize a pile of pills or white powder. The drug barons are still winning their war; the lawmen who care are desperately playing catch-up. Occasionally a policeman gets busted for involvement in the drug trade.

Despite many cultural improvements in the NSW Police Force, there is still corruption in the ranks; there are still bribe-takers and cops who get too close to the criminals. While the endemic levels of corruption this story reveals were largely brought to an end, the crooks in the force, like the crims, have their lines of succession.

But probably the major shift in organised crime is its increased sophistication: it is more likely now that major criminal operations are carefully planned behind closed doors in corporate boardrooms, rather than in grubby hotels like the Lansdowne, the Iron Duke or the long-gone Phoenix in Woollahra.

The next – inevitable – blood-stained wave of criminal activity will wash through society in a different form. No more finger amputations for slow-paying SP punters. But as Sydney has seen at the end of 2009, bloody murder and claims of political corruption are still very much a part of the scene.

This is, after all, Sin City, a society spawned of criminals who ran the first constabulary, which has never – and likely will never – shed its colourful, violent past.

Notes

General

The sources for most of the information in this book are made reference to in the body of the text; these are not repeated here. Over some decades I have conducted numerous interviews with serving and former police, private investigators, lawyers, judges, politicians and criminals, who have all provided information on Sydney's criminal milieu. I have also used as primary reference sources:

- *Can of Worms II*, Evan Whitton (Fairfax Library, 1987)
- *The Prince and the Premier*, David Hickie (Angus & Robertson, 1985)
- *Drug Traffic: Narcotics and Organised Crime in Australia*, Alfred W. McCoy (Harper & Row, 1980).

My thanks go to them for the firm foundation of knowledge they laid, which continues to assist other crime writers.

I have made extensive use of the media coverage of facets of Freeman's story, particularly (but not exclusively) stories published in the *Sydney Morning Herald*.

Contemporaneous electoral rolls and telephone directories provided further information.

I have accessed NSW and federal parliamentary Hansards for references to matters raised in those institutions. I obtained some biographical material of state politicians from the NSW Parliament's website at *www.parliament.nsw.gov.au*.

Freeman's memoir is entitled *George Freeman, an autobiography* (self-published, 1988, edited by Philip Jack). It was not possible to verify the material contained within, some of which was shown to be in conflict with other more reliable sources. (This source indicated by 'GF' in entries that follow.)

Wherever possible, court, royal commission and coroners' inquest documents and reports from the Independent Commission Against Corruption (ICAC) were studied to ensure accuracy. The Australasian Criminal Register (ACR) provided criminal biographies, and was published by the Central Fingerprint Bureau, CIB, Sydney, for Australian and regional police forces.

I obtained some biographical data on police from NSW Police Cadets archives.

The Australian Dictionary of Biography (ADB) (published online by the Australian National University) has provided some biographical data, as has the databases of the NSW Registry of Births, Deaths and Marriages (BDM). Archives of the Australian War Memorial at www.awm.gov.au/research provided military history of our subjects. Most of the obituary data is from the Ryerson Index at www.ryersonindex.org.

Some material came from personal interviews. The people are generally identified in the text, although some requested anonymity, which I have respected.

Other references include:

1. Getting started in the trade

Eric Campbell reference: Keith Amos, 'Campbell, Eric (1893–1970)', Australian Dictionary of Biography, Volume 7, Melbourne University Press, 1979, pp 546–47.

John Kingsley Clarkson escape: National Library of Australia, Historic Australian Newspapers, 1803 to 1954. http://trove.nla.gov.au/newspaper Tamworth Institution for Boys: NSW State Archives.

Marble Bar at Adams Hotel: atmosphere recalled from personal experience.

2. Taking a peep at the big time

McPherson bomb-making data: National Archives of Australia, McPherson, Leonard Arthur (Australian) [Box 537].

McPherson criminal and prison records: copies obtained by author.

Norman Allan: Evan Whitton, 'Allan, Norman Thomas William (1909–77)', Australian Dictionary of Biography, Volume 13, Melbourne University Press, 1993, pp 28–29.

3. Stealing or gambling? George takes an each-way bet

Ray Kelly data: BDM; Whitton; Dickie; Sandra Harvey, 'Kelly, Raymond William (1906–77)', Australian Dictionary of Biography, Volume 14, Melbourne University Press, 1996, pp 615–16.

Western Australia shoplifting spree compiled from ACR entries of participants, court appearances.

4. Reaching for the top – into deals with Mr Big

Freeman/Smith US trip: Moffitt Royal Commission; private research; GF.

5. Hospitality repaid: showing the Mafia our bright lights

Mafia and Joe Testa data: Moffitt Royal Commission; private research.

6. Only a dope would have missed it: drugs make a big hit

Michael Hurley: ACR; media.

Jacky Muller: BDM; ACR; military records; National Archives: title: Muller, John Marcus aka Marcus, John, barcode: 734261.

7. Odds to die for: betting on the drug trade

Bela Hejja: National Archives: title: Hejja Bela – Nationality: Hungarian, barcode: 5496198; media.

Jack McNeill data: BDM; National Archives: title: McNeill Jack: Service Number – 444758, barcode: 5378327; Ryerson; Moffitt Royal Commission; on his authority: Pitfalls of the Introduction of Community Policing, Jeff Jarratt,

Commander, Office of Policy, Planning and Evaluation, NSW Police Service (31/01/2000).

Murray Riley: Moffitt Royal Commission; Sports Reference: www.sportsreference.com/olympics/athletes/ri/murray-riley-1.html.

Nick Paltos: SMH obituary; phone tap transcripts; Whitton.

David Kelleher: ACR, courts, appeal.

8. Odds to die for: betting on the drug trade

Double Bay meetings: personal research; Moffitt Royal Commission; police reports.

Karl Bonnette data: ACR; Whitton; Dickie; Moffitt Royal Commission.

Fred Hanson: Bruce Swanton, 'Hanson, Frederick John (1914–80)', Australian Dictionary of Biography, Volume 14, Melbourne University Press, 1996, pp 380–81; military records; Whitton, Dickie; Ryerson.

9. Drugs not the only racket: racing gets a fix, too

John Regan: ACR; personal research.

Toe cutter gang data: personal research; federal police file.

Freeman's presence in locality of Regan murder: GF.

10. Chips are down as casinos raided: punters take a short break

Neddy Smith: ACR; ICAC; Whitton.

11. A shot in the dark: Freeman cops it in the neck

Freeman's association with Lena Hurley: media; personal interviews.

Freeman shooting: GF; media.

Glen Flack: court transcripts; media; ICAC.

12. A new top cop, the same old game

Merv Wood data: Police Cadets archives; RAAF records (National Archives); police records; media.

Raid on Freeman's home by Commonwealth police: personal interviews.

Murray Riley and Anoa drug importation: police reports; courts; media.

Cessna-Milner affair: court documents; media; Hansard; Stewart royal commission.

13. Punting is easy when you know the winner!

Mr Digby: AJC inquiries; media; ABC documentary The Track.
Warren Lanfranchi killing: coroner; media; Hansard.
Andrew Stathis affair: police phone tap transcripts; court files; Hansard; media.

14. Doc prescribes drugs to ease the pain of his debts

Paltos drugs plan reconstructed from court evidence, phone tap transcripts.

Rogerson bank account data: court evidence; Operation Lavender bugs.

Rogerson lunch to plan Drury hit: court evidence; private interviews.

Rogerson conviction on pervert course of justice charge: Judgment in R v Roger Caleb Rogerson, District Court, 86/11/1440.

Freeman barred from UK: GF.

15. Tall poppies mown down in killing fields

Freeman hired Flannery as bodyguard: personal interviews; Whitton; media.

Daniel Chubb murder: coroner's inquest; police reports.

Michael Sayers murder: coroner; media.

16. NCA targets Freeman – and misses

Flannery shooting: courts; media.

NCA probes: NCA internal memos; federal parliamentary reports.

17. Building a new deal in extortion

Building trade standover: Gyles inquiry.

18. The slaughter goes on

Eustace murder: coroner; police reports; media; personal interview; NCA; phone tap transcripts.

19. The hit man becomes the target
Michael Drury accusation against Rogerson: Police tribunal; court evidence.

Christopher Flannery disappearance: coroner; personal interview; ICAC; Police Royal Commission (Louis Bayeh).

20. McCann clan blown apart
McCann gang members: coroner; court evidence; ICAC.

21. Crims play law games: win more time for crime
Various cases from court papers; media; government reports.

22. Illegal bookie suffers amnesia, writes life story
Freeman book launch: Tony Stephens' story in SMH.

23. Death of a drug addict
Freeman death: coroner; media.

Epilogue
Murray Farquhar schemes: court papers; media.

Index

2

21 Division (Gaming Squad), 18, 32, 82, 85, 92, 93, 105

3

33 Club, The, 55, 76, 79, 84

A

ABC's Four Corners, 82, 92
Abel, John, former MP, 163
Abeles, Sir Peter, TNT, 87-8
Abood, Camille, 89
Adams Hotel, 12, 225
Age newspaper, *The*, 84-5, 86, 101, 124, 187, 199
'*Age* tapes' affair, 84-6, 101, 124, 187, 199
Agius, John, lawyer, 218
Airport Hilton hotel, 168, 170
Allan, Norman Thomas William, commissioner, 20-1, 67
Allen, Colin Ramsay, judge, 179
Anderson, Anthony. *See* Eustace, Tony 'Spaghetti'
Anderson, Charles 'Paddles', 21, 28, 31, 59, 63-4, 72, 149, 167
Anderson, Peter, MP, 82-3
Anderson, Tony. *See* Eustace, Tony 'Spaghetti'
Andy the Greek. *See* Stathis, Andrew
Anoa, 104, 136
Antonopoluos, Peter, 206
Aquino, Corazon, 216, 218
Arantz, Philip, Sgt, 21
Archibald, Bill, reporter, 87
Armarti, David, magistrate, 200
Arncliffe Scots Club, 178
ASIO, 50
Askin, Millie Isabelle née Underhill, 108
Askin, Robin (later Robert), premier, 21, 26-7, 38, 42, 67-8, 71, 73, 77, 80, 88, 108
Aston, John Lawrence, lawyer, 80
Atkinson, Amos, 154
Aussie Bar, Manila, 154
Australasian Criminal Register, 14, 21, 58, 69
Australian Crime Commission, 159
Australian Jockey Club, 113-14, 145
Australian Labor Party, 26, 64, 68, 83, 105, 117, 188, 201
Australian Women's Weekly, The, 221
Avery, John Keith, police commissioner, 131, 137, 172-3, 188

B

Bain, Carolyn, Hardin partner, 162
Baker, Brian, Alpine Scaffolding, 164
Balic, Branko, 43, 161, 184, 206
Ball, Terence Edward, 189
Ballard, Brian, Det-Sgt., 66
Ballard, David Bruce, 161
Bally Poker Machine Co, 42, 44-7, 77
Balmain Rugby Leagues Club, 90
Banks, Keith, jockey, 113-14
Bartley, Mick, SP bookmaker, 25, 27, 32, 36, 46
Bass, Robin Warren, 164-5
Baume, Peter, Senator, 188

Bayeh, Louie Sarkis El, 150-1, 174, 181-2, 186
Bayswater Brasserie, 128, 132
Beck, Merv, Det., 51, 82-4
Beck's Raiders, 82-4
Beirne, Paul, Freeman friend, 213
Birnie, Alexander Magnus, Supt, 86
Bishopgate Insurance, 123
Black, Peter Ernest, 113
Blanch, Reginald Oliver, crown advocate, 131
Bold Personality, Fine Cotton ring-in, 144
Bonnette, Karl Frederick, 64-7, 72, 103-5
Bourbon and Beefsteak bar, 60
Boyd, Brian, 85
Brady, John, 164, 165
Brammer, Mal, Det., 74
Bredmeyer, Theo, judge, 148
Briese, Clarrie, magistrate, 106
Brifman, Shirley, 19
Bristow, Tim, private detective, 160-1
Brock. *See* Bonnette, Karl Frederick
Brown, John, Det, 78
Brown, Malcolm, SMH journalist, 165
Brown, Stephen John, 127, 134
Burt, Darren, 219

C

Caesar's Palace, 61
Callaghan, Jack, 33
Callaghan, Leo 'The Liar', 39, 65
Camilleri, Victor John, 146-7, 184, 193
Campbell, Chris, 29
Campbell, Judith Shirley, shoplifter, 33
Campbell, Michael William, judge, 143
Cannacott, E. E. Supt., 86
Capone, Al, 17
Casey, Daniel Patrick, 152
Cauliflower Hotel, 192

Cessna, Roy Bowers, 105-8, 198, 201-2
Cessna-Milner saga, 105-6, 108, 198, 200-2
Chad, Nelson Rowatt, Det., 126
Chapman, Dr Geoff, horse trainer, 111-12
Charkey Ramon. *See* Ballard, David Bruce
Charlton, Frank, Det-Sgt, 52, 66, 187
Chequers nightclub, 43, 139
Chevron Hotel, 43
Childs, Maureen, 153-4
Chinese David, drug supplier, 193
Chinese Triad, 206
Chowne, Les Det-Sgt., 55
Choyro Maru, 104
Chubb, Daniel Michael 'The Brain', 127, 135, 140-3, 167, 173-5, 178, 194, 211
City Tattersalls Club, 27
Civil and Civic, 161
Clark, Terry (Mr Asia), 2, 79-80, 85
Clarke, Harry, trainer, 113-14
Clarkson, John Kingsley, 4
Clayton, Hilton, 30
Cole, Les, 140
Commonwealth Investigation Service, 50
Cooper, Jackie, 195
Cornwell, Bruce 'Snapper', 79, 104
Court, Robert, judge, 219
Crabtree, William (Bill), MP, 80, 198
Crime Oz Inc, 67
Criminal Investigation Branch (CIB), 8, 19-20, 28-30, 47, 56, 69, 86
Croft, Barry John 'Sugar', 192-4
Crooke, Gary QC, 181
Cross, Peter James, 50, 150, 153-9
CSIRO, 187
Curtains, NCA Refrence No 6, 152-3, 156, 158

D

Daily Mirror, 87
Daily Telegraph, 81
Darlinghurst Police Station, 74
David Jones store, 138
Davies, Cherrie, Chubb neighbour, 140-1
Day, Lloyd, 28
Deaf Mick. *See* Bartley, Mick, SP bookmaker
Delaney, Arthur 'The Duke', 21-2, 39, 43, 59, 65, 72
Delaney, Colin John, police commissioner, 20
Delouney, Bill, 43
Dobell, William, 217
Domican, Thomas Christian, 146-7, 150-3, 155-9, 169, 171, 174, 181, 184-6, 193
Donnelly, Robert Charles, 75
Double Bay Bridge Club, 84, 149
Double Bay meetings, 64, 73
Dowd, John, MP, 117, 142, 188-9
Doyle, Brian Kevin, asst police commissioner, 91
Drury Michael Laurence, Det-Sgt, 130-1, 134, 178-9, 188
Duff, William (Bill), Sgt., 60, 139, 142, 148, 174, 175, 188, 189
Dugan, Darcy Ezekiel, 2, 7, 13, 28, 87, 206
Dugan, Richard, 7
Dunklings Jewellers, 114

E

Edelstein, Geoffrey, doctor, 148
El-Azzi, William, 184
Emont, Dick, 33
Endeavour House. *See* Tamworth Institution for Boys
Erskine, Norman, 213
Eustace, Tony 'Spaghetti', 118-24, 148, 168-74, 178-9, 206, 211
Evans, Wayne, Sgt., 199

F

Farquhar, Murray Frederick, Chief Magistrate, 89-90, 92, 106-8, 198, 201-2, 216-18
Fellows, Warren Edward, 104
Fergusson, Supt. Don, 19-20
Fine Cotton ring-in affair, 143-5
Flack, Glen Roderick, 97-8
Flack, Margaret Elizabeth, 98
Flannery, Christine, 150
Flannery, Christopher Dale, 131-2, 134, 137-9, 147-155, 158-9, 168-171, 174-187, 192, 194-5, 207, 211
Flannery, Kathleen, 138-9, 147, 150, 153-159, 170, 179-180, 183-4, 186, 194, 211
Flock, 'Big' Barry Leonard, 75
Foord, John Murray, judge, 122-5
Forbes Club, 31, 81, 84
Ford, Roger, indemnified witness, 146
Frazer, Graham, Det., 117
Freeman, Adam, 221
Freeman, David, 221
Freeman, George David, 2, 3, 5, 6-15, 17-18, 20-8, 30-44, 46-65, 69-76, 79, 81-7, 89-99, 101-6, 108, 110-15, 117-18, 120-3, 125-8, 132-3, 135-40, 144-5, 147-50, 152-61, 163-8, 170-83, 185-7, 190, 192, 195-8, 204-17, 219-21
1935
born in Annandale 22 January, 5
1947
charged re unlicensed pistol, 8
first children's court appearance, 8
good behaviour bond for stealing, 8
1949
left school aged 14, 6
started job at McLoughlin stables, 9

1951
abandons job at McLoughlins, 9
charged, stealing in Melbourne, 9
charged, theft, sent to Mt Penang, 10
convicted, fare evasion, Coffs Harbour, 9
fined, using insulting words, 9
moved to Tamworth Boys Home, 10
1953
released from Boys Home, 11
1954
found guilty of car theft, 12
three years, first adult gaol sentence, 13
1955
conditional release from gaol, 13
gaoled in Melbourne, 14
1956
gaoled in Sydney, met McPherson, 14
1958
robbed H G Palmer shops, 18
1959
Fred Krahe wants him as informant, 18
three-year gaol for HG Palmer jobs, 18
1961
meets Roger Rogerson, 18
1962
arrested for stealing stockings, 20
teamed up with Arthur 'The Duke' Delaney, 21
1963
married divorcee Marcia McDonald, 23
merged with Mick Bartley's SP business, 25
started in SP bookmaking, 24
1965
claims Askin was paid off, 26
met Mafia's Testa in Sydney, 31

1966
marriage to Marcia breaks down, 32
1967
brief visit to London, 33
plans laid for visit to US, 38
1967-8
uses alias Keane for visit to US, 39
1968
led shoplifting team to Perth, 33
prison term for shoplifting spree in Perth, 34
US visit hosted by Testa, 40
wrist-slap for forged passport document, 40
1969
American Mafia shows interest in Australia, 45
brings Hurley into SP operation, 48
witness at Hurley's wedding to Lena Muller, 49
1970
hit with $23,000 unpaid tax bill, 53
1970s
Hejja amputated fingers in debt collections, 54
Kelleher becomes associated, 60
1971
cop McNeill cuts a deal, 55
forms close friendship with Paltos, 59
sets up company with Testa, 46
syndicate broke Canberra TAB with huge win, 46
Testa's second Sydney visit, 46
Testa's told Freeman is a criminal, 47
wire-tap on his phone, 59
1972
links with US drugs Mafioso Danny Stein, 61
Murray Riley joins forces, 57

peace talks with local crims, 64
1973
appears at Moffitt Royal
   Commission, 40, 41
moves money to US Mafioso
   Stein, 62
1974
link to murder of Regan, 76
named by Moffitt as Sydney's
   leading illegal SP bookie, 73
1975
denial of drugs involvement, 49
Murray Riley collecting his debts,
   73
1976
attends Joe Taylor's funeral, 86
bugged calls implicate McNeill, 85
Insp Watson warns him his phone
   is bugged, 85
no strong ties to Terry 'Mr Asia'
   Clark, 2
talks of casino control with Smith,
   81
1977
at races with Farquhar and Paltos,
   89
Farquhar helps Humphreys, 90
Gaming Squad cover-up, 93
Lauer exiled for report critical of
   Freeman, 92
starts affair with Lena Hurley, 93
1979
discuss Paltos' gambling debt, 94
Jacky Muller shoots him, 95
Jacky Muller shot dead, 95-6
1981
marries Georgina McLoughlin,
   112
1985
implicated in Eustace murder, 170
stand-over activities in building
   trade, 160-1, 163-6
1988
dies after pethidine injection, 212

funeral service at St Stephen's,
   213-14
psychiatric tests reveal drug
   addiction, 211
Freeman, Georgina Catherine, née
   McLoughlin, 112, 132, 184, 195,
   207, 212-13, 215-16, 221
Freeman, Grant, eldest son, 46, 94,
   113, 206
Freeman, Greig David, 215-16
Freeman, Les, brother, 5
Freeman, Rita Eileen née Cooke,
   mother, 5, 6
Freeman, William David, father, 5
Fremantle gaol, 34
Frodsham, Clarence Robert, fraud
   squad Det-Sgt, 90-1
Fryer, Grant, Supt., 106, 199

G

Galea, Bruce (Percy's son), 51, 206,
   216
Galea, Percy, 28, 51, 81
Gambling Man, The, by Kevin
   Perkins, 144
Gaming Squad, 18, 70, 81, 106
Gaudron, Mary, Solicitor-General,
   199
Giordano, Nick, Testa bodyguard, 43
GKN Kwikform scaffolding
   company, 161-5
Glass, Greg, coroner, 142-3, 169-73,
   184-6
Gleeson, Murray, High Court Chief
   Justice, 98
Golconda d'or diamond, 114-15
Goldsmith, Ronald John. *See* Smith,
   Stanley John (Stan 'The Man')
Goodman, Jimmy, 206
Gordon, Wayne, Sen-Const., 169
Gore, Kevin, 75
Goulburn Club, 81, 83-4
Graham, Angus, acting police
   commissioner, 173
Grants Constructions,

Freeman-Testa joint venture, 46-7
Greiner, (Nick) Nicholas Frank Hugo, 83, 84, 160, 201
Grigg, Neville, Insp., 70-1
Gross, Bernard QC, 147
Grove, Russell D, Clerk of the Legislative Assembly, 80
Gulf Frio, 127
Gyles, Roger QC, 160-6, 200

H

Hackett, George Joseph, 29
Haines, Trevor, 123-4
Haitana, Hayden, trainer, 144
Hakim, Fayez (Frank), 78, 196-7
Hand, Derrick Windsor, coroner, 143, 173-4
Hannah, Kevin Samuel, 168
Hanson, Carol Louise, née Whitehall, 88
Hanson, Frederick John, police commissioner, 19, 21, 67-8, 73, 86-8, 90-1, 100-1
Hardin, Bruce, illegal gambler, 81-2, 84, 92, 149, 161-4, 166, 184
Harding, Brian, Det., 117, 193
Harris, Arthur, punter, 27, 113
Harris, William 'Dingy', 169
Hatton, John, MP, 105
Healy, 'Big' Jim, wharf union leader, 50
Heffron, Robert James (Bob), premier, 26
Hejja, Bela, enforcer, 54, 208
Henry, Graham 'Abo', 140, 143, 174, 182
Henson Park Hotel, 25, 74
Hickie, David, author, 26, 110
Higgins, Keith, 10
Hill, Graham, judge, 98
Hills, Patrick Darcy, MP, 68
Hing, Frank, 206
Hitler, Adolf, 4, 7
Holden, Thomas Sinclair, judge, 13
Hollywood Hotel, 29

Houghton, Bernie, 60
Hubbard, Elbert, 68, 214
Hubbard, Sue, Chubb girlfriend, 141
Huckstepp, Sallie-Anne, 195
Humphreys, Kevin Emery, 90-2
Hunt, David Anthony, judge, 194
Hurley, Jeffrey, 115
Hurley, Lena, née Muller, 49-50, 93-5, 98, 209
Hurley, Michael Nicholas, 48-50, 93, 94, 96-8, 114-15, 209, 219-20

I

Ibrahim, John, 221
ICAC inquiries, 78, 97, 168, 174, 205, 222
Independent Action Group for a Better Police Force, 75
Independent Commission Against Corruption. *See* ICAC inquiries
Internal Police Security Unit. *See* IPSU
IPSU, 131
Iron Bar Miller. *See* Petricevic, Milan
Iron Duke hotel, 142, 189, 223

J

James, Greg QC, 200
James, Tass, doctor, 212-13
Jarvis, Richard, 22
Jilly's Roadside Diners, 168
Jones, Harvey, 195
Jones, Kevin Willson, magistrate, 92
Jones, Leslie, 197

K

Karp, Ross John, 94, 126-30, 132-4, 143, 173, 189, 197, 216
Kean, John Eric. *See* Smith, Stanley John (Stan 'The Man')
Keane, Kenneth Laurence. *See* Freeman, George David
Keenan, Andrew, SMH journalist, 172
Kelleher, David, 59-60, 102, 190, 209
Kellett Club, 31, 32

Kelly, Mary née Barnes, 28
Kelly, Ray 'The Gunner', Det., 19, 28-32, 56-8, 73, 116, 189, 205
Kennedy, Ian, Det-Sgt, 142
Kings Cross Aquatic Club, 142
Kinsella inquiry into off-course betting, 25
Kinsella, Edward Parnell, judge, 25
Knebel, Richard, 160-1
Knight, Doug Det-Sgt, 47, 169
Knight, William Harwood, judge, 218
Krahe, Frederick Claude, 18-20, 50, 56, 75, 77, 189
Kron, Gerald, 216-18
Kron, Joanna, 217

L

Landa, Paul, Attorney-General, 119-24, 199
Lanfranchi, Darrell, 116
Lanfranchi, Keith, 115
Lanfranchi, Warren Charles, 115-18, 183, 193, 195
Lansdowne hotel, 146-7, 186, 192, 194, 223
Lansky, Meyer, 61
Latin Quarter nightclub, 30
Lauer, Anthony, Det., 92, 188
Laws, John, broadcaster, 126
Lawton, Donald, 217
Le Grand, Mark, NCA lawyer, 156
Lee, Ronnie, illegal gambler, 31, 39, 43, 81, 138, 168
Lee, Sammy, 30
Lees, James Travers, police commissioner, 198
Lennie the Squealer. *See* McPhersqon, Leonard Arthur
Lewer, Walter 'Wally', magistrate, 51
Lewis, Stanley Raymond. *See* Smith, Stanley John (Stan 'The Man')
Liberal Party, 26, 77, 117, 142, 188, 198
Lloyd, Cecil, shoplifter, 22
Long Bay Gaol, 13-14, 17, 82, 115

Lord, Robert QC, 185
Low, Alexander Keith, shoplifter, 33
Lusher, Edwin Augustus, judge, 81, 137
Lydon, Ned, journalist, 212
Lynch, Frank, racecourse detective, 89

M

Mafia, US, contact with, 17, 31, 40, 42-8, 52, 61-4, 66, 68, 71, 103, 197, 208
Mahoney, John, AJC chief steward, 113, 194
Maloney, William, Toe Cutter gang, 75, 77
Mandarin Club, 186
Mara, Les, 219-20
Marble Bar, 12
Marcos, Ferdinand, Filipino president, 216
Mason, John Marsden, MP, 107, 198-9
Masters, Chris, ABC-TV investigative reporter, 92
Mater, Jack, lawyer, 143
Matthews, Bernie, 10, 11
McCann, Raymond Barry, 145-8, 174-5, 186, 192-4
McCauley, Bruce, 140-1
McClune, 195
McClymont, Kate, SMH reporter, 115, 195, 216
McDonald, Marcia (first wife), 23, 25, 32-3, 94-5
McDonald, Robert, inspector, 128
McFadden, Edward Eric, GKN, 162
McLean, Goldie, 150
McLean, Ian, 150, 154-9
McLoughlin, Charles, 9, 25, 112, 207
McLoughlin, Georgina Cathrine. *See* Freeman, Georgina Cathrine
McNeill, Jack, Det., 32, 42, 47, 48, 55, 56, 57, 58, 66, 68, 80, 85, 86, 104, 115, 187, 205

McNeill, Mary Christina, née Meagher, 56
McPherson, Dawn Joy, née Allen, 16
McPherson, Leonard Arthur, 2, 14-18, 20, 27-32, 34-6, 38-41, 43-4, 47-9, 51-2, 55-66, 69, 71-2, 74, 76, 79, 82, 96-7, 101-4, 108, 114-5, 117-8, 122, 125, 136-7, 149, 152, 160-8, 174-5, 181-3, 186, 190, 195, 197, 204-9, 211-13, 215, 219, 221
McPherson, Marlene, 43, 219
Meissner, Ladisla 'Joe', 84, 152, 169, 174, 193
Menere, Paul Henry, 161
Mengler, Carl, NCA official, 155-6, 158
Miles, Bruce, lawyer, 202
Millar, Frederick, TNT chairman, 88
Milner, Timothy William Lycet, 105-8, 198, 201-2
Moffitt, Athol, judge, 40, 42, 47, 51, 55, 57, 71-3
Montague, Frank, 139
Moore, Rod, Det, 117
Morey, Noel, Det-Sgt., 74
Mount Penang Training School, 10-11, 15
Moylan, Michael jnr, 79
Mr Digby race fix, 112-14, 206
Mr Fix-it. *See* Hakim, Fayez (Frank)
Mr Rent-a-Kill. *See* Flannery, Christopher Dale
Mulherin, Julie, 206-7
Muller, Eseme, née Patmore, 50
Muller, John Marcus (Jacky), 49-50, 93-6, 209
Mulock, Ron, Attorney-General, 124, 173
Murphy, Chris, lawyer, 207
Murphy, Lionel, 87, 106, 119-23

N

National Crime Authority (NCA), 3, 98, 124, 146-7, 149, 151-9, 166, 170, 172, 190
Needham, Garth QC, 71-2
Nelson Hotel, Woollahra, 30
Newington College, 51
Newman, Leonard, deputy police commissioner, 86
Newsome, Debbie, 206
Newtown, Mick, constable, 90
Nielsen, Juanita, 20, 50, 187
Norman the Foreman. *See* Allan, Norman Thomas William, commissioner
Northside Polonia Soccer Club, 57

O

O'Brien, Harold 'Rastus', 22
O'Connor, Raymond Patrick 'Ducky', 30
O'Shane, Pat, magistrate, 143, 194
Olson, Martin, 61
omerta, Mafia 'code of silence', 204-5
Openshaw, John, Det-Sgt., 78, 184, 190
Operation Lavender, 128, 171
Operation Sugar, NCA investigation, 155
Owens, Raymond Arthur. *See* Smith, Stanley John (Stan 'The Man')

P

Paciullo, George, MP, 83, 84, 172, 189, 202
Packer, Kerry, 126
Page, Terry, bookmaker, 114
Painters and Dockers Union, 50, 54, 140
Palmer, Graham George 'Croc', 84, 127-30, 133-4, 143, 171-2, 177, 184, 190, 197
Palmer, H.G. stores, 18
Paltoglou, Nicholas George. *See* Paltos, Dr Nicholas 'Nick'

Paltos, Dr Nicholas 'Nick', 58-9, 84-5, 89, 94-6, 98, 103, 126-30, 132-5, 142-3, 168, 170-3, 177, 180, 184, 189-90, 196-7, 208-10, 212, 216
Paltos, Maria, née Kratzis, 59
Parramatta Gaol, 13, 20
Pash, Graham, STC chairman, 112-13
Pentridge Prison, 14, 146
Perkins, Kevin, author, 144-5
Petricevic, Milan (Iron Bar Miller), 43, 64
Phillip, Capt. Arthur, NSW Governor, 1
Phoenix hotel, 37, 223
Police Royal Commission, 181
Police Tribunal, 142, 148, 188-90
Porter, Chester QC, 131
Presnell, Max, journalist, 111
Prontos restaurant, 168
Puplick, Chris, Senator, 188
Pyrmont Bridge Hotel, 49

Q

Queen Elizabeth II, 12, 73
Queen of the Cross. *See* Freeman, Georgina Catherine

R

Ramon, Charkey. *See* Ballard, David Bruce
Randwick racecourse, 89-90, 96, 101, 112
Ratcliffe, John 'Bronco', 161-2
Rayner, Louis 'Snowy', 29
Regan, John Stewart, 74-7, 96
Richardson, Graham, 152
Richo. *See* Richardson, Graham
Riley, Murray Stewart, 57-8, 65-6, 72, 79, 84, 101, 104-5, 127, 136, 147-8, 209, 219
Rogers, K. *See* Bonnette, Karl Frederick
Rogerson, Roger Caleb, 18, 20, 32, 56, 60, 73-4, 78-9, 96-7, 102, 115-18, 128-36, 138-40, 142, 144, 148-50, 174, 178-9, 182-6, 188-90, 193, 196-8, 205, 209, 220
Rooklyn, Jack, 45, 47, 77
Rowntree brothers, 17
Royal Commissions
1962
Kinsella commission into off-course betting, 25
1973-74
Moffitt Commission into crime in clubs, 40, 42, 47, 51, 55, 57, 71, 72, 73
1977-80
Woodward Royal Commission into drug trafficking, 61, 103, 105
1981-83
Stewart Royal Commission into drug trafficking, 85
1983
Street Royal Commission into Certain Committal Proceedings against K E. Humphreys, 91
1985-86
Stewart Royal Commission into alleged telephone interceptions, 85, 86, 101-2
1990-92
Gyles Royal Commission into the building and construction industry, 160-6
1994-97
Wood Royal Commission into the NSW Police Service, 181
Royal Oak Hotel, 148
Rozelle casino, 82, 149
Rozenes, Michael QC, 151
RSL of crime, 207
Ryan, Morgan, solicitor, 85, 106-7, 122, 124, 199, 201-2

S

Saffron, Abraham (Abe) Gilbert, 2, 63, 68, 93, 118, 168, 190, 209, 221

Sandery, Bruce, 194
Savvas, George, 184, 193-4
Sayers, Michael John, 143-8, 150, 154, 167-8, 178, 194
Sefton, Colin, cab driver, 180
Seymour, Michael, solicitor, 75
Sheehan, Terry, Attorney-General, 201
Shu, Lewton, 195
Sin, Cardinal Jaime, 218
Sinclair, John Bowditch, judge, 201-2
Sinclair, William Charles Garfield, 104
Slippery Sam. *See* Askin, Robin (later Robert), premier
Sloss, Albert Ross, MP, 64-6
Small, Clive, ex-policeman, 52, 79
Smith, Arthur Stanley 'Neddy', 77-9, 96-7, 102, 104, 115-17, 136, 140, 142-4, 148, 175, 182, 187, 188-90, 193-4, 205, 209
Smith, Dennis 'Fatty', 154
Smith, Michael John, 162, 165
Smith, police prosecutor, 199
Smith, Ray, poker machine dealer, 58, 72
Smith, Stanley John (Stan 'The Man'), 6, 8, 11, 12, 15, 30-3, 38-41, 43, 48-9, 51, 52, 55, 57-9, 62-4, 69-72, 74, 79, 81, 85, 102, 104, 108, 114, 118-20, 122-3, 125, 137, 148, 168, 220-1
Smith, Stanley junior, 52
Smorgon, Samuel, 217
Solomon, Karl. *See* Bonnette, Karl Frederick
Spritely minesweeper, 217
Stackpool, Reginald T., asst. police commissioner, 86, 90-2
Stately Stan. *See* Stanley John (Stan 'The Man')
Stathis, Andrew, 118-19, 121-5
Stathis, Andrew, negotiations, 118-25
Stathopoulous, Andreas. *See* Stathis, Andrew

STC (Sydney Turf Club), 112-14
Steele, Robert Lawrence 'Jacky', 30
Steim, Clive, lawyer, 200
Stein, Danny, US Mafioso, 61-2, 208
Steketee, Mike, journalist, SMH, 199
Stevens, William Joseph, shoplifter, 33
Stewart, Donald Gerard, judge, 85-6, 101, 154
Stewart, Murray Lee. *See* Riley, Murray Stewart
Stonner. *See* Smith, Stanley John (Stan 'The Man')
Story, Don, STC director, 113
Strawbridge, Palma, 119,123
Street royal commission, 91
Street, Sir Laurence Whistler, Chief Justice NSW, 91
Strong, Eric, Supt., 189
Stuart, John Andrew, 30
Stuart-Jones, Dr Reginald, illegal abortionist, 28
Sullivan, Gerry, Solicitor-General, 107, 199
Sully, Brian, judge, 146
Sunday Telegraph, 64, 70
Sun-Herald newspaper, 82, 108, 114
Sutherland Hospital, 95, 211
Sutherland United Services Club, 57
Sutherland, Paul, 164
Sweetnam, James Randolph, 51
Sydney Hilton Hotel, 12, 112
Sydney Morning Herald, 5, 83, 115, 143, 165, 172-3, 177, 195, 199-200, 207, 212, 214, 216, 220, 222
Sydney Sun newspaper, 20, 87, 111
Sydney Turf Club. *See* STC

T

Tamworth Institution for Boys, 10-11, 78
Taylor, Joe, illegal gambler, 28, 31-2, 59, 81, 84-6
Tees, Aarne, Det., 61, 117, 159, 174, 180-2, 184, 186

Telford Club, 84
Temby, Ian, ICAC commissioner, 78, 174, 202
Testa, Joseph Dan, US Mafioso, 31-2, 39-44, 46-8, 61, 64, 72, 208
The Duke. *See* Delaney, Arthur 'The Duke'
The Gunner. *See* Kelly, Ray 'The Gunner', Det.
The Track, ABC documentary, 26, 51, 113
Theeman, Frank, 19
Theobold, Kevin Victor, 146, 193
Thomas Nationwide Transport (TNT), 87-8
Thomas, Gordon, 116
Thommo's Two-up School, 59, 86
Thurgar, Roy Lawrence, 193, 195
Toe Cutter gang, 75
Tony's Bar and Grill, 122-3
Toomey, Barry QC, 174-5
Torok, Tony, 81, 83, 149, 170, 206
Torrington, Kenneth, judge, 104
Trimbole, Craig, 147
Trimbole, Robert, 79, 85-6, 110, 124, 126-7, 147, 154

U

Unsworth, Barrie John, MP, 187
Useless. *See* Eustace, Tony 'Spaghetti'

V

Verbal. *See* Kelly, Ray 'The Gunner', Det.

W

Walker, Frank, MP, 119
Walker, George Ziziros, illegal gambler, 81
Walker, Kirk, 160, 165
Walker, Raymond, Sen-Const., 141
Walker, Robert James 'Pretty Boy', 30
Waller, Kevin, coroner, 193, 211-2
Walsh, Norman Francis, coroner, 117
Ward, Barry, author, 20
Ware, Marian, Sayers' girlfriend, 145
Warnock, Steve, journalist, *Sun-Herald*, 82
Waterhouse, Robbie, bookmaker, 144-5
Waterhouse, William Stanley (Bill), bookmaker, 27, 144
Waterman, Sandy, Las Vegas Mafia, 208
Watson, George, deputy DPP, 16-17
Watson, Patrick John, Insp., 85, 106
Western, Phillip, 116
Whelan, Jack, Det., 30
Whiskey Au Go Go, Brisbane, 30
Whitton, Evan, author, 21, 64, 79, 108, 214
Wild, Maurie, Det., 30
Wilks, Alfred Amos, security officer, 50
Williams, Alan David, 130-1, 134, 151, 178-9
Williams, Tennessee, 210
Wilson, Bert, magistrate, 185
Wilson, James Roland, 22
Wilson, Roger, lawyer, 138
Wong, Denis, Mandarin Club, 186
Wood, Joyce née Shelley, 101
Wood, Mervyn Thomas, police commissioner, 58, 67, 87, 91, 100-3, 105-7, 113, 198-202, 220
Woodward Royal Commission, 61, 103, 105
Woodward, Philip Morgan, judge, 61, 103, 105
Wotherspoon, Garry, biographer, 20
Wran, Neville Kenneth, MP, premier, 19, 80, 90-2, 102, 107, 117, 187-8, 198-9
Wren Harry Orrel, 72

www.ingramcontent.com/pod-product-compliance
Lightning Source LLC
Chambersburg PA
CBHW020353170426
43200CB00005B/149